CIVIL PROCEDURE IN TANZANIA: A STUDENT'S MANUAL

B.D. Chipeta

DAR ES SALAAM UNIVERSITY PRESS LTD.

Published by
Dar es Salaam University Press Ltd.
P.O. Box 35182
Dar es Salaam
TANZANIA

ISBN 9976 60 375 4

CONTENTS

Abbreviations for Citations

The following citations have been used in this book.

All E.R.	-	All England Law Reports
E.A.C.A	-	Reports of the Court of Appeal for Eastern Africa (1934 –1955)
E.A.	-	East African Law Reports
A.I.R.	-	All Indian Reporter
K.B.	-	King's Bench Law Reports
A.C.	-	Appeal Cases
H.C.D.	-	High Court Digests (Tanzania)
K.L.R.	-	Kenya Law Reports
L.R.T.	-	Law Reports of Tanzania
T.L.R. (R)	-	Tanganyika Law Reports (Revised)
U.L.R.	-	Uganda Law Reports
Z.L.R.	-	Zanzibar Law Reports
C.P.C.	-	Civil Procedure Code (Tanzania)
T.L.R.	-	Tanzania Law Reports
O.	-	Order in Civil Procedure Code
r.	-	Rule of cited Order

ACKNOWLEDGMENTS

I express my gratitude to the following authors, publishers and copyright holders from whose works, with their kind permission, I have drawn quotations and/or material in writing this book:

Butterworths: *The Eastern/East Africa Law Reports* (E.A.), *The All England Law Reports* (All E.R.), *Halsbury's Laws of England.*
Sweet and Maxwell: "Odgers on Pleading and Practice" "*Res Judicata*" by Spenser-Bower and Turner.
N.M.Tripathi: Publishers – D.P. Mulla's Code of Civil Procedure.
The Hon. The Chief Justice of Tanzania (Mainland): *Tanganyika Law Reports* (T.L.R.) (R).
The Hon. The Chief Justice of Kenya: *Kenya Law Reports* (K.L.R.).
The Hon. Chief Justice of Uganda: *Uganda Law Reports* (U.L.R.).

It is also my duty and pleasure to express my gratitude to the secretarial staff of the High Court Registry who came to my assistance at a crucial stage of preparing the fair copy of the manuscript, to the late Hon. Mr. Justice Y. Rubama for his very useful comments and suggestions, and to my many other colleagues and friends for their suggestions.

Last, but not least, to my wife Ruth, whose patience, tolerance and unwavering encouragement were a source of inspiration at every stage of the preparation of this book.

B.D. CHIPETA
Dar es Salaam
March, 2002

PREFACE

Few areas of the law in East Africa suffer from as much a dearth of local textbooks as the Civil Procedure Law. This is often a handicap to a student; he often has no alternative but to rely on statutory provisions covering the subject and on Indian and English law.

This book is an attempt to fill that void. It is, of course, not an exhaustive work on the subject, but it covers, in as concise a form as possible, most of the basic principles of the law of Civil Procedure as contained in local statues and decisions of superior courts. Inevitably, owing to a dearth of local authorities on some topics, reference has also been made to English and Indian authorities where these have appeared to be sufficiently relevant to East Africa.

As the title suggests, this book has been designed primarily for use by students. However, it is sufficiently comprehensive to be of use to those fresh on the Bench and the Bar and those interested in this area of law in various callings.

Unlike most law textbooks, this book attempts to present the law as it is, and not what it should be. In other words, except in a few instances, jurisprudential questions of the subject have been avoided. The book is largely based on Tanzania statutes, but it is hoped that the reader elsewhere in East Africa will have no difficulty finding equivalent statutes in the other countries.

For the convenience of the reader, footnotes have been avoided. All references to statutes, cases, etc., appear in brackets in the text. In has further been appreciated that some readers of this book may not have ready access to law reports and textbooks referred to here. For this reason, it has been necessary, within the scope of a work of this size, to quote extensively from important authorities. In the case of case law, where the point decided is relatively short or minor, the facts of the case have been omitted, the *ratio decidendi* digested without verbatim quotations, and the citation has been given.

B.D. CHIPETA

CASE INDEX

A

B

C

F

Farrab Incorporated *v.* Brian Robson, (1957) E.A. 441
Fatehali Shah *v.* Muhammad Baksh, A.I.R. 1928 Lahore 516
Fazal *v.* Gulamali (No.1) (1976) L.R.T. n. 35
Fernandes *v.* Commercial Bank, (1969) E.A. 482
Fisher *v.* Owen, (1878) 8 ch. 653
Fernandes *v.* Kara, (1961) E.A. 693
Foum *v.* Registrar of Coop. Socities, (1995) T.L.R. 75
Francis Andrew *v.* Kamyn Industries, (1986) T.L.R. 31
Francis Mwijage *v.* Boniface Kabalemeza, (1968) H.C.D. n. 341

G

G.P. Jani Properties *v.* Dar es Salaam City Council, (1966) E.A. 281
G. R. Mandavia *v.* R. Singh, (1965) E.A. 118
Gajender Pal *v.* Ram B. Sirdaw, (1961) E.A. 344
Gamaha *v.* Lwavu, (1970) H.C.D. n. 257
Gandy *v.* Caspar Air Charters, 23 E.A.C.A. 139
General Manager, E.A.R & H.A *v.* Therstein, (1968) E.A. 354
George & Co. *v.* Pritam's Auto Service,22 E.A.C.A 233
George Shambwe *v.* Tanzania & Italian Petrol Co., (1995) T.L.R. 20
Gilbert *v.* Smith, (1876) 2 C.D. 684
Gulamhussein Fazal *v.* M.H. Gulamali, (1976) L.R.T. n. 35
Gulamhussein Fazal *v.* M.H. Gulamali (No.2) (1976) L.R.T. n. 64
Gunning *v.* Motor Mart, L.R.S. I of 1962
Gurbacham Singh Kalsi *v.* Yowani Ekori, (1958) E.A. 450
Guru Engineering *v.* Coast Region Coop. Union, Dar es Salaam Registry
   Civil Case No. 320 of 1996
Gwamaha *v.* Lwavu, (1970) H.C.D. n. 257

H

Hagod J. Simonian *v.* Johar and Others, (1962) E.A. 336
Haji M. Durvesh *v.* Villain (1957) E.A. 91
Haji Khan *v.* Baldeo Das, (1901), 24 All. 90
Harilal & Co. *v.* The Standard Bank, (1967) E.A. 512
Hasham Suleman *v.* Sayani, (1963) E.A. 603
Hasmani *v.* The National Bank of India 4 E.A.C.A. 55
Hassanali Somji *v.* Kishen Singh 21(1) K.L.R. 29

L

M

N

O

S

V

W

Y

Z

INTRODUCTION

THE OBJECT OF THE LAW OF CIVIL PROCEDURE

To the layman, the rules of Civil Procedure are unnecessary obstacles in the adjudication of substantive matters in law-suits and not worth the paper they are written on. To the law student, the rules of Civil Procedure are unduly intricate and make such "dull" reading that he sees little reason for their existence except to make it even more difficult for him to obtain his law degree.

The rules of Civil Procedure may well be intricate and, possibly, sometimes make "dull" reading. But the inevitable truth is that no practicing lawyer can make much headway in civil litigation without a sound working knowledge of those "intricate" rules. To him those rules are his compasses and roads that guide him and are as indispensable to him as torch light is to a man walking in darkness.

Rules of Civil Procedure are not there to hinder the due administration of justice. On the contrary, the primary object of the rules of Civil Procedure is to show the litigants and courts how the rights of the parties should smoothly be handled. They are a guide as to how pleadings are to be drawn, cases conducted and remedies obtained. They are intended to convenience and protect rather than hinder or encumber the due administration of justice.

Courts have on more occasions than one made this point abundantly clear. In the case of *The Iron and Steelwares Ltd. v. C.W. Martyr & Co.*, (1956) 23 E.A.C.A. 175, Worley, P., said at page 177:

> Procedureal rules are intended to serve as the hand-maidens of justice, not to defeat it....

In the case of *Bhag Bhari v. Mehdi Khan*, (1965) E.A. 94, the same Court said, at page 104:

The rules of procedure are designed to formulate the issues which the Court has to determine and to give fair notice thereof to the parties.

CIVIL PROCEDURE LAW IN EAST AFRICA

The Civil Procedure Law in East Africa is now contained in comprehensive statutes. Uganda has the Civil Procedure Act, Cap. 65; Kenya has the Civil Procedure Act, Cap.5; and Tanzania (Mainland) has the Civil Procedure Code Act No. 49 of 1966.

Before the Civil Procedure Code, 1966 was enacted, the Indian Code of Civil Procedure, 1908, applied to Tanzania (Mainland) by virtue of the provisions of the Indian Act (Application) Ordinance, Cap. 2 of the revised laws. The Civil Procedure Code Act, 1966, came into force on 1st January, 1967.

During the period when the Indian Code of Civil Procedure applied to Tanzania, the courts were nevertheless enjoined to construe its provisions with such modifications as were necessary or proper to suit a particular matter (see section 5 of the Indian Acts (Application Ordinance)).

As a result of that accident of history, there has been little departure by our courts from the Indian and English interpretations of identical or similar provisions of these statutes. Indeed, where there is a dearth of local decisions on a particular point (which is not infrequently the case), East African courts often resort, albeit sometimes grudgingly, to Indian and English authorities for guidance. In doing so, however, they bear in mind (or should) the fact that the interpretation of domestic statutes must be in accord with the local conditions and circumstances.

In other words, our civil procedure law was, in one sense, received from England circuitously via India. We also received it directly from England through the Reception Clause in the Tanganyika Order in Council 1920.

THE SCOPE OF THE CIVIL PROCEDURE LAW

As pointed out above, the object of the Civil Procedure Law is to enable the parties and the courts to know matters which are in dispute between the parties, to guide the courts in the course of determining those issues and to guide and protect the parties. To that end, the statutes on Civil Procedure Law are quite comprehensive. But, human ingenuity and foresight notwithstanding, there are to be found *lacunae* here and there.

The statutes encompass the entire field of litigation processes from jurisdiction of courts to execution of decrees, orders and awards. They provide, for instance, the manner of suing or being sued, the jurisdiction of courts, general rules of pleading, the conduct of trials, the contents of judgments and decrees and modes of execution thereof, and the manner in which appeals are preferred and dealt with. This book gives a bird's eye view of that field.

CHAPTER ONE

MODES OF DISPUTE SETTLEMENT

In all jurisdictions, various modes of settling disputes have been put in place for orderly and efficacious settlement of disputes. These modes are usually created by statutes and in some cases by practice in the relevant tribunals.

In Tanzania, until late 1994, the mode of settling disputes were:

- Adversarial procedures;
- Reconciliatory procedures; and
- Arbitratory procedures.

In some jurisdictions, they apply the modes of inquisitorial procedures. In 1994, there was introduced a fourth mode of settlement of disputes, that is, the Alternative Dispute Resolution (A.D.R.) procedures simply called Mediation. This was done by Government Notice No. 422 of 1994 which amended the First Schedule to the Civil Procedure Code Act, 1966. This mode of settlement of disputes is dealt with in greater detail later in this book.

In the year 2000, mediation was incorporated into the Supreme Law of the Land, that is, the Constitution of the United Republic of Tanzania. That was done by the Thirteenth Amendment of the Constitution. Article 107 A (2) (d) of the Constitution provides (as a free translation):

(2) In deciding civil and criminal cases in accordance with the law, Courts shall abide by the following principles, namely:

(d) To develop and promote mediation (or reconciliation) between parties to disputes.

In Tanzania, the traditional mode of setting disputes is the adversarial system. This system has its strengths and weaknesses. Its great weaknesses are that it encourages delays in settlement of disputes; it is costly in terms of time and finances; it is apt to breed or foster animosity between the parties in that it is a "winner-take-all" process; the rules of evidence and procedure are so intricate that an ordinary litigant does not understand them; and the language is sometimes unintelligible to the common man.

Besides, the decision is imposed on the parties by a stranger, that is, a Judge or magistrate, and relief's are usually confined to the pleadings. By its very character, this mode is perceived by some people to favour the rich, the educated and the articulate.

The mode of settlement of disputes by arbitrary procedures is similar to the traditional adversarial system. The two have almost similar weaknesses.

The settlement of disputes by mediation procedure has several advantage over the traditional adversarial system. Some of such advantages are that the procedure is simple and flexible; the outcome is shaped by the parties themselves and not imposed on them by a stranger; it saves time and money; it takes shorter time than an ordinary trial in that in mediation, no witnesses or assessors are involved; relationships of the parties are preserved and enhanced; and privacy of the matter is maintained. It is also said that by saving time, Judges and Magistrates can then spend more time on questions of law and so develop the law. On this point, in his foreword to the book *Manual for Mediation Training in Tanzania*, retired Chief Justice Francis Nyalali has made the following observation:

> Both research and conventional wisdom show that the majority of cases that currently go to litigation in the Courts do not involve issues of law but concern issues of fact. This means that judges and magistrates who are legally trained and qualified, spend much time deciding disputes without applying their legal training. This is clearly a misuse of a rare human resource and results in the fossilization of the law .... We must move away from this situation to a position where judges and magistrates spend much of their time deciding cases involving the law, and thus developing the law.

It is important to note that not all cases that go to courts are suitable for mediation. By their very nature, some types of cases are inappropriate for the mediation process. Among them are cases in which injunctive relief's are sought, cases in which an interpretation of the law is sought, cases of prerogative remedies; cases for declaratory judgments, and cases in which Constitutional reliefs and interpretation are sought (see Government Notice No. 196 of 1995). Happily, however, these categories of cases form only a small fraction of cases instituted in our Courts. Mediation, therefore, is a very important supplement to the traditional adversarial procedure.

The inquisitorial mode of settlement of disputes is not practiced in Tanzania.

CHAPTER TWO

JURISDICTION OF COURTS AND RES JUDICATA

JURISDICTION

Definition

In simple terms jurisdiction of a court means the extent to which, or the limits within which, a particular court can exercise its powers and what powers. These limits may be territorial or pecuniary or as may be prescribed by statutes or practice. In Mulla's *Code of Civil Procedure*, the following definition of the term jurisdiction is given:

> Jurisdiction means the extent of the authority of a Court to administer justice not only with reference to the subject matter of the suit but also to the local and pecuniary limits of its jurisdiction (13th Edn, p. 125).

The question of jurisdiction is not merely one of form. It is fundamental. Any trial conducted by a court with no jurisdiction to try the same will be declared a nullity on appeal or in revision. There is abundant authority to that effect. Suffice here to refer to only one case, and that is the case of *Melisho Sindiko v. Julius Kaaya*, (1977) L.R.T. no. 18. The facts were that the respondent was the plaintiff in a suit filed by him in the primary court in the West Meru District. He sued the appellant for T.shs. 2,000/= allegedly lent by him (the respondent, and hereinafter referred to as the plaintiff) to the appellant (hereinafter called the defendant). The trial court admirably tried the case and gave the plaintiff judgment for the sum claimed, with costs. Unfortunately, the primary court magistrate was not aware of the fact that the suit was outside the pecuniary jurisdiction of his court. As the Court of Appeal pointed out, this was not surprising, as the normal civil jurisdiction of primary courts, which is T.shs. 2,000/= was limited to T.shs. 1,000/= in the case of suits for the recovery of civil debt by the amendment to section 14(1) of the Magistrates' Courts Act (Cap.537) which is tucked away in the Schedule to the Written Laws (Miscellaneous Amendments) Act, 1968, together with other amendments to ten other Acts.

On appeal to the West Meru District Court, which was vested with the requisite jurisdiction to entertain the suit, the appeal was confined to the merits of the case, and no challenge as to the jurisdiction of the Primary Court was raised. The District Court Magistrate allowed the appeal, and entered judgment for the defendant, with costs. The plaintiff then appealed to the High Court, this time engaging the services of an advocate. At this stage, for the first time, the defendant's advocate raised the question of jurisdiction. The learned Judge had no doubts about the appeal on merits. He held that the District Court Magistrate was not justified in setting aside the judgment of the Primary Court. Against that decision there was no further appeal. The learned Judge dealt with the jurisdiction point in this way: he restored the judgment of the Primary Court in favour of the plaintiff to the extent of T.shs.1,000/=; and gave him leave to bring fresh proceedings in the District Court for the balance of his claim. Against this part of the decision of the High Court, with leave, the defendant appealed to the East African Court of Appeal. Law, VP., said, at page 66:

> Unfortunately it is clear, in my opinion, that this appeal must   succeed. The Primary Court had no jurisdiction to entertain   the plaintiff's suit, and the proceedings in that Court were a nullity. The primary court would only have had jurisdiction if the plaintiff had limited his claim to T.shs. 1,000/=, and   waived his right to claim the balance, which he did not do. Pecuniary limitations to a court's jurisdiction cannot be evaded by bringing a series of suits, each within the court's jurisdiction. The learned Judge's order to this effect cannot be supported, and in my view this appeal must be allowed and the judgment obtained by the plaintiff set aside as a nullity.

To alleviate the plaintiff's plight, after observing that the appeals to the High Court and to it would not have been necessary had the relevant law been brought to the notice of the District Court and of the High Court and as the courts could not be absolved of any responsibility as they are presumed to know the law and may only be reminded of it, the Court ordered that each party must bear his own costs in the Court and in all courts below. It then advised that the plaintiff could bring his suit again in a court having jurisdiction presumably the West Meru District Court, if the suit was not by then barred by limitation.

This case underscores the statement that the question of jurisdiction is fundamental and not one of mere technicality. It is, therefore, the duty of every court to peruse the pleadings in every case and satisfy itself that it has jurisdiction to try the suit before proceeding to do so.

Types of Jurisdiction

i) Terrritorial Jurisdiction

Territorial jurisdiction means the geographical area within which a Court can exercise its powers. Generally speaking, in Tanzania, primary courts and district courts have territorial jurisdiction within the district in which they are established (see sections 4 and 5 of the Magistrate's Courts Act No. 2 of 1984, Cap.537 of Revised Laws, the Fourth Schedule to the Act, and *Sogora v. Khalfan* (1972) H.C.D. No.73). However, the Chief Justice may, by order in the Gazette, authorize a district court to sit outside the district for which it is established when exercising its appellate, confirmatory or revisional powers (see section 10(2) of Act No.2 of 1984).

A court of a resident magistrate has territorial jurisdiction within such areas as are specified by the Chief Justice by an order in the Gazette establishing such court (see s.5 of Act no.2 of 1984). The High Court, on the other hand, has territorial jurisdiction over the entire State. However, according to the High Court Registries Rules, 1961, original proceedings in the High Court may be instituted in the Registry at Dar es Salaam or in the District Registry for the area in which the cause of action arose or the defendant resides (see *Ahmed Ismail v. Juma Rajabu*, (1985) T.L.R. 204).

ii) Pecuniary Jurisdiction

Pecuniary jurisdiction means jurisdiction that is governed by the value, in terms of money, of the subject matter of the suit in question. Primary Courts, for instance, have pecuniary civil jurisdiction in suits for the recovery of civil debts, rent or interest due to the Republic, the Government or any Local Authority, under any judgment, written law (unless jurisdiction therein is expressly conferred on a court other than a primary court), right of occupancy, lease, sub-lease or contract, if the value of the subject matter of the suit does not exceed five million shillings, and any proceedings by way of counterclaim and set-off therein of the same nature and not exceeding such value; or for the recovery of any civil debt arising out of contract, if the value of the subject matter of the suit does not exceed three million shillings, and any proceeding by way of counterclaim or set-off therein of the same nature and not exceeding such value (see section 18 of Act No.2 of 1984).

It should be pointed out in passing that where a suit for the recovery of a civil debt arising out of contract with the value of the subject matter not exceeding T.shs.3,000,000/= has been filed in a primary court, either party to the suit may apply to the court which is seized of the matter to have the proceedings transferred to the district court of the district for which the primary court is established. If, on such application, the primary court is satisfied that the proceeding involves a question of law at issue between the parties, it must transfer the proceeding to the district court for the district for which such primary court in such proceeding has been made or entered. Such decision, judgment or order will not be reversed or altered on appeal or revision on the sole ground that such primary court failed to transfer the proceedings in accordance with the foregoing provisions unless such failure has in fact occasioned a failure of justice.

Primary courts, however, have unlimited pecuniary civil jurisdiction in all proceedings where the law applicable in customary law or Islamic Law, and in administration of deceased's estates where the applicable law is customary or Islamic Law (see *Mohamed Stambuli v. Mwanaharusi Selemani* (1968) H.C.D. no. 357).

A district court, when held by a resident magistrate, a civil magistrate or other description of magistrate has, generally speaking, pecuniary jurisdiction in proceeding for the recovery of immovable property where the value of the property does not exceed twelve million shillings; and in other proceedings, where the subject matter is capable of being estimated at a money value, where the value of the subject matter does not exceed ten million shillings (see section 40 Act No.2 of 1984).

The court of resident magistrate generally has, and exercises, the same pecuniary jurisdiction as a district court held by a resident magistrate or a civil magistrate. The High Court, however, has unlimited pecuniary civil jurisdiction (see also section 13 C.P.C.).

It has been held that where the amount claimed is below the pecuniary jurisdiction of the High Court, then the High Court has no jurisdiction in terms of section 13 of the Civil Procedure Code Act, 1966 (see *Francis Andrew v. Kamyn Industries (T) Limtied*; (1986) T.L.R 31).

iii) Other Types of Jurisdiction

Apart from territorial and pecuniary jurisdiction, jurisdiction of courts may be prescribed by other express statutory provisions. By some express statutory provisions, some courts have and others do not have jurisdiction in particular civil proceedings. For example, a district court has no jurisdiction over matters arising out of the Rent Restriction Act. Under the provisions of section 11 A of the Rent Restriction Act, all claims, proceedings or other matters of a civil nature arising out of the Act must be commenced in a Court of Resident Magistrate of competent jurisdiction (see *Mohamed Ngonyani v. Mtumwa Dodo* (1967) H.C.D. no. 174; *Allarakhian v. Aga Khan* (1969) E.A. 613; *Pili Juma v. Abdullah Khalifa*, (1986) T.L.R. 201) *John Sangawe v. Rau River Village Council*, (1992) T.L.R. 90; *Asha Mohamed v. Zainabu Mohamed*, (1983) T.L.R. 59) *John Agricola v. Rashid Juma* (1990) T.L.R.; *Abifalah v. Kudnap*, (1971) H.C.D. 166; and *Walimu v. Mongo* (1968) H.C.D. n.81).

iv) Appellate and Revisional Jurisdiction

A primary court has appellate and revisional jurisdiction in cases decided by ward tribunals established under the Ward Tribunals Act, 1985. A district court has appellate and revisional jurisdiction in all civil matters originating in primary courts or appeals in cases decided by the primary court on appeal from ward tribunals. The High Court has overall appellate and revisional jurisdiction.

Transfer of Cases for Purposes of Jurisdiction or Otherwise

Where any proceeding has been instituted in a primary court, the Primary Court may, at any time before judgment, transfer the proceeding to the district court, or a court of a resident magistrate having jurisdiction, or to some other primary court. But such transfer must be with the consent of such district court or court of a resident magistrate.

Similarly, a district court or a court of a resident magistrate within any part of the local jurisdiction (i.e. territorial jurisdiction) of which the primary court is established, may lawfully transfer the proceeding from the primary court to itself or to some other magistrate's court. The High Court, too, has power to order the transfer of the proceeding to itself or to some other magistrate's court.

It should be noted that while a primary court can only transfer a proceeding to another court with the consent of the district court, or a court of a resident magistrate, the district court or a court of resident magistrate, or the High Court, does not need to have the consent of the primary court seized of the matter. Once an order of transfer of the proceeding has been made at any time before judgment by the district court or a resident magistrate or the High Court, such primary court must comply with the order.

The power of transfer will be exercised:

a) Where it appears that the circumstances or gravity of the proceeding make it desirable that the proceeding should be transferred; or

b) Where there is reasonable cause to believe that there would be failure of justice were the proceeding to be heard in the primary court; or

c) Where the subject matter of the proceeding arose outside the local limits of the primary court's jurisdiction or is not within its jurisdiction, or in any case in which the law applicable is a customary law which is not a customary law prevailing within such primary court's local jurisdiction; or

d) Where the proceedings seek to establish or enforce a right or remedy under customary law or Islamic law, or are an application for the appointment of an administrator of the estate of a deceased person, and the court is satisfied that the law applicable is neither customary nor Islamic Law, or that the question whether or not customary law or Islamic law is applicable cannot be determined without hearing or determining the proceedings.

A court exercising the power to transfer a proceeding, however, must record in its record its reasons for making such order. Besides, if the proceeding in question is one which is required by any law to be commenced in a primary court, then the transfer of such proceeding must be to some other primary court. Furthermore, such transfer must not be made to a court which has no jurisdiction in respect of the subject matter, however constituted it may be (see section 47 of Act No.2 of 1984).

Conversely, where any proceeding in respect of which primary courts have jurisdiction is instituted in a district court, a court of a resident magistrate or the High Court, it is lawful at any time before judgment for such court to transfer the proceeding to any primary court having jurisdiction where it is satisfied that such transfer of the proceeding will not be contrary to the interests of justice or cause undue inconvenience to the parties, and in such a case, it must record its reasons for making the order of transfer (see section 48 of Act No.2 of 1984).

In addition to transfer of cases from one court to another, primary courts may, with the consent of the parties, transfer a proceeding in a civil suit to an arbitration tribunal.

Leave of the High Court

Where a matter must be tried in a primary court, the High Court may, usually on application, grant leave to the applicant to file his intended suit in a court other than a primary court (see ss.44 and 63 M.C.A. see also *Ng'unda v. Ng'unda*; (1995) T.L.R. 155; and *Kulthum Kara v. Yasin Osman*, (1968) H.C.D. n.340).

Ouster of Jurisdiction of Courts by Statutory Provisions

It is quite often that the legislature enacts laws which, explicitly or by necessary inference, exclude courts of law from exercising jurisdiction in a given dispute. Such enactments are sometimes referred to as "finality" or "exclusion" clauses. The statute may expressly or inferentially provide that a decision, say by a minister or some statutory body, is final and conclusive and not subject to review by, or appeal to courts of law.

Case-law tends to suggest that courts of law are jealous of their jurisdiction and so do not always take kindly to such ouster clauses. Where the ouster clauses are not clearly worded, courts of law quite often circumvent them either by resorting to judicial review or by holding that the language used by the legislature did not oust the jurisdiction of courts of law.

In his book, *Administrative Law*, Professor Wade states, at page 48:

> At the root of the matter is jurisdiction, or more simply power. The principle is that if an administrative authority is acting within its jurisdiction,

... and no appeal from it is provided by statute, then it is immune from control by a court of law. But if it exceeds its power, or abuses them so as to exceed them, a court of law can quash its decision and declare it to be legally invalid (2nd Edition, Oxford).

In the English case of *Congreve v. Home Office*, (1976) A.C. 629, Lord Denning had this to say:

> When the licencee has done nothing wrong at all, I do not think the minister can lawfully revoke it without giving reasons, or for no good cause. If he should revoke it without giving cause, or for no good reasons, the court can set aside his revocation and restore the licence. It would be misuse of the power conferred on him by Parliament: and these courts have the authority and I would add, the duty - to correct a misuse of power by a minister or a department, no matter how much he may resent it or warn us of the consequences if we do.

In the case of *Mtenga v. University of Dar es Salaam*, (1971) H.C.D. n. 247, the High Court of Tanzania almost equally icely stated:

> It is trite to observe that the Court is, and has to be for the protection of the public, jealous of its jurisdiction, and will not lightly find its jurisdiction ousted. The Legislature may, and often does, I am afraid far too often, oust the jurisdiction of the Court in certain matters, but for the Court to find that the Legislature has ousted its jurisdiction, the Legislature must so state in no uncertain and in the most unequivocal terms.

In the case of *J. Yusuph v. Minister for Home Affairs*, (1990) T.L.R. 80, the High Court quashed the Minister's deportation order on the ground that the minister had acted *ultra vires* his powers conferred on him by section 24 of the Immigration Act, 1972.

Effect of Lack of Jurisdiction

As pointed out earlier, the question of jurisdiction is not a matter of mere technicality. It is fundamental. Any trial of a proceeding by a court which has no jurisdiction to try it will be declared a nullity on appeal or revision. The case of *Melisho Sindiko v. Julius Kaaya* (supra) sufficiently underscores this point.

Even the fact that it would be convenient for the parties to have a proceeding heard in a particular court is not enough to confer jurisdiction on such court if it in fact has no jurisdiction to try the suit. Indeed, it makes no difference that the parties to the suit have agreed that their proceeding be heard in a particular court if such a court has no jurisdiction to hear and determine the matter. Parties cannot confer jurisdiction on a court by consent. As was stated by the East African Court of Appeal in the case of *Shyam Thanki and Others v. New Palace Hotel*, (1972) H.C.D. n.92 at page 23:

> All the courts in Tanzania are created by statute and their jurisdiction is purely statutory. It is an elementary principle of law that parties cannot by consent give a court jurisdiction which it does not possess.

RES JUDICATA

Definition

The doctrine of *res judicata* states that once a court or judicial tribunal of competent jurisdiction to determine the matter in issue in any suit or proceeding between the parties thereto has finally decided those matters, such decision, unless reversed on appeal or revision, is conclusive, so that the parties thereto or their privies are precluded from disputing or questioning in any later litigation the correctness of such earlier decision, in law or in fact, as against any other party or privy thereto. The doctrine also acts as an estoppel to such parties to relitigate those same matters in any subsequent suit because the doctrine, apart from binding the parties as to the matter decided, also puts to an end the particular cause of action on which the former litigation between the parties was founded.

In the words of Sir Udo Udoma, C.J., in the case of *Karshe v. Uganda Transport Co.*, (1967) E.A. 774, at page 777:

> In general terms, the impression I form from these cases seems to me to be this: that once a decision has been given by a court of competent jurisdiction between two persons over the same subject matter, neither of the parties would be allowed to relitigate the issue again or to deny that that decision had in fact been given, subject to certain conditions.

In the English case of *Stiftung v. Rayner and Keeler Ltd.*, (1966) 2 All E.R. 536. Lord Guest had this to say, at page 564:

> The rule of estoppel by *res judicata*, ... is that where a final decision has been pronounced by a judicial tribunal of competent jurisdiction over the parties to the subject-matter of the litigation, any party or privy is stopped in any subsequent litigation from disputing or questioning such decision on the merits.

In Tanzania, the principle of *res judicata* is embodied in section 9 of the Civil Procedure Code Act, 1966, which provides:

> No court shall try any suit or issue in which the matter directly and substantially in issue has been directly and substantially in issue in a former suit between the same parties or between parties under whom they or any of them claim litigating under the same title in a court competent to try such subsequent suit or the suit in which the issue has been subsequently raised and has been heard and finally decided by such court.

The Rationale of the Doctrine of Res Judicata

The doctrine of *Res Judicata* has found expression into two Latin maxims:

i) *"Interest rei publicae ut sit finis litium,"* which means: the interest of the general public requires that there must be an end to litigation; and

ii) *"Nemo debet bis vecali, si constat curiae quod sit pro una et eadem causa,"* which means: no man should be twice sued or twice prosecuted upon one and the same set of facts, if there has been a final decision of a competent court (see Earl Jowit's *Dictionary of English Law,* 1959 Edition).

In their book *Res Judicata,* Spenser-Bower and Turner paraphrase the two maxims in the following terms:

> There are two theories (which, however, in analysis, may perhaps be regarded as merely two aspects or sides of one and the same theory) whereupon the doctrine of *estoppel per res judicatam* is commonly justified: *viz.* First, the general interest of the community in the termination of disputes, and in the finality and conclusiveness of judicial decision; and, secondly, the right of the individual to be protected from vexacious multiplication of suits and prosecutions at the instance of an opponent whose superior wealth, resources and power may, unless curbed down by judicially declared right and innocence. (2nd Edition, at page 107).

In Karshe's Case (supra), His Lordship expressed the rationale of the doctrine in the following terms, at page 777:

> This court is not oblivious of the cardinal principle that the doctrine of *res judicata* is not a technical doctrine applicable only to records. It is a fundamental doctrine of all courts that there must be an end to litigation as a matter of public policy.

This statement was also made by the Court of Appeal for East Africa in the case of *G.R. Mandavia v. Rattan Singh,* (1965) E.A. 118, in which the Court stated, as page 121:

> *Res Judicata* ... is a matter of pleading and can be raised only at the trial. The principles underlying the doctrine of *res judicata* are *"Interest rei publicae ut sit finis litium"* and *"Nemo debet bis vexari pro eadem causa* (per Crabbe, J.A.)

In the case of *New Bruswick Railway Co. v. British* and *French Trust Corporation Ltd.,* (1938) 4 All E.R. 747, Lord Maughan, L.C. said, at page 754:

> The doctrine of *estoppel* is one founded on considerations of justice and good sense. If an issue has been distinctly raised and decided in an action in which both parties are represented, it is unjust and unreasonable to permit the same issue to be litigated afresh between the same parties, or persons claiming under them.

Essential Elements of the Rule of Res Judicata

Since a judicial decision is, by the operation of the doctrine of *Res Judicata,* final and conclusive as between the parties and their privies on matters raised and decided in a particular litigation and so puts to an end the particular cause of action, a plaintiff or his privy cannot sue on the same cause of action in a subsequent suit nor can he raise matters which were finally decided in the former suit. If he does so, the defendant is entitled to plead *Res Judicata.*

In order to succeed on a plea of *Res judicata,* therefore, it is essential to show not only that the cause of action was the same, but also that the plaintiff has had an opportunity of recovering, and that but for his own fault might have recovered, in the first action what he now seeks to recover. It must be shown that there was an actual merger in the decision of the cause of action or that the same point has been decided between the same parties.

A close examination of section 9 of the Tanzania Civil Procedure Code Act, 1966, reveals the following essential elements of the doctrine of *res judicata:*

1) That the judicial decision was pronounced by a Court of competent jurisdiction;

2) That the subject matter and the issues decided are the same or substantially the same as the issues in the subsequent suit;

3) That the judicial decision was final; and

4) That it was in respect of the same parties litigating under the same title.

i) That the Decision was Made by a Court of Competent Jurisdiction

For a plea of *res judicata* to succeed, one of the essential elements that must be shown is that there has been a judicial decision which has been duly pronounced by a Court or judicial tribunal of competent jurisdiction. Jurisdiction here means jurisdiction in every respect to make the decision in respect of the subject-matter and the parties thereto. The question of jurisdiction must be determined irrespective of the question whether there is a right of appeal from the decision of that court (see explanation 2 to section 9 of the Civil Procedure Code).

So long as the decision was pronounced by a court of competent jurisdiction, and so long as such decision has not been reversed or altered on appeal, it operates as *res judicata*.

ii) The Same Subject-matter as in the Former Suit

Another essential element of the doctrine of *res judicata* is that the subject-matter pleaded in the subsequent suit should be the same as that decided in the former suit. Let us take a simple example. On 12th January, 1990, A, driving his own car, collided with a lorry belonging to B and driven by C a driver of B. On 20th February, 1990, C sues A in Iringa District Court for damages for injuries which C sustained in the accident alleging that the sole cause of the accident was A's negligent manner of driving. On 27th February,1990 A sues B and C in the High Court at Mbeya for damages to his car and for injuries which A sustained in that same accident. On 14th July, 1990, after a full trial, the High Court pronounces judgment in favour of A holding that C was wholly to blame for the accident. In those circumstances, the suit of C against A, if still pending, will be *res judicata* on the question as to who, between A and C, was to blame for the accident, although it was filed prior to A's suit against B and C.

Having shown that the decision was in a "former suit," it must next be shown that the subject-matter involved in the subsequent suit is the same or substantially the same as in the former suit. In other words, it must be shown that the cause of action and the issues in the subsequent suit were alleged by one party and either denied or admitted, expressly or impliedly, by the other (see Explanation 3 to section 9 of the Code).

A problem that often arises is to define the phrase "matter in issue." The meaning of this phrase was considered by the Court of Appeal for Eastern Africa in the case of *Jadva Karean v. Harman Singh Bhogal*, (20 E.A.C.A. 74). Construing that phrase as used in section 6 of the Kenya Civil Procedure Ordinance (Cap. 5), which is identical with section 9 of the Tanzania Civil Procedure Code Act, 1966, the Court stated, at page 76:

> The authorities are clear that the "matter in issue" in section 6 of the Ordinance (which corresponds to section 10 of the Indian Civil Procedure Code) does not mean any matter in issue in the suit but has reference to the entire subject in controversy; it is not sufficient that one or some issues are in common. The subject matter of the subsequent suit must be covered by the previously instituted suit and not *vice versa.*

In Mulla's *Code of Civil Procedure*, it is stated at page 40-41.

> It is not enough to constitute a matter *res judicata* that it was in issue in the former suit. It is further necessary that it must have been in issue directly and substantially. A matter cannot be said to have been "directly and substantially" in issue in a suit unless it was alleged by one party and denied or admitted, either expressly or by necessary implication, by the other. It is not enough that the matter was alleged by one party. At the same time it is not necessary to constitute a matter 'directly and substantially' in issue that a distinct issue should have been raised upon it; it is sufficient if the matter was in issue in substance (13th Edition).

These comments by the learned author were referred to with approval by the Court in Karsan's case (supra) in which the Court added, at page 77:

> To bar the second action there must have been a merger of the cause of action in the judgment and "there will be no merger unless the cause of action is the same and the plaintiff had an opportunity of recovering in the first action what he seeks to recover in the second. Otherwise the defendant is not twice vexed for the same cause." A plaintiff is allowed to bring successive actions in respect of the very same circumstances, provided that those circumstances give rise to different causes of action.

In order to determine whether the matters decided in a former suit are the same as those in a subsequent suit, a court will have to look to the pleadings and judgment or final order in the former suit. But if the formal order of the Court is in unambiguous terms, the reason therefor cannot be looked at for the purpose of excluding from the scope of the former order any matter which, according to the issues raised on the pleadings and the terms of the order itself, included in the formal order. *Ipso facto*, if the declaration made in a judgment is unambiguous, regard cannot be had to the pleadings in the suit or to the history of the case for the purpose of attributing another meaning to the declaration.

If any matter might or ought to have been a ground of defense or attack in the former suit, it is deemed to have been "a matter directly and substantially in issue" in such suit (see explanation 4 to section 9 of the C.P.C.). Such matter, therefore, is deemed to have been controverted. This rule, however, does not cover cases in which a defendant in a former suit failed to raise the matter by way of counterclaim or set-off. Karshe's case (supra) affords a good illustration. In that case, the facts were that in a former suit the plaintiff, Karshe, had been sued by the defendants, Uganda Transport Co., Ltd. for damages for negligence arising out of a road accident. In that suit Karshe filed no counterclaim. The Judge in that suit found both parties fifty per cent to blame, and gave the defendants judgement for half its claim. After that judgment was delivered Karshe filed a suit claiming fifty per cent of the damages suffered by him as a result of the accident. In the subsequent suit a question arose as to whether the suit was caught by *res judicata*, that is, whether the subject matter in the subsequent suit was the same as in the former suit.

The defendants argued that the plaintiff was stopped by the judgment in the previous suit from bringing the suit because he had failed to counterclaim in the previous suit. After considering several English and Indian authorities on the interpretation of explanation 4 to section 11 of the Indian Code of Civil Procedure (which is identical with explanation 4 to section 9 of the Tanzania Civil Procedure Code Act, 1966), the Court held that if the parties had an opportunity of controverting the point which it was sought to presume as having been constructively a matter directly and substantially in issue, and such point properly belonged to the subject of the litigation and which the parties exercising reasonable diligence might have brought forward at the time then the matter is *res judicata*. But the Court went on to hold that the provisions of the explanation did not cover situations where a claim in a suit might have been pleaded by way of set-off or counterclaim in a previous suit.

On the larger question as to whether the plaintiff's suit was *res judicata* on the ground that the matters in issue had been raised and decided in the former suit, the Court pointed out that the issues between the parties in the former suit were:

1) Who was negligent as between the parties;

2) To what extent did the plaintiffs in that suit contribute towards the defendant's negligence if any; and

3) Whether the plaintiffs in that suit suffered the loss and damages claimed as a result of the collision, and if they contributed to the negligence, to what proportion of such loss and damage were the plaintiffs entitled.

Having referred to those issues, the Court went on at page 783:

> The issues set out above and which had been decided by the court in the previous suit are of course *res judicata* and cannot be enquired into again by any court. The result of this is that the defendant in the present suit is stopped from denying that it was fifty per cent responsible for the accident occasioned by it. Similarly the present plaintiff is stopped from denying that he was fifty per cent responsible for the accident! The issue of loss or damage suffered by the present plaintiff was never enquired into by the court in the previous suit and therefore is not caught by the plea of *res judicata* (see also *Zaruki Mbokemize v. Swaibu Omari*, (1988) T.L.R. 160).

And suppose in a suit relief has been claimed in the plaint but it is not expressly granted by the decree. What, then, is the position? In such a case, such relief must, for the purpose of *res judicata*, be deemed to have been refused (see explanation 5 to section 9 C.P.C). It would, however, appear that explanation 5 does not mean that *res judicata* would operate where a court has expressly left an issue open. In the Indian case of *Bapana v. Jaggiah*, A.I.R. 1939 Madras 818, a subordinate judge expressly left open one of the issues. He stated:

> I ... refrain from giving any finding on issue 9.

The question, then, was whether such issue could be said to have been *res judicata*. The Court there stated:

Explanation 4 imports a fiction into section 11 C.P.C. Having provided that a matter which might and ought to have been made a ground of defense or attack in a former suit it introduced a fiction that it shall not only be deemed to have been raised, but also to have been directly and substantially in issue in that suit. This would not have been however enough for the purpose of section 11 C.P.C. until the matter was presumed to have been decided. In view of the express order by the Court that the matter would be left open, it is impossible to permit any such fiction to be introduced in this case.

If, however, a point has been decided by necessary implication in the former suit, it will operate as *res judicata* in a subsequent suit (see *Chattar Singh v. Roshan Singh*, A.I.R. (33) 1945, Nagpur 277).

Now, suppose that the applicability or non-applicability of a rule of law is not in question and does not affect the rights claimed and denied in a litigation. In such a case, it would appear that, any decision on such abstract question of law, dissociated from and unconnected with such rights in the litigation, can never be of any importance or value to the parties and to the decision of the case and cannot, therefore, be deemed to have been substantially in issue. It was so held in the case of *Chattar Singh v. Roshan Sing (supra)* where the Court quoted with approval *Chitaley and Rao's Code of Civil Procedure*, 1944 edition, in which the authors state:

> In order to understand and solve this apparent conflict of views, it is necessary to see what exactly is meant by "that point of law in issue in a previous suit." It is submitted, with respect, that what is meant is only that the applicability or non-applicability of a rule of law to a given set of circumstances was in question in the previous suit. Parties to a litigation have absolutely no concern in raising questions as to the existence of a particular rule of law or as to the nature thereof, except so far as such questions affect the rights claimed or denied in such litigation. An abstract question of law dissociated from and unconnected with such rights in litigation can never be of any importance or value to the parties and to the decision of the case and cannot therefore be deemed to have been substantiality in issue.

The provisions of explanation 4, it has been held, do not cover cases in which there are inconsistent or mutually destructive pleas. In the case of *Gurbacham Singh Kalsi v. Yowani Ekori* (1958) E.A. 450, the Court of Appeal for Eastern Africa held that the fact that a party had previously brought an unsuccessful action based upon an allegation of nonfeasance did not stop him from bringing a second action based upon misfeasance which, in the circumstances of that case, could not have been joined with the first.

The Tanzania High Court has also held that *res judicata* does not operate where the suits are based on different rights and where different principles of law are involved because a person may use any or all the legal means of enforcing his rights (see *Nduke v. Mathay* (1970) H.C.D. n.96).

While on this point, it is pertinent to point out that the rule of *res judicata* as applied to civil litigation has the same rationale as the pleas of *outrefois* acquit and *outrefois* convict in criminal proceedings. It must be noted, however, that compensation awarded in criminal proceedings cannot constitute *res judicata* in a civil suit for civil redress in respect of the same act or omission that gave rise to the criminal proceedings. In the case of *S.K. Meghji v. Odhiambo*, (1951) 24 K.L.R. 84, the Court said, at page 85:

> There can, in our opinion, be no shadows of doubt that any person who sustains bodily harm at the hands of another person is entitled to set in motion both the criminal and civil law either contemporaneously or otherwise.

In the case of *Cosmas v. Faustini* (1971) H.C.D. n.349, the Tanzania High Court had this to say:

> That the parties were before a civil court and a criminal case based on the same facts cannot bar a subsequent civil claim based on the very same facts ....
> It need hardly be pointed out that the respondent's argument that the matter between him and the appellant was *res judicata* in view of his acquittal was wrongly upheld.

The same Court also so held in the cases of *Abdullah Ramadhani v. Asinate Kimomwe* (1969) H.C.D. n.24, and *Ramadhani Hassani v. Ramadhani Iddi* (1972) H.C.D. n.129.

That the Judicial Decision was Final

It is not enough to show that the subject matter and issues in the suit are the same as in the previous suit, and that a court of competent jurisdiction pronounced a decision. It must further be shown that the decision finally decided the matters in dispute. As was stated by Lord Porter in the Indian case of *Bhagwasti v. Ram Kali* (A.I.R.) 1939 P.C. 133:

In order to successfully establish a plea of *res judicata* or *estoppel* by record it is necessary to show that in a previous case a court having jurisdiction to try the question came to a decision necessarily and substantially involving the determination of the matter in the later case.

The decision, therefore, must be on the merits, and it must be clear that the parties were heard or were given an opportunity to be heard before the decision on the merits was pronounced. If, therefore, a suit is dismissed on a preliminary point, which does not finally decide the rights and liabilities of the parties, then the plaintiff cannot be said to have been heard on the merits, and so a subsequent suit is not *res judicata*.

But what is the position where a judgment was pronounced under rule 4 of O.15 of the Civil Procedure Code Act (see infra)? In the case of *Sahim A.H. Zaidi v. Faud Hussein Humeidan* (1960) E.A. 92, the court considered this question and held that if a judgment is pronounced for failure to produce evidence, such a judgment is deemed to be a judgment on merits and operates as a *res judicata*. After referring to several Indian cases and learned authors, Forbes, V.P. stated at page 98:

> Similarly, in terms of O.15, r.4, of the Indian Rules if a plaintiff fails to produce evidence, the court can pronounce judgment. It does not dismiss the suit for non-prosecution .... Equally, I think, when the court, acting under r.178 of the Rules of Court "pronounces judgment" it must be a judgment on the merits on the material before it.

His Lordship went on:

> It is well settled in India that the dismissal of a claim under O.17, r.3, on account of the plaintiff's default in producing evidence to substantiate his case has the effect as a dismissal founded upon evidence, and that the subject of such a claim will be *res judicata* .... Since decision is deemed to be a decision on the merits, this is a logical conclusion. And it seems to me that a judgement pronounced against a party under O.15, r.4 must, on the same principle, operate as *res judicata* .... I see no reason to differ from the Indian decision on the effect of a decision under O.17, r.3, and I think the same reasoning and conclusion applies equally to a "judgment pronounced" against a plaintiff under r.178 of the Rules of Court; that such a judgment must be deemed to be a decision on the merits and must have the same effect as a dismissal upon evidence; that accordingly the matters in issue on the suit must be deemed to have been heard and

determined; and that the decision operates as *res judicata* (see also: *George Shambwe v. Tanzania Italian Petroleum Co. Ltd.*, (1995)T.L.R. 20).

On the basis of this principle, it has been held that a consent judgment is as good as one obtained on contest, especially if it is between the same parties to the suit in which the consent judgment was obtained, and that if a party did not choose to raise any grounds of attack or defence on the previous suit which would have been raised had the judgment not been by consent, such a party cannot be allowed to re-litigate that matter in a subsequent suit which is between the same parties litigating under the same title (see *Shamsul Nisa v. Md. Jaffar and Others* (A.I.R.) 1935 Lahore 487). It has also been held, however, that such a judgment cannot stop parties other than those who consented to it (see *Kora Mal Gurdial v. Fazal Ali and Others* (A.I.R.) 1934 Lahore 759).

It has similarly been held that a matter will be said to have been heard and finally decided if the decision was made *ex-parte*. In the case of *Radha Mohan and Others v. Eliza Jane Hilt*, (A.I.R. (34) 1947 Allahabad 147, a mortgage suit was decided *"ex-parte."* A subsequent suit on the same matter was held to be *res judicata*. The Court stated:

> A date was fixed for the decision of the suit in the previous case and that meant that the parties were given an opportunity to be heard if they wished to be heard. The defendant did not appear and the suit was decided ex-parte against him. It cannot be said that the suit was not heard and decided for the purposes of applying the rule of *res judicata* (see also *Tanganyika Motors v. Transcontinental Forwarders*, (1997) T.L.R. 158).

It is, however, important to note that the decision must have been one on the merits of the suit. So, if a suit is dismissed, say, for lack of jurisdiction of the trial court, such a decision is not *res judicata* because it cannot be said that the parties were heard or given an opportunity of being heard on the substantive issues or the merits of the case. Similarly, where a suit is dismissed on the ground that there is a misjoinder or non-joinder of parties, multifariousness, or that the plaint is technically defective, such dismissal will not render a subsequent suit on the same cause(s) of action *res judicata* because the dismissal was not on the merits of the suit.

What is the position where the decision in the former suit was not necessary to the determination of that suit? On this point, in Mulla's Code of Civil Procedure it is stated:

A matter directly and substantially in issue cannot be said to have been heard and finally decided, 'unless the finding on the issue was necessary to the determination of the suit. A finding on an issue cannot be said to be necessary to the decision of a suit unless the decision was based upon that finding ... it is not sufficient to attract the bar of res judicata that an issue has been framed on the question. It is further necessary that there must be a decision on the issue expressed or implied which forms the basis of the decree.'

It is also necessary to note that for purpose of *res judicata* it is immaterial or irrelevant to show that the decision relied upon to found *res judicata* is itself correct or well founded in law or fact. A final decision pronounced by a court of competent jurisdiction and of whatever status in the judicial hierarchy, and which decision has not been reversed on appeal or revision, will operate as *res judicata* as betweens the same parties or their privies in respect of the same subject matter. In the case of *Kotak v.Kooverji* (1969) E.A. 295, it was argued on behalf of the appellant that where a ruling was on a point of law, the doctrine of *res judicata* did not apply. Georges, C.J. dismissed this argument and stated, at pages 296-297:

The purpose of the doctrine, as I understand it, is that there should be an end to litigation. Where a court has investigated an application and has concluded that whatever be the merits, the law provides no remedy, it cannot really be said that the application has not been determined on its merits .... Once it is, as this particular rule of law is applicable to a particular factual situation between parties, then as far as these parties are concerned in the identical factual situation, the fact of the applicability of the rule is *res judicata* and can be challenged only on appeal.

If, however, subsequent events show that although the matter was decided in a former suit, the decision on the former suit was based on fraud and evidence of such fraud has become available which was not known to the party at the time of the first suit, even though it "might" have been discovered, and which raises an issue which was not determined in the first suit, such decision will not operate as *res judicata* (see *Rashid Allarakhia Janmohamed & Co., v. Jathalal Valabhadas & Co.*, 23 E.A.C.A. 255). But as was stated by Sir John Rolt in *Patch v. Ward*, (1867) L.R. 3 Ch. D.203:

The fraud must be actual, positive fraud, a meditated and intentional contrivance to keep the parties and the court in ignorance of the real facts of the case and obtaining that decree by that contrivance.

But if the fraud complained of in a subsequent suit was included and adjudged in a former suit, such subsequent suit will be *res judicata*. In the case of *Ramdev Malik v. Lionel Albert Callow*, (1958) E.A. 99, the facts were that in an action before a magistrate at Tanga, judgment was given for the respondent for arrears of salary claimed by him from the appellant. The appellant did not appeal. Instead he brought a new suit against the respondent alleging that the judgment in the earlier suit had been obtained by a fraudulent false statement made by the respondent in the course of his evidence to the effect that certain forms had been signed by him, regarding the completion of certain works. It was contended that his evidence was most material to the court in coming to a decision. The appellant then asked, *inter alia,* that the judgment be set aside. The magistrate ruled that the second suit was *res judicata*. On appeal, the High Court dismissed the appeal and held that the alleged fraud was included in something which had already been adjudged, and that to entertain the new action would be to re-open the issue already decided and to test again the evidence of the respondent and that of the appellant and his witnesses thereon which the appellant could have done in the earlier suit. The Court reviewed several Indian and English decisions and quoted with approval the case of *L. Chinnaya v. Ramanna* (1915), 38 Mad. 203. There the Court stated, at page 208:

> The test to be applied is, is the fraud complained of not something that was included in what has already been adjudged by the court, but extraneous to it? If, for instance, a party be prevented by his opponent from conducting his case properly by trice or misrepresentation, that would amount to fraud .... Where two parties fight at arm's length it is the duty of each to question the allegations made by the other and to adduce all available evidence regarding the truth or falsehood of it. Neither of them can neglect his duty and afterwards claim to show that the allegation of his opponent was false.

In the case of *Mohamed Golab v. Sulliman* (1894), 21 Cal. 612 which was quoted in the *Malik* case (supra), Petheram, C.J., said:

> The principle upon which these decisions rest is that where a decree has been obtained by a fraud practiced upon the other side, by which he was

prevented from placing his case before the tribunal which was called upon to adjudicate upon it in the way most to his advantage, the decree is not binding upon him and may be set aside in a separate suit, and not only by an application made in the suit in which it was passed but also to the court by which it was passed but I am not aware that it has ever been suggested in any decided case, and in my opinion it is not the law, that because a person against whom a decree has been passed alleges that it is wrong and that it was obtained by perjury committed by, or at the instance of, the other party, which is of course fraud of the worst kind, that he can obtain a re- hearing of the questions in dispute in a fresh action by merely changing the form in which he places it before the court and alleging in his plaint that the first decree was obtained by the perjury by the person in whose favour it was given. To so hold would be to allow defeated litigants to avoid the operation, not only of the law which regulates appeals, but that which relates to *res judicata* as well.

To mention the obvious, if a decree is appealed from, the decree that must be looked to for purposes of *res judicata* is the appellate court's decree and not that from which the appeal was preferred. Should the appeal be pending, then the original decree cannot be said to be final, and the matter will be said to be *res sub judice*. So, if a subsequent suit is filed in a matter to which the doctrine of *res judicata* would, but for the pendency of an appeal from the former decree, be pleaded, the best thing to do is to stay the second suit pending the determination of such appeal. It was so held by the Privy Council in the *Ceylon case of Annamalay Chetty v. B.A. Thornhill,* (A.I.R. P.C. 26) In that case the appellants sued the respondent in 1924 on an account and obtained a decree on 17th January, 1927. The respondent filed an appeal two days later and the appellant, to avoid a possible bar of limitation, filed a fresh suit on the same cause of action on 2nd June, 1927. The suit was dismissed as *res judicata* although the respondent's appeal in the first suit was pending. In allowing the appeal, the Privy Council advised, at page 264:

> The appellant maintained that, under this provision no decree, from which an appeal lies and has in fact been taken, is final between the parties so as to form *res judicata*, while the respondent contended that such a decree was final between the parties and formed *res judicata* until it was set aside on appeal. In their Lordships' opinion the former view is the correct one, and where an appeal lies the finality of the decree on such appeal being taken, is qualified by the appeal, and the decree is not final in the sense that it will form res judicata as between the parties.

The Privy Council also added:

> Their Lordships regret that the second action was not adjourned pending
> the decision of the appeal in the first action, as that could have simplified
> procedure and saved expense.

That it was in Respect of the Same Parties Litigating Under the Same Title

It is an essential element of the doctrine of *res judicata* that it must be
shown that the former suit was between the same parties or their privies
and litigating under the same title. Generally speaking, a judgment cannot
operate as *res judicata* to complete strangers. The case of *Salehe bin Kombo
v. Administrator General* (1957) E.A. 191, is a good illustration. In that
case the facts, in so far as they are material, were that in a former suit the
Administrator General, in his capacity as administrator of the estate of
one late Hassanbhai Dadabhai, a clove shamba owner, was the plaintiff
and sued Saleh bin Kombo (the plaintiff in the subsequent suit). In the
subsequent suit by Kombo, Kombo sued the Administrator General as
administrator of deceased broker named Kassasmali Alibhai to whom
Kombo claimed to have paid moneys as purchase price for certain shambas
which the deceased Kassamali, as broker, sold by auction on behalf of
the estate of Hassanbhai Dadabhai, the owner of the shambas.

The defendant, the Administrator General, relied on *res judicata*. In
rejecting the plea of *res judicata* the court (Windham, C.J.) said at page
192:

> The defendant's contention must, however, fail on one point, namely that
> although in each of the two cases the Administrator General was a party
> he was not in both cases "litigating under the same title" for the purpose
> of section 6 of the (Zanzibar) Civil Procedure Decree, which deals with
> res judicata. For in the former case he sued as administrator of the estate
> of the clove 'shamba' owner Hassanbhai Dadabhai, whereas in the present
> case he is sued as administrator of the broker Kassamali Alibhai.

Citing Mulla's *Commentary on the Indian Civil Procedure Code* (9th edition)
with approval, His Lordship went on:

> (Mulla) makes it clear ... that the expression "the same title" in S.11 of the
> Indian Code (which is reproduced in s.6 of the Zanzibar Decree) means
> "the same capacity," that is to say the same representative capacity. The

Administrator General having been a party in a different representative capacity in the two cases, the defence of res judicata must fail, notwith - standing that the matter is indeed *res judicata* in a *Stiftung v. Rayner and Keeler Ltd.* (1966) 2 All E.R. 536 very other respect (see also *Mateka v. Anthony Hyera*, (1988) T.L.R 188).

In the English case of *Marginson v. Blackburn Borough Council*, (1939) 1 All E.R. 273, the plaintiff sued the defendants for damages in respect of injuries received by his daughter and himself, and in respect of the death of his wife, arising out of a collision between a car driven by the plaintiff's wife and an omnibus driven by the defendant's servant. Prior to the commencement of this action, 3 persons whose premises had been damaged as a result of this accident had, in a county court, sued both the present plaintiff and the defendants, each of whom then served a third-party notice upon the other claiming indemnity and contribution in respect of any sum which the plaintiffs in the county court action might recover. In addition, the present defendants had claimed damages against the present plaintiff in respect of damage to their omnibus. In this prior action judgment was given against the present plaintiff and present defendants jointly and severally, and it was ordered that they should be liable for the sum and costs in equal shares. With regard to the claim relating to the omnibus, it was also found that both parties were to blame, the judge treating that claim as a separate action. The question in the second suit was whether by reason of the action in the county court the plaintiff was stopped from proceeding in the second action, which was on the same facts as was the action in the county court. The Court of Appeal said, at page 272:

> In the county court proceedings, the claim on the third party notice was against him in his personal capacity, and, therefore, being, in the two capacities, in the contemplation of the law two separate and district persons, it is clear that a decision against him in his personal capacity is not conclusive against him in his representative character .... Therefore, no estoppel arises. The same observations apply in the case where he is proceeding as administrator of the person deceased under Fatal Accidents Act 1845 S.2.

The Court then quoted with approval *Kingston's (Duches) case* (1776) 21 Digest, 159, 253, in which it was stated:

It must be observed that a verdict against a man suing in one capacity will not estop him when he sues in another capacity, and, in fact, is a different person in law.

It should be noted, however, that a matter may be *res judicata* as between co-plaintiffs or co-defendants. For example, if A sues B and C for damages resulting from a motor accident in which C was the driver of B, and it is necessary to decide the question whether C was an employee of B and was driving in the course of his employment at the material time for purpose of holding that B is vicariously liable to A, then a decision that C was an employee of B and was driving in the course of his employment at the time will operate as *res judicata* in a subsequent suit between B and C in which C sues B for damages for injuries sustained in that accident. But as was stated by the Privy Council in the Indian case of *Swed Mohamed Saadat Ali Khan v. Mirza Wiguar Ali Beg and Others*,(A.I.R.) (3) 1943 C.P.C. 115, three conditions must be fulfilled before a decision can operate as *res judicata* between co-defendants; it was there stated, at page 120:

> In order that a decision should operate as res judicata between co-defendants three conditions must exist. There must be a conflict of interest between those co-defendants, (2) it must be necessary to decide the conflict in order to give the plaintiff the relief he claims, and (3) the question between the co-defendants must have been finally decided.

When Should a Plea of *Res Judicata* be Raised?

Res judicata is a question of pleading, and so any party wishing to set up *res judicata* must do so at the first available opportunity by pleading it, or, if that is not possible, at the trial or hearing (see *G.R. Mandavia v. Rattan Singh*, (1965) E.A. 118, 121). English courts have held, however, that mere failure to set it up in the pleadings will not necessarily defeat the *estoppel* if the same is not raised at too late a stage in the proceedings (see *Winnan v. Winnan* (1949) p. 174).

If, however, a party does not take precaution to give in good time notice to the opposite party of his intention to rely upon *res judicata,* he will be deemed to have impliedly represented to the other party that he has waived his right to insist on the plea, unless he can prove that he had no opportunity to plead it, say, that the fact of there having been an earlier decision on the matters in issue came to his knowledge very late. In that event it is his duty to raise it as soon as he has the opportunity to do so.

Consequences of Failure or Success of Plea of *Res Judicata*

Where a preliminary issue alleging *res judicata* fails, that is, where a court before which the plea of *res judicata* is raised comes to a decision that the plea is without merits, then the matters in controversy are still open, and so the court will proceed to determine the matter on the merits. If, however, the plea of *res judicata* succeeds, such decision amounts to a bar for the plaintiff of establishing his claim, and so, the case will be dismissed. This was made abundantly clear in *Mandavia's* case (supra) in which Crabbe, J.A., said, at page 123:

> Where in any suit *res judicata* is pleaded the court can do one of two things – (1) it may uphold the plea and dismiss the suit, or (2) dismiss the plea and hear the suit on merits. In the first, the result is that the plaintiff is debarred from establishing his right to the relief which he seeks or from litigating an issue, and in my view it is an adjudication which conclusively determines a right upon a matter or matters in controversy in the suit. In the second, the matters in controversy are still at large, since there has been no adjucation affecting the rights of the parties, and all issues remain alive.

CHAPTER THREE

==

PARTIES TO SUITS

Generally speaking, a suit is a contest between two or several parties. The person who institutes a suit is called a "plaintiff." A plaintiff, then, may be defined as every legal person who asks for any relief in a court of law (not being by way of counterclaim as a defendant) against any other legal person by way of a civil proceeding. Conversely, a defendant may be defined as any legal person against whom a civil proceeding is instituted or directed.

JOINDER OF PARTIES

A person may sue on his own behalf, but subject to certain conditions, several persons may sue jointly. Similarly, a person may be sued alone, but again subject to certain conditions, several persons may be sued jointly in a single suit.

Let us now examine the circumstances in which there can be proper joinder of parties, and the consequences of misjoinder or non-joinder.

Joinder of Plaintiffs

As pointed out above, several persons may sue jointly in a single suit. Where that happens, the persons so suing are joint plaintiffs. This is called *"joinder of plaintiffs."*

The question is: who may be joined as plaintiffs? Put differently, in what circumstances will the joinder of plaintiffs be permitted? The rule is that all persons may join in one suit as plaintiffs in whom any right to relief in respect of or arising out of the same act or transaction or series of acts or transactions is alleged to exist, whether jointly, severally or in the alternative, where, if such persons brought separate suits, any common question of law or fact would arise. (O.1, r. 1C.P.C.).

The essential requirements that must be fulfilled for a proper joinder of plaintiffs were stated in the case of *Stround v. Lawson* (1898) 2 Q.B. 44, in which the Court said, at page 52:

> It is necessary that both these conditions should be fulfilled, that is to say, that the right to relief alleged to exist in each plaintiff should be in respect of or arise out of the same transaction, and also that there should be a common question of fact or law, in order that the case may be within the rule (see also *Bangue De Mosccu v. Midland Bank* (1939) 2 All E.R. 354).

In the case of *Yowana Kahere and Others v. Bunyo Estates Ltd.* (1959) E.A. 319, the facts were that each of the six plaintiffs claimed to be a tenant of the defendant company. They sued as joint plaintiffs for interference of their right to possession. The plaintiffs, however, were not joint tenants of the same holding, but each claimed to be a tenant of a separate holding. The second, third, fourth and fifth plaintiffs claimed that they were unlawfully evicted from their holdings on different dates and that their houses and crops were destroyed. The first and six plaintiffs were still in possession of their holdings, but alleged that their crops and houses were destroyed. Objection was taken by the defendant company that there was misjoinder of parties and causes of action. Sustaining the objection, Bennett, J. said, at page 321:

> In my judgment, the causes of action set out in paragraph 8 of the plaint do not arise out of the same act or transaction or series of acts or transactions. They arise out of wholly distinct and independent acts of dispossession or interference with the right to possession. Nor on the plaint as it stands, does any question of law or fact arise which is common to the claims of the several plaintiffs. The only matter which is common to their claim is the fact that they are all suing the same defendant.

The elements of the rule of joinder of plaintiffs, then, are the following:

1. That each of the plaintiffs must be suing or be entitled to sue the same defendant;

2. That the right to relief alleged to exist in each plaintiff should be in respect or arise out of the same acts or transactions; and

3. That there should be a common question of law or fact, that is to say, that it must be shown that if such persons filed separate suits any common question of law or fact would arise (see *T.P.C. v. Minister of Labour*, (1996) T.L.R. 303).

It is important to note that these requirements are not to be taken in the alternative. All of these must exist for there to be a proper joinder of plaintiffs.

To illustrate the rule, let us take one example. A is involved in a motor accident in which his car which he is driving collides with a lorry belonging to B and driven by C. As a result of the collision, a house belonging to D is damaged. In such a case D and A may jointly sue B and C because each of them is entitled to sue B and C; the rights to relief in A and D are in respect of or arise out of the same accident; and there would arise common questions of law and fact, namely, the question as to who was negligent and the question whether B is vicariously liable.

It should be noted here that it is not necessary that the joint plaintiffs must have the same cause of action. Several persons may join as plaintiffs in one suit although their causes of action are separate and distinct, so long as the right to relief alleged to exist in them arises out of the same act or transaction or a series of acts or transactions, against the same defendant, and the case is of such a nature that if each of them brought a separate suit, any common question of law or fact would arise.

It has also been held that it is immaterial that not all questions of law or fact arising in the case are common to the suits. In the Indian case of a *Sitaram v. Rajendra Chandra* (A.I.R.) (43) 1956 Assam 7, the court considered the interpretation of the phrase *"any common question of act or law"* in O.I. r. I of the Indian Civil Procedure Code and said, at page 8:

It is not necessary that all questions arising in the case should be common to two suits if plaintiffs co-shares had instituted separate suits. If even one question of law or fact common to both the suits could arise, there would be justification for joinder and the requirement of r.I of O.I would be satisfied.

It has been held further, that a plaintiff may sue in double capacity under the rule of joinder of parties (see *Bolton v. Salim Kambi* (1958) E.A. 360).

However, even where there has been proper joinder of plaintiffs, where it appears to the court that any joinder of plaintiffs may embarrass or delay the trial of the suit, the court may, in its discretion, ask the plaintiffs to elect separate trials or it may itself order for such separate trials (O.1 r. 2 C.P.C.)

Joinder of Defendants

As with plaintiffs, all persons may be joined as defendants against whom any right to relief in respect of or arising out of the same act or transaction or series of acts of transactions is alleged to exist, whether jointly, severally or in the alternative, where if separate suits were brought against such persons, any common question of law or fact would arise. (O.1, r. 3.C.P.C.).

It is not necessary for the joinder of defendants that every defendant should be interested as to all the reliefs claimed in any suit against him, or as to every cause of action included in any proceeding against him (O.1 r 5 C.P.C.). In other words, it is immaterial that the causes of action against the defendants are different. A plaintiff is entitled under this rule to join several defendants in respect of several and district causes of action. Where the court is of the opinion that the joinder would embarrass a defendant or put him to unnecessary expense, it will order separate trials (see *The Bank of India v. Shah* (1965) E.A. 18; and *Uganda General Trading Co. v. Jinja Cash Stores* (1965) E.A. 469).

As a general rule, then, where claims against different parties involve or may involve a common question of law or fact bearing sufficient importance in proportion to the rest of the action to make it desirable that the whole of the matter be disposed of at the same time, a court will allow the joinder of the defendants subject, of course, to its discretion as to how the action should be tried. It was so held in the English case of *Payne v. British Time Recorder* (1921) All E.R. 388 in which Scrutton, L.J., stated, at page 393:

.... Broadly speaking, where claims by or against different parties involve or may involve a common question of law or fact bearing sufficient importance in proportion to the rest of the action to render it desirable that the whole of the matters should be disposed of at the same time, the court will allow the joinder of plaintiffs or defendants subject to its discretion as to how the action should be tried.

In the case of *Bank of India v. Shah* (supra), the plaintiff bank sued five defendants jointly and severally as guarantees of monies lent on an overdraft to a company. The claim was for T.shs. 289,291/44 guaranteed by six guarantees of the defendants executed between March, 1955, and March, 1961. The first defendant was only a party to two guarantees, namely, one dated March, 14, 1955, and executed by him and the second defendant for a total of T.shs. 450,000/= and interest, and another dated May, 27, 1958 executed by him with the second and third defendants for a total of T.shs. 300,000/= and interest. The 2nd, 3rd, 4th, and 5th defendants submitted to judgment. A preliminary objection was taken for the first defendant that there was a misjoinder of parties and of causes of action on the ground that each guarantee created a distinct cause of action. The Court held that there was no misjoinder of defendants and stated, at page 20:

> Here can not it be said that the six guarantees arose out of the same act or transaction or series of acts and transactions? Although the word ''same' must govern the words "series of acts or transactions", as they are the same here, it is not necessary that every defendant should be interested in all the reliefs claimed in the suit, but it is necessary that there must be a cause of action in which all the defendants are more or less interested although the relief asked against them may differ... here the main question to be investigated is the state of the company's account with the plaintiffs, and it would defeat the purpose of the rule, which is to avoid multiplicity of suits and needless expense, if this had to be done in five or six separate suits against the different guarantors" (see also *Peter & Co. Ltd v. Mangalji*, (1969) E.A. 80).

The Civil Procedure Code also provides that a plaintiff may, at his option, join as parties to the same suit all or any of the persons severally, or jointly and severally, liable on any one contract, including parties to bills of exchange and promissory notes (O.1, r. 6 C.P.C.) (see also *Fernandes v. Kara*, (1961) E.A. 693).

Where the plaintiff is in doubt as to the person from whom he is entitled to obtain redress, he may join two or more defendants. Judgement may be given against such one or more of the defendants as may be found to be liable, according to their respective liabilities (O.1, r. 4 C.P.C.). But joinder on appeal is not permissible (see *Magu District Council v. Nkwabi*, (1997) T.L.R. 286).

Representative Suit

In a case where there are numerous persons having the same interest in one suit, one or more of such persons may, with the permission of the court, sue or be sued, or may defend, in such suit, on behalf of or for the benefit of all persons interested. If the court should give such permission, then it must give, at the plaintiff's expense, notice of the institution of the suit to all such persons either by personal service or, where from the number of persons or any other cause such service is not reasonably practicable, by public advertisement, as the court in each case may direct. However, any person on whose behalf or for whose benefit a suit is instituted or defended under these provisions may apply to the court to be made a party to such suit (O.1, r.8 C.P.C.).

Let us take an example. Fifty persons own houses in Area F. of Dodoma City. Access to Area F from the city is by one dirt road. Subsequently, City authorities allocate a plot right across that road to a construction company which intends to construct a huge industrial complex on the plot, and thus deny the fifty persons of access to the city by that road. In an application for an injunction to restrain the City authorities and the industrial company from proceeding with their plans, anyone of the fifty persons may, with the leave of the Court, institute and prosecute the application on behalf of the others, provided that due notice is given.

This rule, it will no doubt be noted, is an exception to the general rule that all persons interested in a suit must be made parties to such suit. The object of the rule is convenience. It is there to save trouble and expense. However, there has to be a common cause of action. A person who has no interest in the suit cannot represent others. There must be common interest and a common grievance, and the relief sought must in its nature be beneficial to all those suing or being sued and those they claim to represent.

In the case of *Daudi Abdulla and Osman Haji Ladha* (on behalf of the *Cutchi Lohar Wadha Jamat) v. Ahmed Suleman and Two Others* (13 E.A.C.A), the facts were that the President and Secretary/Treasurer of a religious association called Cutch Lohar Wadha Jamat brought a suit for damages against the three trustees of the association. As the association was not a legal entity and could not sue in its own name, the suit was brought by the President and Secretary/Treasurer in their own names and on behalf of the members of the association under O.1, r.8 of the Kenya Civil Procedure Rules. On the application of one of the defendants the plaint was ordered to be struck out on the grounds that O.1 r.8 did not apply to a claim for damages in tort and that all the members of the association did not have identical interests in the suit.

On appeal, the Court of Appeal said:

> As was said by Fletcher Moulton, L.J. in Markt. & C. Knight Steamship Co. (1910) L.J.K.B. 939, at p.950, in dealing with Order 16 Rule 9 of the English Rules (which corresponds with Order 1 rule 8 of the Kenya rules), we have, in this case to consider the language of order 1 rule 8, and be guided by it and not attempt to extend or limit what according to its natural construction appears to be the ambit of the rule. The rule authorizes the bringing of a representative action "where there are numerous persons having the same interest in one suit." It says nothing whatever about suits founded in contract or in tort or any other kind of suit. The sole test is whether the plaintiffs and the persons whom they claim to represent have the same interest in the suit.

The Court quoted with approval Lord Macnaghten's words in *Duke of Bedford v. Ellis* (1901) 70 L.J. Ch. where he said at page 105:

> Given a common interest and a common grievance, a representative suit is in order if the relief sought is in its nature beneficial to all whom the plaintiff proposes to represent.

The Court then went on to hold that on the plaint, the plaintiffs and those whom they proposed to represent had a common grievance and common interest, that the relief sought was beneficial to all of them, and that consequently a representative suit under O.1 r. 8 was in order.

In order that this rule should apply, therefore, it must be shown: (1) that there is a common interest and a common grievance between the plaintiff and those he claims to represent; (2) that the parties are numerous; (3) that the relief sought is beneficial to all of them; and (4) that the permission of the court has been sought and granted and notice duly given.

It has also been held that in the case of a club or other association, a chairman, president or secretary of the club or association can not sue alone in respect of a matter in which the association is interested. The suit must be brought by all the members of the club or association, or by him on his own behalf and on behalf of the other members of the association (see *Compos v. De Souza* (1933) 15 K.L.R. 86).

It hardly need to be pointed out that an application for leave to bring a representative suit must be filed in the court which will hear and determine the suit in due course (see *Mussa Hamisi and Others v Dar es Salaam City Council*, (1996) T.L.R. 201; and *Lujuna Ballonzi v. C.C.M.* (1996) T.L.R. 203).

Consequence of Misjoinder and Non-Joinder of Parties

The mere fact that there has been a misjoinder or non-joinder of parties is not necessarily fatal to a suit, and the court may in such suit deal with the matter in controversy so far as regards the rights and interests of the parties actually before it (O.1, r.9 C.P.C.) If, however, an application for joinder is made at a very late stage, the court may, in its discretion, refuse to allow such joinder (see *Allah Ditta Qureshi v. Patel (1951)* 18 E.A.C.A.).

It is well to note, as we shall see later, that this rule cannot be brought in aid where there has been misjoinder of parties as well as to causes of action. Indian courts have also held that as regards non-joinder of parties, a distinction ought to be drawn between non-joinder of a person who ought to have been joined as a party and the non-joinder of a person whose joinder is only a matter of convenience; and so, if the decree can not be effective without the absent parties, the suit is liable to be dismissed. Cases of partnership accounts in which some partners have not been joined are typical examples. But if they are not necessary parties, non-joinder is not fatal.

If, however, there has been a misjoinder of parties as well as of causes of action, the suit cannot be saved on the basis of this rule (see *Yowana Kahere's* case (supra).

Striking Out and Adding Parties

Where a suit has been instituted in the name of the wrong person as plaintiff or where it is doubtful whether it has been instituted in the name of the right plaintiff, the court may, at any stage of the suit, if satisfied that the suit has been instituted through a *bona fide mistake,* and that it is necessary for the determination of the real matter in dispute so to do, order any other party to be substituted or added as plaintiff upon such terms as the court thinks just (O.1.r. 10(1) C.P.C.).

Similarly, the court may, at any stage of the proceedings, either upon or without the application of either party, and on such terms as may appear to the court to be just, order that the name of any party improperly joined, whether as plaintiff or defendant, be struck out, and that the name of any person who ought to have been joined, whether as plaintiff or defendant, or whose presence before the court may be necessary in order to enable the court effectively and completely to adjudicate upon and settle all the questions involved in the suit, be added (O.1.r.10(2) C.P.C.).

However, a person must not be added as a plaintiff suing without a next friend or as the next friend of a plaintiff under disability without his consent (O.1. r.10(3) C.P.C.).

If the person added be defendant, the plaint must be amended accordingly unless the court should otherwise direct. When such amendment has been made, the amended copies of the plaint and summons must be served on the new defendant and, if the court thinks fit, on the original defendant. In such an event, and for the purpose of the law of limitation, the period starts to run against such added defendant from the date of service of the summons (O.1. r. 10(4) and (5) C.P.C.).

It has, however, been held that where there has been delay in making an application for adding a party as a defendant where such delay would deprive such party of his vested right, such as limitation, then it would be unjustifiable for the court to exercise its discretion under O.1. r. 10 of the Civil Procedure Code (see *Mehta v. Shah* (1965) E.A. 321). In the case, the court quoted with approval from the judgments of Scrutton, L.J. and Greer, L.J. in the case of *Mabro v. Eagle Star and British Dominions Insurance Co* (1932) I.K.B. 485.

There Scrutton, L.J., had this to say:

> In my experience the court has always refused to allow a party or a cause

of action to be added where, if it were allowed, the defence of the Statute of Limitations would be defeated. The court has never treated it as just to deprive a defendant of a legal defence.

Greer, L.J. said:

> Whether the matter is one of discretion or not, it appears to me inconceivable that we should make an order which would have the effect I have mentioned. It has been the accepted practice for a long time that amendments which would deprive a party of a vested right ought not be allowed.

Now, what is the meaning of the term "mistake" in this rule? The wording of the rule makes it plain that the mistake must be bona fide or honestly made. Such bona fide mistake may be of a matter of fact or a matter of law, and it has been held that an amendment not sought in a lower court may be allowed on appeal (see *Hassanali Somji v. Kishen Singh* (21) (1) K.L.R. 29), and that so long as it was a *bona fide* mistake, it is immaterial that it was as a result of negligence (see *Lombard Banking Kenya Ltd v. Shah Bhagwanji (1960* E.A. 969).

It is important to note that sub-rule (2) of Rule 10 concerns parties who have been wrongly joined and so should be struck out, or who ought to be joined or added. In the words of *Sir Ralph Windham, C.J., in the case of Parry v. Carson* (1962) E.A. 515, at page 517:

> The rule is thus concerned with parties who have been wrongly joined, or who ought to be joined or added. To "join" or "add" a party is not synonymous with making a person a party. To be joined or added presupposes a co-defendant (or plaintiff) sought to be joined or added can be joined or added.

It has also been held that in a suit for tort a defendant can not be added if the plaintiff opposes the addition (see *Santana Pernandos v. Kara Arjan & Sons* (1969) E.A. 693). Order 1 r. 10 (2) can not apply unless the removal of the plaintiff or defendant to the suit would still leave the suit intact.

From the Indian and East African authorities, it is clear that a party can only be added under this rule when he ought to have been joined as plaintiff or defendant, and is not so joined, or when, without his presence, the questions in the suit can not be completely decided. The test was stated in the Indian case of *Sampat Bai v. Madhu Singh* (A.I.R.) 1960 Madhya Pradesh 84 in which the court said:

> The test is not whether the joinder of the person proposed to be added as a defendant would be according to or against the wishes of the plaintiff or whether the joinder would involve an investigation into a question not arising on the cause of action averred by the plaintiff. It is whether the relief claimed by the plaintiff will directly effect the entervenor in the enjoyment of his rights. It is not enough that the plaintiff's right, and rights which the person desiring to be made a defendant wishes to assert should be connected with the same subject – matter. The intervener must be directly and legally interested in the answers to the questions involved in the case. A person is legally interested in the answer only if he can say that it may lead to a result that will affect him legally that is by curtailing his legal rights.

In that case the court quoted with approval the case of *Amon v. Raphael Tuck and Sons* (1956) All E.R. 273, in which Devlin J. stated, at page 287:

> The only reason which makes it necessary to make a person a Party to an action is so that he should be bound by the result of the action, and the question to be settled, therefore, must be a question in the action which can not be effectually and completely settled unless he is a party.

His Lordship added:

> It is not enough that the intervener should be commercially or indirectly interested in the answer to the question; he must be directly or legally interested in the answer. A person is legally interested in the answer only if he can say that it may lead to a result that will affect him legally – that is by curtailing his legal rights. That will not be the case unless an order may be made in the action which will operate on something in which he is legally interested.

From the foregoing, it is logical that if the circumstances are such that the adding of a party would introduce quite a new cause of action, or if it would alter the nature of the suit, such party must not be joined.

Consequences of Striking Out a Party

Where a party has been improperly impleaded, a court will strike out the name of such party. Such striking out of the names of the persons on the ground of misjoinder amounts to an exoneration of such parties, so that thereafter they cease to be parties to the suit. In the case of *Pandra v. Dola Behara and Others* (A.I.R.) 1933 Madras 435; Beasley, C.J., said, at page 436:

> It is quite clear that, where parties have been wrongly joined and then suit against them is given up by the plaintiff or upon that ground he exonerates them, or there is a finding come to that they have wrongly joined them the correct procedure is to strike out their names as having been improperly impleaded. On the exoneration of the striking out the names of the person on the ground of misjoinder, they cease to be parties to the suit.

It is important to note that all objections to non-joinder or misjoinder of parties must be taken at the earliest possible opportunity and in all cases where issues are settled, at or before such settlement, unless the ground of objection has arisen subsequently, and any objection not so taken will be deemed to have been waived (O.1., r. 13 C.P.C.).

THIRD PARTY PROCEDURE

The Procedure to be Followed

Where a defendant in a suit claims against any person not a party to the suit (usually referred to as the third party) any contribution or indemnity, or any relief or remedy relating to or connected with the subject matter of the suit and substantially the same as a relief or remedy claimed by the plaintiff from such defendant, such defendant may apply to the court for leave to present to the court what is called a third party notice, that is, a claim in the suit by the defendant for any such contribution or indemnity from the third party (O.1., r., 14(1) C.P.C.).

If a defendant so chooses to do, he must file the application ex-parte unless the court should direct otherwise, accompanied with an affidavit in which he should state: (1) the nature of the claim made against him by the plaintiff in the suit (2) the stage which the proceedings in the suit have reached; (3) the nature of the claim made by him against the third party and its relation to the plaintiff's claim against him (i.e. the defendant); and (4) the name and address of the third party (O.1., r., 14(2) C.P.C.).

On receipt of the application supported by the affidavit containing the matters set out above, the court will make an order granting the defendant leave to present a third party notice if the court is satisfied that the defendant's claim against the third party is in respect of any contribution or indemnity, or any relief or remedy relating to or connected with the subject matter of the suit and substantially the same relief or remedy claimed by the plaintiff. Even when the court is satisfied on those matters, it will not grant the application unless it is further satisfied that having regard to all the circumstances of the case it is reasonable and proper to grant leave to the defendant to present a third party notice.

When the court is satisfied on these matters, it will then make the order on such terms and conditions as it may think just. Such order will contain directions as to the period within which such third party notice should be presented and any other matters the court may think just (O.1, r., 14(3) (4) C.P.C.).

Let us take one example. A sues B for damages to his house resulting from a motor accident between two vehicles driven by B and C. In such a case, B may apply for a third party notice against D, his insurance company, because B's claim against D is connected with the subject matter of the suit between B and A and relates substantially to the relief claimed by A from B.

In order that a third party may be legally joined, therefore, the subject-matter between the plaintiff and defendant and the original cause of action must be the same. As was stated by Leon, J., in the case of *Yafesi Walusimbi v A-G (1959)* E.A. 223, at page 225.

> In my opinion two things are clear in third party procedure: (1) in order that a third party may be legally joined the subject matter of the suit must be same and (2) the original cause of action must be the same.

Now, what is the meaning of the term "indemnity" and when does it arise? In *Yafesi's* case (supra) His Lordship said, at page 226:

> In case this matter may arise hereafter I express the view that the word "indemnity" in O.1.r. 14 does not include any right to damages arising from either a breach of contract or a tort.

The House of Lords was even more specific in the case of *Eastern Shipping Co. v. Quak Beng Kee* (1924) A.C. 177 in which their Lordships stated, at page 182:

A right to indemnity exists where the relation between the parties is that either in law or in equity there is an obligation upon the one party to indemnify the other.

In the case, Bowen, L.J. said:

> But it is quite certain to my mind that a right to damages ... is not a right to indemnity as such. It is the converse of such a right. A right to indemnity as such is given by the original bargain between the parties. The right to damages is given in consequence of the breach of the original contract between the parties. It is an incident which the law attaches to the breach of a contract and is not a provision of the contract (see also *Champion Motor Spares v. Barclays Bank & Another* (1964) E.A. 385).

What circumstances a court will consider reasonable to justify granting an application for third party notice will depend on the facts and circumstances of each case (see below). Once leave to file a third party notice has been granted to a defendant, the defendant will then present a third party notice which should contain the following matters:

1) The nature of the plaintiff's case against the defendant;
2) The nature of the defendant's case against the third party;
3) The relief claimed by the defendant vis-à-vis the third party;
4) The period within which the party should present his defence; and
5) The consequences of failure by the third party to present his defence within such period (O.1., r., 15 C.P.C.).

When the defendant has filed the third party notice, the court will then cause a copy of it to be served on the third party and other parties to the suit in accordance with rules of service of summonses (see infra). (O.1., r., 16 C.P.C.). It will then be up to the third party to file a written statement of defence either denying liability of the defendant to the plaintiff or his own liability, as the case may be. Such written statement of defence must be filed within 21 days or such longer period as the court may direct (O.1., r., 17 C.P.C.).

Thereafter the court will then fix a date for what is called giving directions. On the date fixed for giving directions, the court will consider whether there is a proper question to be tried as to liability of the third party in respect of the matter. If the court is satisfied that there is such a question it will order the question to be tried in such manner, at or after the trial of the suit, as it may direct. If, however, the court is not so satisfied, it will pass such decree or make such order as the nature of the case may require (O.1., r., 18 C.P.C.).

Let us take one example. In the example given above, D, the Insurance company, may file a written statement of defence denying liability to the defendant on the ground that the policy covering him or his car had expired, or that at no time did B insure with them. In such an event the court may well hold that there is a proper question to be tried, the question being whether B is covered by insurance policy with D against personal accidents and/or damage caused to his insured property, because if that question be answered in the affirmative, D will be liable to indemnify B in a suit by A against B. That question will then be tried either before or after the main suit has been disposed of.

Consequences of Failure by Third Party to File Written Statement of Defence or to Appear

If, after due notice, a third party fails to file a written statement of defence within the time allowed for doing so, or having presented his written statement of defence in due time, he defaults in appearing on the date fixed for giving directions, then, if judgment is entered against the defendant by default (see infra), the defendant may at any time after satisfaction of that judgement or, with leave of the court, before the satisfaction, apply and prove his claim ex-parte against the third party, and the court will enter such judgment against the third party as the nature of the suit may require. If, on the other hand, the defendant has judgment entered against him after trial of the suit against him, the court may at or after the trial of the suit, enter such judgment for the defendant against the third party as the nature of the suit and the claim made in the third party notice may require; but in that event, the execution of any decrees so passed must not be issued without the permission of the court, until after satisfaction by the defendant of the decree passed against him. If, on yet the other hand, judgment is entered against the defendant by consent in favour of the plaintiff, the court may, on application of the defendant and on ex-parte proof by him or his claim against the third party, enter such judgment in favour of the defendant against the third party as the nature of the suit may require. In such an event, however, execution of a decree passed against the third party must not be issued without the permission of the court, until after the satisfaction by the defendant of the decree passed against him (O.1, r., 19(1) C.P.C.).

Nevertheless, the court has discretion at any time to set aside or vary judgment entered against a third party under the foregoing provisions on such terms as it may think just (O.1., r., 1992) C.P.C.).

In all cases of third party procedure, the court has a discretion to, and often must, decide all questions of costs between a third party and other parties to the suit. It may therefore, make such orders as to costs as it may think just (O.1., r., 20 C.P.C.).

Law of Limitation to Third Parties

For purposes of the law of limitation, the rules apply, *mutatis mutandis*, in relation to third party notice and to proceedings begun thereunder as if the third party notice were a summons to a defendant; that is, as if the defendant were a plaintiff and the third party a defendant, and as if the date fixed for directions were a hearing date. Similarly, an ex-parte judgment entered under the third party procedure will be treated as if it had been entered against a defendant in a suit. (O.1., r., 21 C.P.C.).

It should also be noted that a third party who has been served with a third party notice has the same right to present a third party notice against some other party not a party to the suit as if he were a defendant in that suit (O.1., r., 22 C.P.C.). In other words, a third party may have his own third party in the same way that he is a third party *vis–a–vis* the defendant in the suit.

Third Party Claiming Indemnity or Contribution From Another Party

If in any suit a defendant claims against another defendant in the same suit, i.e. a co-defendant; (a) any contribution or indemnity; (b) any relief or remedy relating to or connected with any subject – matter of the suit and substantially the same as a relief or remedy claimed by the plaintiff against the defendant, such defendant may present a third party notice against the co-defendant in the same manner and subject to the same conditions as if the co-defendant were a third party and the same procedure will be adopted for the determination of the claims made against the co-defendant as if the co-defendant were a third party (O.1., r., 23 C.P.C.).

Practical Application of the Provisions

Having looked at the provisions of third party procedure in outline, let us now look at their practical application. To start with, we shall look at the question - when may directions be given? It has been held that ordinarily, directions must be given as soon as the third party has filed his written statement of defence and before the disposal of the suit. However, in the case of *Brooks v. Isher Kaur and Others* (1932) 14 K.L.R. 103, it was held that directions may be sought or given even though judgment has already been entered against the defendant.

The requirements that a court must first give directions before a defendant can have judgment against the third party is not one of form. In the case of *Patel v. The Universal Timber Co.* (1952) 19 E.A. 29), the appellant was second defendant in an action by the plaintiff on a promissory note made by the first defendant and endorsed by the second defendant. Judgment was entered against the first defendant and the decree was satisfied. Previous to that, the first defendant had applied for a notice of indemnity on the second defendant. The court granted leave to serve this notice of indemnity on the second defendant. The second defendant entered an appearance, but no defence was filed within the prescribed time but directions were not given. A Deputy Registrar entered judgment against 2nd defendant. In that case, the court quoted with approval the English case of *Tritton v. Bankart* (1967) L.T.R. 306, and stated, at page 31:

> … the provisions of Order 1, rule 18, must surely mean what they say and in my opinion the Supreme Court of Kenya should follow the practice approved in *Tritton v. Bankart*. As was noted by Kekewich, J., it is true that the application for direction is at the discretion of the defendant seeking indemnification but if he wants the issue between him and his co-defendant tried and determined he must first seek the direction of the court.

It has also been held that since third party notice is limited to the issue of indemnity, a counterclaim in the pleadings of a third party is improper and would have to be struck out (see *Total Oil Products Ltd. v. Malu and Others*, (1966) E.A. 164. But, as was appreciated in that case, there would appear to be no logical reason for drawing any difference between indemnity of contribution and set-off or counter claim. Set-off and counterclaim can conveniently be investigated in the same way as claims of indemnity or contribution.

Finally, let us turn to the principles upon which costs in third party notices are ordered. There is a dearth of authorities on this point, but the case of *Kenya Meat Commission v. Jackson and Hill and Others*, (1958) E.A. 719, sets out the principles lucidly. In that case, the court said that what should be taken into consideration are: (1) whether the third party was embroiled into the case against his will at the instance of the defendant; (2) whether any liability against third party has been established by the defendant; (3) whether the issues between the defendant and the third party have been tried or otherwise determined, and at what stage; and (4) whether the normal rule that costs should follow the event should be applied.

CHAPTER FOUR

THE FRAMING OF SUITS AND JOINDER
OF CAUSES OF ACTION

Where a party has or believes he has a cause of action against another and that he will need the Court to give him redress, it is his duty to file a suit in a Court of competent jurisdiction and before the expiry of the period of limitation.

Definition of "Cause of Action"

Now what is a "cause of action?" A lucid definition of what constitutes a cause of action is given in Mulla's *Code of Civil Procedure* in the following terms:

> Cause of action means every fact which, if traversed, it would be necessary for the plaintiff to prove in order to support his right to the judgment of the court. It is not limited to the actual infringement of the right to sue on but includes every piece of evidence which is necessary to be proved to entitle the plaintiff to a decree. Everything which if not proved would give the defendant a right to an immediate judgment must be part of the cause of action. It is, in other words, a bundle of essential facts which it is necessary for the plaintiff to prove before he can succeed in the suit (Page 144, 13th Edition) (see also *John Byombalirwa v. A.M.I.* (1983) T.L.R. 1.).

Let us look at an example. A sues B for the balance of the price on goods sold and delivered by A to B. The "bundle of essential facts" for A to allege are: (1) that the goods were sold by A; (2) that they were sold to B; (3) that A delivered the goods to B at an agreed or reasonable price; and (4) that B has since not paid the balance alleged to A. All those four points constitute A's cause of action against B. It is immaterial that B has a good defence. What must be looked at to find if there is a cause of action is what the plaintiff has alleged in the plaint itself, as we shall see later (see *Byombalirwa's* case (Supra).

It should be noted here that a plaint must disclose when the cause of action arose (see *Juma Kadala v. Laurent Mnkande,* (1983) T.L.R. 1203).

The Rule Against Splitting of Claims

As a general rule, a suit must include the whole claim which the plaintiff is entitled to make in respect of the particular cause or causes of action. However, a plaintiff may relinquish a portion of his claim so as to bring the suit within the jurisdiction of the court in which the suit is to be filed. But if he chooses to relinquish a portion of his claim, he can not thereafter sue for the portion so relinquished. Similarly, if he is entitled to more than one relief in respect of the same cause of action, he may sue for all such reliefs; but if he omits to claim any of such reliefs, he can not, except with the permission of the Court, afterwards sue for any relief so omitted (O.2, r.1 and 2 C.P.C.; *Merisho Sindiko's* case, supra).

If, for instance, A has a cause of action against B in which he is entitled to general damages and special damages, say, resulting from injuries he sustained in a motor accident, A is entitled to sue for both reliefs. If he opts to sue only for general damages, he may not, unless with the leave of the court, afterwards sue for special damages.

The purpose of those provisions, it is plain, is to ensure that, as far as is possible, all matters in dispute between the parties relating to the same cause or transaction are determined in one suit in order to avoid a multiplicity of suits, or, as stated in rule 1 of O.2, *"to prevent further litigation concerning them."*

Indian courts have held, however, that the rule against the splitting of claims applies only where the plaintiff intentionally omits or relinquishes his claim in respect of the same cause of action or where he was aware of the claim but accidentally or involuntarily omits to claim the same. It has no application where the plaintiff was unaware or was not informed of the claim or the facts which would give him a cause of action. In the case of *Venkata Chamdikamba v Kanala* (A.I.R.) 1936 Madras 699, the court said, at page 700:

> It is now well established that to constitute omission by the plaintiff within the meaning of O.2. r.2 Civil Procedure Code, it is necessary that the claim must have been known to him. It is only a claim or remedy known at the time of the institution of the suit of which a subsequent litigation will be barred.... A litigant cannot be required to include in his suit the claim of relief based upon facts of which he is ignorant.

It is submitted that that is also the law in East Africa. What, then, is the position where the plaintiff files simultaneous suits for the two claims? There appear to be no East African authorities on this point, and Indian courts are at variance. One view is that in such a case the plaintiff must be asked to choose as to which of the two suits he should prosecute and which one he should abandon. The second view is that the court should strike out the one that bears the later number in the register because this will be taken to have been filed "afterwards" and so deemed to have been relinquished. A third view is that the court should consolidate them.

It is submitted that of three views, the third would appear to be the better view in that it would not cause injustice to the plaintiff or to the defendant, as opposed, say, to the second view which in some cases would work to the detriment of the plaintiff.

The next important point to bear in mind is that the rule against the splitting of claims applies to claims in which the cause of action is the same, and in respect of the same parties. It does not apply where the causes of action are different. Where the causes of action are different, two distinct suits must be filed, and it is irrelevant that the causes of action are against the same defendant.

This would appear to be so even where the different causes of action arise out of the same transaction. In the case of *Mutungi v. Kabuchi*, (1966) E.A. 454, the plaintiff was involved in a motor accident, with the vehicle owned by the second defendant and driven by the first defendant, in which the plaintiff suffered personal injuries and his motor vehicle was damaged. Two separate actions were filed on the same day against the defendants, in the first a consent judgment was entered for the claim for personal injuries. The second suit for the damage to the vehicle was defended. The plaintiff could have recovered damage to the vehicle in the first action.

On the hearing of the second action a preliminary objection was taken on behalf of the defendants that the suit was contrary to law because it contravened the maxim *"Interest rei publicae suit finis litium"* It was held that the plaintiff had two distinct and separate causes of action, and so he was not barred from bringing two suits against the defendants.

Joinder of Causes of Action

We have seen that all persons may join in one suit as plaintiffs in whom any right to relief in respect of or arising out of the same act or transaction or series of acts or transactions where, if such persons brought separate suits, any common question of law or fact would arise. The same applies to defendants, *mutatis mutandis.*

Similarly, subject to certain exceptions, as we shall see presently, a plaintiff may unite in the same suit several causes of action against the same defendant or the same defendants jointly; and any plaintiffs having causes of action in which they are jointly interested against the same defendant or the same defendants jointly may unite such causes of action in the same suit (O.2. r. (1) C.P.C.).

But for there to be a proper joinder of causes of action, the rights to relief must arise out of the same transaction. They must not be so disconnected as to form the basis of separate suits. If the causes of action arose not from the same but similar transactions there would be misjoinder (see *Barclays Bank D.C.O. v. Patel and Others* (1959) E.A. 214). As was stated by Collins, M.R. in the English case of *Saccharone Corporation Ltd. v. Wild,* (1903) 1 Ch. 416.

> *Prima facie* a dozen causes of action cannot be combined in one writ; they must be so intimately connected as to justify their being included in one writ (see also *Yowana Kahere v. Lunyo Estates,* (1959) E.A. 319 – supra).

Let us take simple examples to illustrate the point. P a cyclist, is knocked down by a motor vehicle belonging to D and driven by E who is D's driver. As a result of that accident, P sustains personal injuries and his bicycle is damaged and E sustains injuries too. From that single transaction – the collision – two distinct causes of action have arisen: (a) personal injuries, and (b) damage to the bicycle. In such a case, P may unite those causes of action in one suit against D and E jointly. If on the other hand, P was to blame for the accident in which E received personal injuries and

D's vehicle was damaged, then D, whose cause action is damage to his vehicle, and E whose cause of action are his injuries, may sue P jointly and unite their causes of action in one suit because the causes of action arose out of the same transaction, and because D and E are jointly interested.

The provisions as to joinder of causes of action, it has been held, must be read subject to the provisions regarding the joinder of parties. In the case of *Pioneer Investment Trust Ltd v. Amarchand and Others.* (1964) E.A. 703, the Court of Appeal for East Africa quoted with approval *Mulla's Commentary* on the application of these rules, in which the learned author states:

> This rule, however, is to be read subject to the provisions of O.1, r.3, which relates to joinder of defendants. Hence, two or more defendants may be joined as parties in one suit, though there are two or more causes of action, provided the right to the relief claimed arises from the same act or transaction and there is a common question of law or fact; and this is so although they may not all be jointly interested in all the causes of action. But if the right to relief claimed does not arise from the same act or transaction, or if there be no common question of law or fact, the defendants cannot all be joined in one suit unless they are jointly interested in the causes of action as provided by this rule.

The rule regarding joinder of causes of action, it is apparent, is not mandatory. It is merely aimed at avoiding unnecessary multiplicity of suits. In such situations, the role of the court is to prevent vexation or oppression. It does not operate to exclude a second suit on a different cause of action (see *Mutungi's* case (supra); *Brusden v. Humphrey* (1884) 14 Q.B.D. 141 and *Shah v. Mohamed Haji Abdulla* (1962) E.A. 769). In *Brunsden's* case, Bowen, L.J., said at page 151:

> It may be said that would be convenient to force persons to sue for all their grievances at once and not to split their demands; but there is no positive law... against splitting demands which are essentially separable, although the High Court has inherent power to prevent vexation or oppression, and by staying proceedings or by apportioning the costs, would have always ample means of preventing any injustice arising out of the reckless use of legal procedure.

In *Mutungi's* case, the plaintiff was denied his costs in the second suit on the basis of this principle. What, then, constitutes "same transaction?" The meaning of these words was considered by Lord Wright, M.R., in the case of *Bendir v. Anson* (1936) 3 All E.R. 326, in which he said, at page 330:

> The phrase "transaction or series of transactions" is not a term of art, and I cannot find in the authorities any precise definition of the exact scope of those words. But it is quite clear that the tendency of the decisions has been to give a literal interpretation to the rule and to apply it in any cases where you have a claim of relief by more than one person in respect of what has been treated as the effect of the words "transaction or series of transactions, whether the relief claimed is jointly, severally, or in the alternative." The word "transaction," I think, necessarily means an act, the effect of which extends beyond the agent to other persons.

Effect of Joinder of Causes of Action on Jurisdiction

If causes of action are united, the pecuniary jurisdiction of the court as regards the suit must depend on the amount of value of the aggregate subject – matters at the date of the institution of the suit. (O.2, r.3 (2) C.P.C.). For example, if a plaintiff unites claims for personal injuries, for which the claims T.shs. 12,000/=, and those for damages to his motor vehicles, for which he claims T.shs. 10,000/= the aggregate amount (i.e. T.shs. 22,000/=) will determine the pecuniary jurisdiction of the court.

Exceptions to the Rule of Joinder of Causes of Action

There are cases in which the joinder of causes of action cannot be done without leave of the court – even if other requirements of such joinder should be fulfilled. For instance, no cause of action can be joined with a suit for the recovery of immovable property, without the leave of the court, except (a) claims for mesne profits or arrears of rent in respect of the property claimed or any part thereof; (b) claims for damages for breach of contract under which the property or any part of it is held; and (c) claims in which the relief sought is based on the same cause of action. Where, however, a party in a suit claims for foreclosure or redemption, this rule will not prevent him from asking to be put into possession of the mortgaged property. (O.2. r. 4 C. P.C.). The provisions of this rule, it should be noted, must be read together with those of rule 2 of Order 2. No leave to unite causes of action will be granted if other essential requirements to unite the causes of action are lacking.

The second exception to the rule as to joinder of causes of action is that no claim by or against an executor, administrator or heir, as such, must be joined with claims by or against him personally unless the latter claims are alleged to arise with reference to the estate in respect of which the plaintiff or defendant sues or is sued as such executor, administrator or heir, or such as he was entitled to, or liable for, jointly with the deceased person whom he represents. (O.2., r. C.P.C.).

When should such leave be sought or given? As a general rule, it should be sought before the suit is instituted. But in the case of *Buike Estate Coffee Ltd. v. Lutabi and Another* (1962) E.A. 328, the Uganda High Court following the decision in the case of *Lloyd v. Great Western Dairies Ltd.* (1970) 2 K.B. 727, held that such leave can be given in proper cases after the institution of the suit. In the Buike case, leave was given after the Court was of the opinion that the case was such that uniting the causes of action would avoid a multiplicity of suits, and that the claim, which was for possession, would hinge upon a matter regarding the validity of the action of defendants as directors.

Power of the Court as to Joinder of Causes of Action

Apart from the power of the court to grant leave for uniting certain causes of action, where it appears to the court that any causes of action otherwise properly joined in one suit can not be conveniently tried or disposed of together, the court may order separate trials or make such other orders as may be expedient (O.2, r. 6 C.P.C.).

It should be noted that this rule refers to cases in which there has been proper joinder of causes of action. It has no application where there has been misjoinder of such causes of action. In Mulla's *Code of Civil Procedure*, the application of this rule is summed up thus:

> This rule does not apply to cases of misjoinder, but to cases where several causes of action have been properly joined in one suit and the causes of action so joined cannot be conveniently tried together. In such a case the court cannot require the plaintiff to file separate plaints but can only order separate trials and for that purpose can require the plaintiff to amend his plaint in such a manner that the allegation against the different sets of defendants may be set out separately in order that the issues may be separately framed for the purpose of separate trials.

In the Indian case of *Rantij Kumar v. Urari Mohan* (A.I.R) (45) 1958 Calcutta, 710, the court stated, at page 713:

> The rule of mutifariousness is a rule of convenience and it is primarily in the discretion of the court to decide whether the plaintiff should be allowed to proceed with the different causes of action in the same suit upon consideration of all the facts and circumstances of the case.

In other words, it is no right of a party who has united his causes of action to elect to have separate trials of the different causes of action. That is for the court to decide.

Objections to and Consequences of Misjoinder of Causes of Action and of Parties

As with misjoinder of parties, all objections to misjoinder of causes of action must be taken at the earliest possible opportunity and in all cases where issues are settled or at or before such settlement, unless the ground of objections has arisen thereafter. If such objection is not so taken, it is deemed to have been waived (O.2. r. 7 C.P.C.).

Now, what are the consequences of misjoinder of causes of action and of parties. As we have seen, the test for proper joinder of causes of action and parties is that the causes of action must arise out of the same transaction or a series of the same transactions and that parties so joinded are jointly interested in the sense that there is a common question of law of fact to be decided in respect of all or some of the causes of action. If, say, the defendants are not jointly interested in the causes of action in any of them, the suit is said to be bad for multifariousness; and if neither the defendants nor the plaintiffs are jointly interested in the causes of action, the suit is said to be bad for double misjoinder.

So when a suit is bad for misjoinder of causes of action, the court should return the plaint with an order that it should be amended. If, however, there has been misjoinder of causes of action, as well as of plaintiffs, such misjoinder cannot be cured by the provisions of rule 9 of Order 1 of the Civil Procedure Code. It was so held in *Yowana Kahere's* case (supra) where Bennett, J., said, *inter alia*:

> The matter is not curable under O.1, r. 9 because that rule applies only to misjoinder or non-joinder of parties. I have been asked to strike out the

plaint under O.6, r. 17 but I am not disposed to adopt that course although agreeing with the defendant's counsel that the plaint in its present form is embarrassing. It is also, in my view, an abuse of the process of the court.

He then gave leave to the plaintiff to withdraw the suit and to institute a fresh suit or suits, gave costs to the defendants and stayed the suit. This decision was in line with the decision in *Barclays Bank D.C.O. v. C.B. Patel and Others (Supra)*.

Failure to Disclose Cause of Action

Where a plaint does not disclose a cause of action, the result should not be to dismiss the suit but to either allow the plaintiff to amend it so that it discloses a cause or causes of action or to strike out the plaint (See *J.B. Shirima and Others v. Humphrey Meena t/a Comfort Bus Services* (1992) T.L.R. 290).

CHAPTER FIVE

RECOGNIZED AGENTS AND ADVOCATES

Except where otherwise expressly provided by any law to the contrary, any appearance, application, or act in or to any court required to be done by a party in such court, may be made or done by the party in person or by his recognized agent, or by an advocate duly appointed by such party to act or appear on his behalf. But a court has discretion to direct that such appearance must be made by the party in person (O.3, r. 1 C.P.C.).

So, if a party seeks to file a suit in court against another, such intending plaintiff may file the suit in person, or may do so through his recognized agent or an advocate whom he has duly instructed. Conversely, a defendant who has been summoned to appear in answer to a summons in a suit or application may do so in person or through his recognized agent or an advocate whom he has duly instructed, unless the court should otherwise direct.

Recognized Agents of Parties

Who are "recognized agents of parties?" There are two classes of recognized agents; (1) those persons holding powers of attorney, authorizing them to make and do such appearance, applications or acts on behalf of the parties who have given them the powers of attorney; and (2) those persons carrying on trade or business for and in the names of parties not resident within which limits the appearance, application or act is made or done, in matters connected with such trade or business only, where no other agent is authorized to make and do such applications, appearances or acts (O.3, r. 2 C.P.C.).

Indian courts have held that the phrase "appearance, application or act" does not include the right to plead. So a recognized agent has no right of audience and cannot plead, nor can a person holding a power of attorney. In the case of *In re Eastern Tavay Minerals Corporation* (A.I.R.) 1934 Calcutta 563, the right of audience was claimed by a Mr. Harcourt, one of the directors of the company who held a power-of attorney which authorized him "to appear for and on behalf of the company in the proceeding etc." It was held that he had no right of audience. The learned judge there stated:

> To plead is not to make or do an appearance, or an application or an act and is not in my judgment within the order and rules cited (O.3, r. 1 and 2 Indian Civil Procedure Code). I am glad to find that in this matter I am supported by so high an authority as the late Sir Lawrence Jenkins, C.J., who held that a recognized agent as such has no right of audience. I hold that Mr. Harcourt has no right of audience and I can not hear him on this application (see also *J. Petro v. C. Raphael*, (1983) T.L.R. 346).

With regard to the second category of recognized agents mentioned above, it should be noted that the provisions only apply where the matter in question is in connection with the trade or business of the agent's principal. If, for example, the matter in question be one of a personal nature which has no rational connection with the trade or business of the principal, then such agent is not "recognized agent" within the meaning of the rule.

The power of a court to direct that a party must appear in person is discretionary, and it being a judicial discretion, it has to be exercised judicially, and so must not be made without very good reason. In the case of *Pandur v. Hira*, (A.I.R.) 1936 Nagpur 85, the court held that a party is not bound to attend the court in person when he has engaged a pleader or has a recognized agent.

Service of Processes on Recognized Agents

In the same way that an appearance, application or act made or done by a recognized agent is deemed to be an appearance, application or act by the party himself, court processes served on agents are, unless otherwise directed by the court, as effective as if they have been served on the party in person (O.3, r. 3 C.P.C.).

Apart from such recognized agents, any person who resides within the jurisdiction of the court may be appointed an agent to accept service of process. Such appointment may be special or general, but it must be by an instrument in writing signed by the principal and such instrument or, if the appointment is general, a certified copy of it, must be filed in court (O.3, r. 6 C.P.C.).

Appearance by, and Service of Process on, Advocates

The appearance of a party may be made by an advocate who has been duly appointed by such party to make an appearance on the party's behalf. An advocate is a special agent in that in addition to the fact that he can, if so appointed, enter an appearance, make an application or do an act on behalf of a party, he is authorized by law to plead and so has the right of audience in all courts unless the law should otherwise provide. In Tanzania, an advocate has the right of audience in all courts except in primary courts. Section 33(1) of the Magistrate's Court Act, 1984 expressly bars an advocate from appearing or acting for any party in a primary court.

Even in courts where advocates are authorized to appear and plead for a party, the court may require an advocate claiming to act on behalf of any party who has not appeared in person or by his recognized agent to produce, within such time as is reasonable, a written authority signed by such party or his recognized agent authorizing such advocate to act on behalf of such party (O.3, r. 4 C.P.C.). This is a discretion which courts very rarely exercise. It is recognized that advocates usually adhere to strict professional ethics as required of them by their profession, and so courts often assume that advocates who appear before them have in fact been duly appointed by the party they claim to represent and that they have been fully instructed to appear or act in the particular matter on behalf of such party.

As we shall see later in this book, the provisions of O.3, r.3 must be read together with O.9, r.6 (1) (a) (ii) B and O.17, r.2 and O.5, r. 5 (b) of the C.P.C. It was so held in the case of *William Andrea Shangarai v. Farm Vehicle Ltd.,* 1969 H.C.D. n.16. In that case the plaintiff sued the defendant for a sum of money for goods sold and delivered and work done. On the date set for hearing, the defendant was personally absent but was represented by his advocate who stated that he had been fully instructed and was prepared to proceed with the case. The trial court gave judgment for the plaintiff holding that O.17 r. 2 and O.9, r. 6 (i) (a) (ii) (b) of the Code required appearance by the defendant personally and not merely by his advocate. On appeal, the High Court allowed the appeal and stated:

> The provisions of O.17, r. 2 and O.9, r. 6(I) (a) (ii), which deal with the procedure to be followed when a defendant fails to appear, must be read together with the provisions of 0.3 and 0.5....

In that case, the court cited with approval the case of *The Land Officer v. Abdurasul Jivraj*, I.T.I.R (R) 410, in which it was held that when a recognized agent of one of the parties to a suit is present in court when the suit is called for hearing, the question is whether he intended to appear and did in fact appear for his principal by virtue of Order 3 Rules 1 and 2 of the Code.

With regard to service of process, any process served on an advocate of any party or left at the office or ordinary residence of such advocate, and whether the same is for the personal appearance of the party or not, is presumed to be duly communicated and made known to the party whom the advocate represents, and, unless the court otherwise directs, is as effectual for all purposes as if it had been given or served on the party in person (O.3 r. 5 C.P.C.). It has in fact been held that where an advocate has duly withdrawn from acting for a defendant, and such defendant has not furnished any other address of service of process, then service of hearing notice at the address of the advocate is effectual (See *Elkan v. Patel and Another*, (1960) E.A. 340).

In the case of an ordinary agent, the authority given to the agent by the principal lapses at the death of the principal (see *Imerimaleva v. Dima Nhorongo* (1991) T.L.R. 1).

CHAPTER SIX

GENERAL RULES OF PLEADING

In the preceding chapters, we have dealt with the jurisdiction of courts and *res judicata*, the joinder of parties and of causes of action, the frame of suits and agents of parties. In this and the following chapters, we shall look deeper into that important province of civil procedure law, namely, the rules that generally govern pleadings, and the consequences of failure to observe those rules. In order to avoid possible confusion, let us know the definitions of terms which we are going to use in this and the following chapters.

Definitions

Foremost among those terms is the term "plaint." A plaint may be defined as a written statement drawn by a plaintiff which contains in a concise form all the material facts on which the plaintiff relies for the relief which he seeks in a suit. As we shall see later, a plaint contains the names and addresses of the parties, the facts constituting the cause of action, the facts giving the court jurisdiction to take cognizance of the suit and the relief claimed.

A "Statement of defence," or "written statement of defence," as it is usually called, is a written statement, drawn by a defendant to a suit, which contains in a concise form the material facts on which he relies for his defence to the claim.

A "pleading" has been defined as meaning a plaint or a written statement of defence, including a written statement of defence filed by a third party, and such other subsequent pleadings as may be presented in accordance with rule 13 of Order 8 of the Civil Procedure Code (O.6, r. 1 C.P.C.). To put it broadly and in simple terms, a plaintiff's pleading is his plaint, and a defendant's pleading is his written statement of defence. All those statements are called "pleadings."

Function and General Rules of Pleading

It is a general rule of pleading, and this is the fundamental rule, that every pleading must contain, and contain only, a statement in a concise form of the material facts on which the party pleading relies for his claim or defence, as the case may be, but the evidence by which they are to be proved must not be pleaded. When necessary, the pleading must be divided into paragraphs numbered consecutively (O.6, r. 3 C.P.C.).

What this means, then, is that generally speaking, only (but all) material facts must be pleaded, and in a concise form. Immaterial facts, matters of law, or the evidence by which the material facts are to be proved must not be pleaded.

What facts constitute "material facts" and the degree of conciseness of a pleading will, of course, depend on the nature and complexity of a given case. Pleadings must state material facts and in a concise form, but that is far from suggesting that materiality and conciseness should be achieved at the expense of lucidity or omission of other material facts.

This fundamental rule of pleading is designed to ensure that as far as possible parties are put on their guard and know what exactly they have to meet at the trial, and also to avoid unnecessary prolixity of pleading and waste of time. In the English case of *Thorp v. Holdsworth* (1876) 3 Ch. D. 637, Jessel, M.R., stated the rationale of this rule in the following terms, at page 639:

> The whole object of pleadings is to bring the parties to an issue, and the meaning of the rules of this Order is to prevent the issue being enlarged, which would prevent either party from knowing, when the cause came on for trial, what the real point to be discussed and decided was. In fact, the whole meaning of the system is to narrow the parties to definite issues, and thereby to diminish expense and delay, especially as regards the amount of testimony required on their side at the hearing.

It cannot, therefore, be over-emphasized that a pleading must contain all the material facts and all the reliefs claimed or facts denied. Once a pleading has been presented to the court, the party pleading it will not, except by way of amendment, and with leave of the court, he able to raise any new ground of claim or raise any allegation of fact which is inconsistent with his previous pleadings. (O. 6, r. 7 C.P.C.). In other words, a party is bound by his pleadings and his case is confirmed to the issues raised in those pleadings unless and until they have been amended.

It is on this ground that it has been held that as a general rule, relief which is not founded on the pleadings will not be given because relief must be given within the limits of the pleadings, the allegations made at the hearing and the issues framed. In the case of *Gandy v. Caspar Air Charters Ltd.* (23 E.A.C.A.) 139 Sinclair, V-P, said, at page 140:

> "The object of pleadings is, of course, to secure that both parties shall know what are the points in issue between them, so that each may have full information of the case he has to meet and prepare his evidence to support his own case or to meet that of his opponent. As a rule relief not founded on the pleadings will not be given."

His Lordship then quoted with approval a dictum of Scrutton, L.J., in the case of *Blay v. Pollard and Morris*, (1930) I.K.B. 682 which states:

> "Cases must be decided on the issues on the record; and if it is desired to raise other issues they must be placed the record by amendment. In the present case the issue on which the Judge decided was raised by himself without amending the pleadings, and in my opinion he was not entitled to take such a course."

It has, however, been held that an incorrect description of a particular fact should not be fatal where the particulars of the claim have been given with reasonable precision. In the case of *Pushpa Patel v. The Fleet Transport co. Ltd.*, (1960) E.A. 1025, Gould, J. said, at page 1034:

> "It is of course a salutary and necessary rule that a party is bound by his pleading. If, however, particulars are given in undue detail and what is proved varies from them in ways which are immaterial, it remains the duty of the court to see that justice is done and leave to amend will be given at any state. If, on the other hand, the particulars given have misled the defendant or led to his shaping his case in a certain way that is a very different matter."

Similarly, relief may be granted where allegations at the hearing are not inconsistent with the pleadings and are within the issues framed. It was so held in *Stanley & Sons Ltd. v. Saleh Alibhai* (1963) E.A. 594. In that case, the court quoted with approval the statement of Lord Tomlin in the case of *Sagarmull Nathany v. John Galstaun* (193) A.I.R. P.C. 205, in which in a suit based on an agreement, a subsequent variation of the agreement was not pleaded but was put in issue. Lord Tomlin there said:

> Their Lordships are satisfied that notwithstanding the form of the plaint the suit was fought by the parties deliberately upon issues substantially as framed by the trial judge and ought upon that footing to be determined.

In the Indian case of *Haji Khan v. Baldeo Das* (1901), 24 All, 90, which was also quoted in the *Stanley and Sons* case, Chamier, J., said:

> I am most unwilling to bind a plaintiff too closely to his plaint in a case of this kind, and I agree with the opinion expressed by Aikman, J., that a suit like the one before us should not be dismissed merely because the plaintiff fails to prove that he leased the premises to the defendant, and that if a court sees that the plaintiff is entitled to the relief which he claims, although on grounds other than those put forward in his plaint, the court should give that relief, if the defendant would not thereby be taken by suprises. (see also *Odd v. Mubia*, (1970) E.A. 476.).

On the rule that facts and not law should be pleaded, the Tanzania High Court held, in the case of *Narsinh Valji v. Shukla* (L.R.S. No. 1 of 1967, p.9), that it is not necessary to plead compliance with statutory procedural requirements as there is no duty on a plaintiff to anticipate a defence. It has, however, been held by the Kenya Supreme Court that where a plaintiff's cause of action, or his title to sue depends upon a statute, he must plead all facts necessary to bring him within that statute. That was in the case of *New Era Stores v. Ocean Trading Co.* (1950 24 91) K.L.R., 53). The facts in that case were that the defendant company changed hands between the time of the contract of sale of goods on which the suit was based, and the date of suit, and further changed hands between then and the trial. The law that gave the plaintiffs the title to sue was the Fraudulent Transfer of Business Ordinance (Kenya) which, however, was not pleaded. On appeal to the Supreme Court, The Court said, at page 54:

It is elementary law that a plaint must contain a statement in concise form of the material facts on which the plaintiff relies for his claim (0.6,v.1) otherwise the object of pleadings which is (to) secure that the parties shall know what are the real points in issue between them will be defeated. On the application of that principle it has been held that if a plaintiff's cause of action, or his title to sue, depends on a statute he must plead all facts necessary to bring him within that statute (c.f. *Byombalirwa's* case – supra).

Cases in Which Specific Facts Must be Pleaded

Where Party Relies on Fraud, Misrepresentation, Influence, etc.

There are cases in which the Civil Procedure Code specifically provides what particular facts must be pleaded. For instance, in all cases in which the party pleading relies on any misrepresentation, fraud, breach of trust, wilful default, or undue influence, such particulars – including dates and items if necessary – must be pleaded (O.6, r. 4 C.P.C.).

On the basis of these provisions, it has been held that in a claim based on trade usage, the precise nature of the usage must be pleaded *(Harilal & Co. v. The Standard Bank Ltd.* (1967) E.A. 512); and in a case based on contract, it has been held that consideration, unless implied by law, is a fact which must be pleaded *(Patel v. Central African Commercial Agency)* (1959) E.A. 903). Similarly, in a suit for damages for defamation of character, it is always necessary to set out the exact words alleged to be defamatory.

Besides, it is open to the court, usually on the application of the opposite party, to order that the party must furnish further and better particulars of the statement of the claim or defence or of any particulars of any matter stated in his pleading (O.6, r. 5 C.P.C.). When such an order has been given, the party to whom the order refers must furnish such further and better statement or particulars. For example, if in a suit for damages resulting from a road accident between two motor vehicles, the plaintiff omits to state in his plaint the particular road along which the accident occurred, he may be ordered to furnish further and better particulars of the *locus in quo*.

Where Party Relies on Condition Precedent, Performance, etc.

Where a party relies on any condition precedent, the performance or occurrence of which is intended to be contested, the party pleading such performance or occurrence must distinctly specify it in his pleading. But subject to that, an averment of the performance or occurrence of all conditions precedent necessary for the case of the plaintiff or defendant will be implied in his pleading (O.6, r. 6 C.P.C.).

In a Suit Based on a Contract

Where a contract is alleged in a pleading, an opposite party's bare denial of it will be taken to mean a denial in fact of the express contract alleged or the matters of fact from which it may be implied; it will not be taken to mean a denial as to the legality or sufficiency in law of such contract (O.6, r. 8 C.P.C.). In other words, where a contract is alleged in a pleading and the opposite party challenges, for instance, its legality or sufficiency in law, such party must specifically plead such illegality or insufficiency and not merely deny the existence of the contract.

Where Suit is Based on Contents of a Document

In a claim where the contents of a document are material, it is not, in general, necessary to set out the whole or part of such contents. It is sufficient to state the effect of it as briefly as possible, unless the precise words of the document or any part thereof are material (O.6, r. 9 C.P.C.). Exceptions to this rule include suits for defamation of character where the exact words used in the document alleged to be defamatory must be specifically stated.

Malice, Fraudulent Intention and Other Conditions of Mind

If it is material in a pleading to allege malice, fraudulent intention, knowledge or other condition of the mind of any person, it is sufficient to allege it as a fact without setting out the circumstance from which it is to be inferred (O.6, r. 10 C.P.C.).

In the case of *Panjwani v. A.P. Hirji and Company* (1971) H.C.D. n. 177, the plaintiff claimed from the defendant company damages for fraudulent misrepresentation in a contract. The plaintiff alleged that he was induced to enter into agreement by false and fraudulent representations of the defendant. It was submitted for the defendant company that the pleadings were defective in that there was no averment that the plaintiff was induced to enter into the contract by misrepresentation. It was held that as it had been alleged that most of the terms of the contract were fraudulently misrepresented, the omission to plead expressly that he was so induced was not fatal to the claim as pleaded, for the fact that the plaintiff was induced to enter into the contract by fraudulent misrepresentation arose by necessary implication from the pleadings.

In the case of *Hasham Suleman Ltd and Another v. N.R. Sayani* (1963) E.A. 6093, in a suit for damages for defamation, the plaintiff pleaded that the slanderous words were published "falsely and maliciously," but malice was not expressly pleaded. It was held that it was not necessary for the plaintiff to plead express malice in their reply because their allegation of malice in the plaint was sufficient to entitle them to prove it.

Where Notice of Matter of Fact is Material

When it is material to allege notice to any person of a fact, matter or thing, it is sufficient merely to allege such notice as a fact, unless the form or the exact terms of such notice, or the circumstances from which such notice is to be inferred, are material.

The application of these provisions was considered in the case of *African Overseas Trading Co. v. Bhagwanji* (1960) E.A. 417. In that case the plaintiff sued in a district court on a dishonored promissory note. The plaint contained no averment whether notice of dishonour had been given. The magistrate held that the plaint was defective and so rejected it. On appeal, the High Court said at page 419:

> Order 6, r. 11 requires that when notice to any person of any fact, etc., is material, it shall be sufficient to allege such notice as a fact with certain exceptions, which are not relevant in the instant case. It would not seem to require a negative averment in such a case, i.e. when notice of a fact is not necessary. It is also unnecessary to plead matters of which the court takes judicial notice – such matters include the law of the territory including Ordinances enacted in the territory. It would seem, therefore, that if notice of dishonour in the case of a promissory note is not necessary under the relevant law in Tanganyika namely, the Bills of Exchange Ordinance, Cap 215, the court can take judicial notice of that fact without it being averred in a plaint.

If, however, it is material to allege such notice, and it is not alleged, the plaint, it has been held, is defective, and no amendment can cure it (see *Hasmani v. The National Bank of India*, 4 E.A.C.A. 55).

Implied Contract of Relation from a Series of Letters or Conversations

In a case of contract, whenever any contract or relation between any persons is to be implied from a series of letters or conversations or otherwise from a number of circumstances, it is sufficient to allege such contract or relation as fact and to refer generally to such letters, conversations or circumstances without setting them out in detail. If the person pleading wishes to rely, in the alternative, upon more contracts or relation than one as to be implied from such circumstances, he is at liberty to state the same in the alternative (O.6, r. 12 C.P.C.). The reason for this rule is obvious. It is intended to avoid unnecessary prolixity in pleadings.

Matters of Fact Which the Law Presumes in a Party's Favour

In addition to the foregoing, in any pleading no party need plead any matter of fact which the law presumes in his favour or as to which the burden of proof lies upon the other side, unless such fact has specifically been denied; say, consideration for a bill of exchange where the plaintiff sues only on the bill, and not for the consideration as substantive ground of claim (O.6 r. 13 C.P.C.). So, if A sues B for the value of a dishonoured cheque drawn by B in favour of A for T.shs. 500/=, the law will presume that the cheque was drawn for a consideration, and so A need not plead consideration.

Pleadings to be Signed and Verified

When the pleading has been drawn, the party pleading or his advocate must sign such pleading. If, however, a party pleading is, by reason of absence or for other good cause, unable to sign the pleading, it may be signed by any person duly authorized by him to sign the same or to sue or defend on his behalf (O.6, r. 14 C.P.C.). Besides, unless otherwise provided by any law, every pleading must be verified at the foot and signed and dated by the party or parties pleading, or by some person proved to the satisfaction of the court to be acquainted with the facts of the case. The person verifying must specify the reference to the numbered paragraphs of the pleadings what he verifies of his own knowledge and what he verifies upon information received and believed to be true. The place at which the verification was made must be stated (O.6, r. 15 C.P.C.). (Also see *Nimrod Mkono v State Travel Services*, (1992) T.LR. 24; and *Aloys Lyenga v. I.G.P.*, (1997) T.L.R. 101). A verification is normally stated thus:

I certify that the contents in paragraphs 1,2,3,5 and 7 are true to the best of my personal knowledge, and the contents in paragraphs 4 and 6 are true to the best of my information and belief.

Now, what is the consequence of failure by a party to sign and/or verify his pleading? Indian courts have held that the requirements are mere matters of procedure, and that if, say, a plaintiff or his authorized agent omits to sign or verify the pleading, and the defect is discovered before judgement, the plaintiff may be ordered to amend the plaint by signing it; so too if the defect is discovered on appeal. In other words, the omission to sign or verify a plaint is not a defect that would nullify a pleading or affect the jurisdiction of the court (see *Ma Ngwe v. Ma Hme* (AIR) 1923 Rangoon 206).

There is reason to believe that that is also the law in East Africa. In the case of *Transgem Trust v. Tanzania Zoisite Corp Ltd.* (1968) H.C.D. n. 501, the plaintiffs had not signed the plaint, but they undertook to sign it later. Plat, J., held that signing of a plaint was a matter of procedure and that the defect does not affect the merits of the case or the jurisdiction of the court.

Power of the Court to Strike Out, Order Amendment or Reject Pleadings

Striking Out Pleadings

A court may, at any stage of the proceedings, order that any matter in any pleading which may be unnecessary or scandalous or which may tend to prejudice, embarrass or delay the fair trial of the suit be amended or struck out (O.6, r. 16 C.P.C.).

There is usually no difficulty in deciding what matter is unnecessary. The difficulty lies in deciding what matter is scandalous, embarrassing or prejudicial to a fair trial of the suit. A matter is said to be scandalous if it is indecent or needlessly offensive, or is an allegation made for the malignant purpose of abusing or prejudicing the opposite party (see *Re. R. (deceased)* (1950) 2 ALL E.R. 117, 119). It is also said to be embarrassing if it is so drawn that it is not clear what case the opposite party has to meet. The rationale of the rule against pleading scandalous matters is, of course, that as the courts have a duty to discharge to the public and parties to suits, they must take care that court records are kept free from irrelevant and scandalous matters (see *Christie v. Christies* (1873) L.R. 8 Ch. 499). In *Story's "Equity Pleadings,"* the rationale is expressed thus:

> (Courts' records must not be made) the means of perpetuating libelous and malignant slanders; and the court in aid of public morals is bound to interfere to suppress such indecencies, which may stain the reputation and wound the feelings of the parties and relatives and friends (10th Edition, Sec. 270).

If, however, the matter complained of as being scandalous is relevant to the pleadings, it will not be struck out for, in the words of Cotton, L.J. in *Fisher v. Owen* (1878) 8 Ch. D. at page 653, "nothing can be scandalous which is relevant." In *Christie v. Christie* (supra) it was held that allegation of dishonesty and outrageous conduct are not scandalous if they are relevant.

And what matter is embarrassing? Lord Pickford, L.J. in *Mayor etc., of London, v. Horner* (1914) 111 L.T. said, at page 514:

> I take 'embarrassing' to mean that the allegations are so irrelevant that to allow them to stand would involve useless expense, and would also prejudice the trial of the action by involving the parties in a dispute that is wholly apart from the issues.

English courts have further held that the mere fact that an allegation in a pleading is unnecessary is no ground for striking it out, nor is a pleading embarrassing merely because it contains allegations which are inconsistent or stated in the alternative (see *Re Morgan* (1887) 35 Ch. D. 492).

The power of the court under this rule, it has been held, must be exercised with great caution. It is a discretionary power and should be exercised only in plain and obvious cases (see *Hubbuck & Sons v. Wilkinson* (1899) Q.B. 86, (1). As stated in *Odgers on Pleadings*, at page 151 of the 19th Edition:

> Unless the pleading as it stands is really and seriously embarrassing, it is often better policy not to attack it; you only strengthen your opponent's position by compelling him to reform and thus to improve his pleading,

for parties are entitled to plead in the manner they think best. If, on the other hand, the allegations are both unnecessary for the purpose of the reliefs claimed and scandalous, the pleading may be struck out for being scandalous and embarrassing (see *Booking v. Maudslay* (1886) 55 L.T., 345; and *Murray v. Epsom Local Board* (1897) I Ch. 35).)

But, as was stated in *Lakhani v. Bhojani* (17 E.A.C.A. 7), once a court has exercised its discretion and struck out a matter in a pleading, an appellate court will entertain an appeal against the exercise of such discretion only where it is plain that the discretion was wrongly exercised. The exercise of the discretion must be shown to be:

> Based on some embarrassment or other injustice of substance caused by a wrong exercise of that discretion by the Court below. This court and the court below are courts of justice and not mere academics of pleading.

The court may exercise this discretion on its own motion or on application made by chamber summons. And when should such an application be made? The answer in the rule is: "at any stage of the proceedings." But it would appear to be now settled that an application under this rule must be made promptly. In the case of *Manji and Another v. Singh* (1962) E.A. 557, the respondent sued the appellants for the balance alleged to be due under a building contract. The appellants filed a pleading which they called "set-off and defence" to which no objection was taken at the time. There were several adjournments of the hearing at one of which the trial judge intimated to counsel for the appellants that the "set-off and defence" was defective.

Subsequently the advocate for the appellants sent to the advocate for the respondent a document giving further and better particulars of the defects in the work done by the respondent. Some 19 months after the filing of the "set – off and defence," the hearing began, and the advocate for the respondent submitted that the defence was not a defence in law, that the set-off implied an admission of the plaintiff's claim and that the purported particulars could not be looked at. He opposed any application for amendment, applied for the defence to be struck out and asked for judgment. The trial judge refused to treat the purported particulars as part of the pleadings, held that the appellants' pleadings were clearly embarrassing and bad, refused to allow an amendment thereof on the ground of delay and entered judgment for the respondent. On appeal, Forbes, V-P., stated, at page 562:

It is not proper for a party, who is entitled to further information from the other side, to sit by and do nothing till the trial and then seek to have a pleading struck out. Even if he is entitled to have a pleading struck out, the application should always be made promptly.

His Lordship added:

Technically, I do not think these particulars could be said to form part of the pleadings unless the respondent had elected to treat them as such; which he did not. But I do not think that the respondent is entitled, not merely to refrain from asking for further and better particulars himself, but, when particulars are supplied without request, to shut his eyes to them and then come into court asking for the appellant's pleadings to be struck out. The respondent had failed to take the steps which he ought to have taken if he found himself embarrassed, and I think, with respect, that in the circumstances the learned judge acted on a wrong principle in striking out the defence (or such part of it as he did strike out) for lack of particulars at that stage in the proceedings.

It would, therefore, seem to follow that the better practice is to make an application before the pleadings have been concluded or before the trial starts. At any rate, the application must be made promptly.

It has also been held that this rule does not relate to the striking out of any pleadings as a whole. In the case of *Hagod Jack Simonian v. Johar and Others* (1962) E.A. 336, the Court considered the application of rule 17 of Order 6 of the Kenya Civil Procedure Act, which is identical with rule 16 of Tanzania Civil Procedure Code. Crawshaw, J.A., there said, at page 34:

Rule 17 does not, as I see it, relate to the striking out of any pleadings as a whole, but only to such matter in the pleadings as may be "unnecessary or scandalous or which may tend to prejudice, embarrass or delay the fair trial of the action."

In the case of *Tildesley v. Harper* (1878) C.D. the court said, at page 396:

My practice has always been to give leave to amend unless I have been satisfied that the party applying was acting mala fide, or that, by his blunder, he had done some injury to his opponent which could not be compensated for by costs or otherwise. (See also *Eastern Bakery v. Castelino* (1958) E.A. 461,

462, *Manji v. Singh* (1962) E.A. 55); *Shambwe v. Attorney – General,* (1996) TLR. 334; and *Agrovety v. Kleb*, (1995) T.L.R. 168.).

In the case of *Motohov v. Auto Garage Ltd, and Others* (1971) H.C.D. n. 81, Biron, J., summed up the principle in the following terms, at page 54:

> Very few cases are altogether alike, and each must be decided on its own merits. The overriding principle is laid down in the very rule itself, that 'The court may at any stage of the proceedings allow either party to alter or amend his pleadings in such manner and on such terms as may be just, and all such amendments shall be made as may be necessary for the purpose of determining the real question in controversy between the parties.' The making of amendments is not really a matter of power of a court but its duty, so that substantial justice may be done.

The test, then, is this: will the proposed amendments help to raise the substantial questions in controversy between the parties, and be made without causing injustice to the other side which can not be compensated for by way of costs or otherwise?

Since the rule imposes a duty on the court, as Biron, J., pointed out in *the Motohov case (supra)*, it has been held that the court can order amendments on its own motion. In the case of *General Manager, E.A.R. & H.A. v. Therstein* (1968) E.A. 354, Harris, J., said, at page 358:

> ... there is nothing in the rules which purports to deprive the court of its essential and inherent jurisdiction to allow or direct of its own motion at the hearing of the action, and upon terms if necessary, all such amendments to the pleadings as may be or become requisite to secure the ends of justice, and the second part of 0.6, r. 18 makes it incumbent on the court without necessarily awaiting an application in that behalf by either party, to ensure that the pleadings are in a suitable form to enable the 'real questions in controversy' between the parties to be determined.

But if an application seeks to substitute one distinct cause of action for another or change the character of the suit, the amendment may be refused. In the case of *Eastern Bakery v. Castelino* (supra), Crawshaw, J.A. said, at page 462:

> It will be sufficient, for purposes of the present case, to say that amendments

to pleadings sought before the hearing should be freely allowed, if they can be made without injustice to the other side, and that there is no injustice if the other side can be compensated by costs....The court will not refuse to allow an amendment simply because it introduces a new case... but there is not power to enable one distinct cause of action to be substituted for another, nor to change, by means of amendment, the subject – matter of the suit.... The court will refuse leave to amend where the amendment would change the action into one of a substantially different character... (see also *Patel v. Joshi*, 19 E.A.C.A. 42; and *Shivji v. Pellegrini*, (1972) H.C.D. n. 76).

From the authorities, it would appear that the court may refuse leave to amend where the party applying is acting *mala fide*, or where the intended amendment is not necessary for determining the real questions in controversy between the parties, or if it would take away from the other party a legal right which has since accrued to him, say, by lapse of time; or where the party applying has been guilty of unconscionable and substantial delay in making the application.

In *Thiersteins's* case (supra), however, Harris, J., said, at page 359:

The plaintiff's final ground of objection is that, if any amendments were to be made, the plaintiff could not be adequately compensated by an order for costs in his favour. This may well be true, but, when the circumstances of a case require an amendment of the pleadings, the fact that the order directing the amendment will not, in dealing with costs, have the effect of depriving the party whose pleading is to be amended of the entire fruits of the amendment is not necessarily in itself a sufficient reason for declining to direct the amendment. By analogy, an application by a party for leave to amend which is proper to be allowed will not be refused merely because it would not be possible by an order as to costs to deprive the applicant of the fruits of the amendment, else no purpose would be served by a party obtaining leave to amend.

It has also been held that leave to amend may be granted on appeal in certain circumstances. In the case of *Jupiter General Insurance Co. v. Rajabali Hasham & Sons* (1960) E.A. 592, it was held that an amendment may be allowed on appeal even if the omission was due to inadvertence however regrettable, subject to a suitable order as to costs if all the necessary material was available before the appellate court. In the case of *Cheleta Coffee Plantation Ltd v. Eric Mehlesn* (1966) E.A. 203, it was held that leave to amend may be granted on appeal if the issue sought to be raised is not fundamental, and if the material for a decision is before such court and it is shown that the matter came to be known by the party after the judgment was pronounced; but if the amendment would raise a fundamental issue and no question of inadvertence is involved, and further pleadings and evidence could be required, an application for leave to amend pleadings on appeal will be refused. The court added, however, that an application for amendment should be made at the earliest possible moment. In *Jani Properties Ltd. v. Dar es Salaam City Council* (1966) E.A. 281, the Court of Appeal for East Africa summed up the position thus, at page 285:

> There can be no doubt that this court has power to allow such an amendment even at this late stage. A similar position arose in *Jupiter General Insurance Co. Ltd. v. Rajabali Hasham & Sons* (2) when an application was made for leave to amend a written statement of defence at the hearing of the appeal. The reasons which prompted the court to grant the indulgence sought were, *inter alia:*
>
> a) That the subject matter of the amendment became known to counsel only after judgment had been pronounced in the court; and.
>
> b) That all the material to enable the new ground of defence to be considered was before the Court of Appeal so that there was no need to remit the matter for further evidence or for re-trial in the High Court.
>
> The instant case is clearly distinguishable. The subject matter of the proposed amendment was in the mind of the counsel when the suit was tried in the High Court.... The issue now sought to be raised is fundamental, and should have been raised long ago. No question of inadvertence is involved, and the matter was mentioned in argument at the trial. Further pleadings would almost certainly be required, and possibly further evidence.

The application was accordingly refused. It should be noted that an amendment to pleadings by a party must be read together with the earlier pleadings. In other words, once the amendment, say, to the defence, has been made, the defence must be read as whole as if the amendment had been incorporated from the beginning (see *Uganda Credit & Savings Bank v. Yosamu Muzei Kirya and Others* (1960) E.A. 660).

Consequences of Failure to Amend

If a party who has obtained an order for leave to amend his pleadings does not amend them accordingly within the time limited for the purpose by the order, or, if no time is thereby limited, within 14 days from the date of the order, he will not be permitted to amend after the expiry of such 14 days or other time specified in the order unless the time is extended by the court (O.6, r. 18 C.P.C.).

The final question is: as from what date does an amendment to a plaint speak? In the case of *Eastern Radio Service v. Patel* (1962) E.A. 818, Sir Trevor Gould, J.A., expressed the view, which is in accord with English authorities, that an amended plaint relates back for all purposes to the date of the original plaint. But Newbold, J.A., was of the contrary opinion, while Sir Ronald Sinclair preferred to leave the question open. The Court of Appeal almost settled this question some five years later, when it had the opportunity to do so in the case of *South British Insurance Co. v. Samiullah* (1967) E.A. 659, but did not make a firm statement. Law, J.A., there said, at page 662:

> I do not feel it necessary to express any definite opinion on the point in this case, because even if an amended plaint does relate back to the date of the original plaint for some purposes, such relating back can not in my view operate so as to preclude a judge from taking notice of the date of the amendment, if such date is material to the issues for decision, as it undoubtedly was in this case.

The question, therefore, is far from clearly answered. But it is submitted that the preponderant (and I dare say better) view is that generally speaking, an amendment of a plaint speaks from the date of the original plaint, for otherwise, there would be no logic in the principle that once the amendment to a pleading has been made, such pleading must be read as a whole as if the amendment had been incorporated from the beginning (see *Shah v. Queensland Insurance Co. – (Supra)*.

CHAPTER SEVEN

THE PLAINT AND THE INSTITUTION
OF SUITS

INSTITUTION OF SUITS

Every suit must be instituted by presenting a plaint to the court or such officer as the court may appoint in this behalf (S. 22 and O.4, r. 1 (i) C.P.C.), and every plaint must be drawn in compliance with the general rules of pleading and the rules governing the drawing up of plaints (See infra; O.7 C.P.C.) as far as they are applicable (O.4 r.1 (i) C.P.C.).

Order IV, rule 3 of the Civil Procedure Code Act, as amended by Government Notice No. 422 of 1994 provides that after the suit has been duly filed, a Judge or Magistrate incharge of the court must, within four days thereafter, cause the suit to be assigned to a specific Judge or magistrate under what is loosely referred to as "the Individual Calendar."

The plaint must be filed in duplicate or with several copies. The original is to be kept in the file, and the copy or copies will be sent to the defendant/ defendants together with the summonses. The court or proper officer will then cause any book or account filed with the plaint to be marked for purposes of identification, or certified copies thereof, as the case may be, as provided by O.7, r.17, of the Civil Procedure Code.

The particulars of a plaint which should be entered in the civil register are:

1) The year number of the suit;
2) The names of the parties;
3) The nature of the claim and relief claimed; and
4) Date of filing the suit or date when summons was issued.

The Civil Register also contains columns of particulars which are completed after the disposal of the suit. These include date of judgment, brief statement of the result of the case, and the name of the Judge or magistrate who tried the suit.

As we have seen, the plaint must be filed in a court with competent jurisdiction to try the same. Section 13 of the Civil Procedure Code states that a "Court" means a court of a resident magistrate and a district court, both of which are courts of the same grade, and a suit must be instituted in the court of the lowest grade competent to try it.

It has been held, however, that this rule is merely one of procedure and not of jurisdiction. It does not, therefore, deprive higher courts of jurisdiction which they already possess. It is merely a rule of convenience: it is intended to avoid overcrowding in higher courts. So where the lowest courts have concurrent jurisdiction to try a suit, such suit will not be defeated merely because it has been filed in a higher court, unless there is an express provision preventing such a course (see *Francis s/o Mwijage v. Boniface s/o Kabalemeza* (1968) H.C.D. n. 341.

But in the case of *Francis Andrew v. Kamyn Industries* (supra), a contrary view was expressed. The better view would appear to be that expressed in *Mwijage's* case (supra).

THE PLAINT

As already noted, a plaint is a written document drawn by a plaintiff or his advocate, which contains, in a concise form, all the material facts on which the plaintiff relies for the relief he claims in a suit. We have also discussed the general rules that must be followed in all pleadings. We now proceed to look at the rules specifically governing plaints.

Form and Content of a Plaint

A properly drawn plaint must contain the following essential matters:

1) The name of the court in which the suit is to be filed;
2) The name or names and description of the place or residence of the plaintiff(s);
3) The name(s) of the defendants) and description of the place of his/ their residence so far as these can be ascertained;
4) Where the plaintiff or defendant is a minor or a person of unsound mind, a statement to that effect;

5) The facts constituting the cause of action and when it arose
6) The facts showing that the court has jurisdiction;
7) The relief which the plaintiff claims;
8) Where the plaintiff has allowed a set-off or relinquished a portion of his claim, the amount so allowed or relinquished; and
9) A statement of the value of the subject – matter of the suit for the purposes of jurisdiction and of court fees, so far as the case allows (O. 7, r. 1 C.P.C.).

A plaint must show all these essential matters, if relevant, because it has to show the foundation of the right alleged to have been violated unless the right in question in the circumstances is one implied by law. In the case of *Charles Cottar v. A.G. and Another* (5 E.A.C.A. 18), the appellant claimed for a declaration that he was entitled to a mining lease in respect of a certain claim or location. The plaint contained certain averment of fact but did not aver by what right the appellant claimed to be entitled to lease or whether the action was founded on contract or on one or other of the Mining Ordinances. It was held that the plaint did not disclose a reasonable cause of action in as much as it did not disclose what right the plaintiff had to obtain the lease to which he claimed to be entitled and whether such right arose by contract or under one or other of the Mining Ordinances. The court added that where a plaintiff relies on some breach of a statutory duty arising independently of a contract the statute should be referred to and the facts which bring the case within it sufficiently pleaded. In a case where the plaintiff's claim is for breach of contract, for instance, his pleading should set out the terms of the contract, its date, the parties to it and the breach with all necessary details.

The rationale of this principle is that a plaintiff can not succeed upon a cause of action not alleged in the plaint and which is inconsistent with his pleadings and his evidence and also because a plaintiff must, in his pleadings, give sufficient notice of his complaint against the defendant (see *Henry H. Ilanga v. M. Manyoka* (1961) E.A. 705). In the words of Willers, J., in *Cautret v. Egerton,* (1867), L.R. 2, C.P.C. 317:

The plaintiff must, in his declaration, give the defendant notice of what his complaint is. He must recover secundum allegata et probata.

A plaint, however, must not be read literally. In the case of *Sullivan v.*

Alimohamed Osman (1939) E.A. 219), the respondent instituted a suit against the appellant claiming damages for trespass on his vehicle. In the plaint the respondent alleged:

> On September, 5, 1957, the defendant (an agricultural officer), without the authority or consent of the plaintiff, wrongfully and wilfully interfered with and exercised control over the plaintiff's motor – lorry DSA 985 at or near Songea, Tanganyika, by wrongly ordering the driver employed by the plaintiff, one Hamisi Matola, to drive the said vehicle unlawfully along the main Songea/Lindi Road to the police station, Songea.

One of the grounds taken upon appeal was that the plaint disclosed no cause of action in that it failed to state (a) that the respondent's driver complied with the appellant's order to drive the lorry, (b) that, even if this be taken as implied, the order was accompanied by either force or duress, and (c) that the interference with the respondent's use of the vehicle or control over the lorry, occasioned by the order, was a direct interference. In respect of this ground of appeal, the court stated (per Windham, J.A.) at page 241:

> The first of these three objections is correct in so far the allegation is merely that he was ordered to do so, and this is consistent with a refusal by the driver to obey that order. This omission would of course be fatal to the claim if the correct approach to the plaint were the literal one. But it is not. That which is necessarily implied from its context must be read into the plaint. And the statement that the appellant ordered the driver to drive the lorry to police station, the respondent was deprived of the use of it… necessarily implies, to my mind, an allegation that the driver complied with that order.

This, however, is not to be taken to mean that a party must draw up his plaint perfunctorily in the hope that other facts will be implied and read into the plaint. A necessary fact which has not been pleaded can not be implied merely because otherwise another necessary fact pleaded could not be true. Let us now look at each of the contents of a plaint in turn.

Name of the Court in Which the Suit is to be Filed

It is necessary that the plaint must contain the name of the court in which the suit is to be filed. The reasons for this are obvious. One reason is that since suits must be instituted in the court of the lowest grade to try it, the plaint will show whether that is in fact the lowest court competent to try the suit. Another reason is to identify the court of first instance for purposes of appeals and citation of authorities.

Names of the Parties, Their Addresses, Their Relation and Interest

It is essential that the names of the parties to a suit must be clearly stated in the plaint. The reason is plaint enough. A cause of action as between two parties necessarily means that it is those parties and no others who are the contestants. A mistake in the name of, say, the defendant, may, therefore, be fatal.

With regard to the addresses of the parties, these are necessary for at least two reasons: the first is to enable the court to decide whether or not it is the correct court to take cognizance of the suit (post). The second is to enable court processes to reach the parties.

On this point, it is well to note that the addresses must be as complete as possible. For instance, it is not enough to describe a defendant's address as being Dar es Salaam, Kampala or Nairobi. As much information as possible must be given – the house or plot number or street or location of his place of residence and his postal address, are all necessary and must be given where possible. If the address of the defendant is insufficient, the court process will be returned unserved for insufficiency of the address for service.

With regard to the relation and interest of the plaintiff, where the plaintiff sues in a representative character, the plaint must show (1) that he has an actual existing interest in the subject matter; and (2) that he has taken steps (if any) necessary to enable him to institute the suit concerning it (O.7, r, r. 4, C.P.C). If these provisions are not complied with, the plaint will be rejected.

A typical example of the application of these provisions is where the plaintiff sues as a representative or administrator of a deceased's estate.

In the case of *Tulipilike Sandube Mwakatobe v. Martia Tassos Alexion t/a "Etiennes Hotel" and Another* (Dar es Salaam Civil Case No. 125 of 1976 – unreported), the plaintiff, the mother and personal legal representative and/or administratirix of the Estate of one Leston Mwakatobe (deceased) sued the defendants on behalf of herself as a dependant and on behalf of other dependants and for the benefit of the estate of the deceased for damages arising out of a motor accident resulting in the death of the said Leston Mwakatobe. Counsel for the defendants raised a preliminary point to the effect that the suit be dismissed on the ground that the plaintiff did not show that the plaintiff had taken necessary steps to enable her to institute the suit as required by O.7, r. 4 of the Civil Procedure Code and so should be dismissed.

Patel, J., ruled that O.7, r. 4 refers to the plaint and not to the evidence, and added, after quoting both O.7, r. 4 and O.7 r. 11:

> Thus it is clear that O.7, r. 4 does not provide for dismissal of plaint but merely provides for rejection of plaint and such rejection shall not be a bar or preclude the plaintiff from presenting a fresh plaint in respect of the same cause of action under O.7, r. 4.

He accordingly ruled that as the plaint did not show that the plaintiff had taken steps to have herself appointed adminsitratrix of the estate of the deceased, the plaint contravened the provisions of O.7, r. 4, but that it was open to the plaintiff to seek amendment of the plaint under O.7, r. 11 of the Civil Procedure Code.

Besides the relation and interest of the plaintiff in the subject – matter of the suit, the plaint must also show that the defendant is or claims to be interested in the subject – matter, and that he is liable to be called upon to answer the plaintiff's demand (O.7, r. 5 C.P.C.).

The Facts Constituting the Cause of Action and When it Arose

This is one of the most important rules to remember in drawing a plaint. A plaint must show the foundation of the right alleged to have been violated, unless such right, as we have seen, is one implied by law. If a plaint does not disclose a cause of action, therefore, the suit will be rejected because, as we have seen, a plaintiff can not succeed upon a cause of action which he has not alleged in the plaint and which is inconsistent with his pleadings and his evidence. As was stated in the case of *Motohov v. Auto Garage*, (1971) H.C.D. n. 81 (supra):

> It is trite to observe that a plaint must set out with sufficient particularity the plaintiff's cause of action… This fundamental rule of pleading would be nullified if it were to be held that a necessary fact not pleaded must be

implied because otherwise another necessary fact that was pleaded could not be true (see also *Sullivan v. Alimohamed Osman* (1959) E.A. 239, (supra).

In addition to disclosing a cause of action, the particulars as to when the cause of action arose must also be pleaded in the plaint. The importance of this is that from the date given the court will know whether or not the suit is barred by the law of limitation, and the defendant will be under no illusion as to the date or time the events complained of allegedly occurred. Indian courts have held, whoever, that a plaintiff is not absolutely bound by the statement in the plaint as to the date and that the court is entitled to determine the date from the facts alleged in the plaint (see *Fatehali Shah v. Muhammad Baksh and Others* (A.I.R.) 1928 Lahore 516).

Facts as to Jurisdiction

As we have seen earlier, the question of jurisdiction is not one of form. It is fundamental. A plaint, therefore, must contain a statement of facts which show that the court in which it is sought to be filed has jurisdiction to hear and determine the suit. As already stated, the nature of the claim, the value of the subject matter of the suit, where the cause of action arose, the defendant's place of business or residence, etc., are matters that show the fact of jurisdiction. These must be stated in the body of the plaint and it must also be stated how the particular court has jurisdiction to hear and determine the suit. The statement as to local jurisdiction, for example, may be stated thus:

> The cause of action arose at Dodoma, within the jurisdiction of this honourable court.

Where the plaintiff relies on the value of the subject – matter of the suit for the purposes of showing that the court has jurisdiction (in addition to other matters), the determination of the question as to whether the court has jurisdiction to try the suit will be based on the substantive relief to which he is entitled on the fact alleged and not on the prayer which he has chosen to make in his plaint. Costs are not to be taken into account.

If the plaintiff relies on the defendant's residence or place of business as conferring jurisdiction on the court the facts of it must be stated in the body of the plaint. The statement of these facts in the title to the suit is not sufficient because the title to the suit is not covered by the verification clause (see *Motibhai v. King & Co.,* (1959) E.A. 270, 279).

It must be noted that it is not enough to simply allege in the plaint that the court has jurisdiction. The provisions of the rule require that you must state the facts showing that the court has jurisdiction. In the case of *Assanand & Sons v. E.A. Records* (1959) E.A. 360, Sir Kenneth O' Connoner, P., had this to say, at page 364:

> Paragraph (f) of O.8, r. 1 (1) places upon a plaintiff the obligation of pleading "the facts showing that the court has jurisdiction." That is a matter of great importance; for, if the court has no jurisdiction, any judgment which is given is a nullity. A mere assertion by the plaintiff that the court has jurisdiction is not enough. The rule requires the facts showing that the court has jurisdiction to be stated.

As to the objects of the rule, the Court stated:

> The objects of this requirement would seem to be, first, that the court should be able to exercise some critical function and to draw a reasonable inference that if the facts alleged are established, it would appear to have jurisdiction and, second, that the defendant should know what facts were alleged and have an opportunity of controverting them, if desired.

If the suit is for immovable property, there must be sufficient description of it so that it is capable of identification. If the suit is over the ownership of a building under the Land Registration Ordinance, the plaint must describe its location and Registration number. It is not enough, for example, to merely state that 'the immovable property is within Moshi Township" (O.7, r. C.P.C.).

Amount of Money to be Stated Precisely

If the plaintiff seeks to recover money, the plaint must state the precise amount claimed. But where he sues for mesne profits, or for an amount which will be found due to him on taking unsettled accounts between him and the defendant, the plaintiff must state approximately the amount sued for (O.7, r., 2 C.P.C.).

Relief Which the Plaintiff Claims

R.7 of O.7 of the Civil Procedure Code provides that every plaint must state specifically the relief which the plaintiff claims either simply or in the alternative, although it is not necessary to ask for general or other relief which may always be given at the discretion of the court to the same extent as if it had been asked for.

If the plaintiff seeks relief in respect of several distinct claims or causes of action founded upon separate and distinct grounds, these must be stated, as far as possible, separately and distinctly. For instance, in a suit for arrears of rent, mesne profits and vacant possession, these reliefs must be stated separately, and distinctly.

As we have seen earlier, it is important that a plaintiff should specifically ask for all the reliefs he claims in the suit as stated in the rule against the splitting of claims.

When Suit Instituted After Period of Limitation

If the suit is to be instituted after the period of limitation has elapsed, the plaint must show the ground upon which exemption from such law of limitation is claimed (O.7. r.6 C.P.C).

The grounds for exemption from the law of limitation in Tanzania are contained in sections 14 to 30 (inclusive) of the Law of Limitation Act, 1971. The question that arises is whether these must be specifically pleaded. There is no East African case on this point. However, Indian Courts have held that a plaint should not be rejected merely because the exemption is not claimed specifically. All that the rule requires is that the plaint shall show the ground of exemption. In other words, if facts in the plaint disclose grounds for exemption from the law of Limitation, that is sufficient compliance with the requirements of the rule. In the case of *Subramonian v. Kalyanarama* (A.I.R) (45) 1958 Kerala 243, the plaintiff did not specifically plead exemption from the law of limitation on the ground of acknowledgment in a suit on a promissory note. The court there held that in a suit on a promissory note, the omission in the plaint to formally rely on the acknowledgement as a ground for exception for saving limitation is not fatal where relevant facts have been mentioned.

What, then, is the consequence of failure by the plaintiff to plead facts as to exemption from the law of limitation? In such a case, either the plaint will be rejected or the plaintiff may be allowed to amend the plaint so as to plead the ground for the exemption – if there be such exemption.

Documents Relied on in Plaint

Should the plaintiff be suing on a document in his possession, he must produce such document or copy of it in Court at the time of presentation of the plaint. Such a document is usually referred to in a plaint as an "annexture" (O.7, r.14(1) C.P.C). If, for instance, he sues on a promissory note, the promissory note or a copy thereof must be annexed to the plaint.

If he relies on any other documents (whether in his possession or power or not) as evidence in support of his claim, he must prepare a list of such documents and annex them to the plaint (O.7, r.14(2)C.P.C.). If any of such documents are not in his possession or power, he must, if possible, state in whose possession or power they are (O.7, r.15 C.P.C.).

If in a suit founded upon a negotiable instrument, it is proved that the instrument is lost, and an indemnity is given by the plaintiff to the satisfaction of the court against the claims of any other person upon such instrument, the court may pass such decrees as it would have passed if the plaintiff had produced the instrument in court when the plaint was presented, and had at the same time delivered a copy of the instrument to be filed with the plaint (O.7, r.16.C.P.C.).

Where the document on which the plaintiff relies is an entry in a shop book or other account in his possession or power, and subject to the provisions of the Evidence Act relating to Bankers' books, the plaintiff must produce the book or account at the time of filing the plaint together with a copy of the entry on which he relies. The court or an authorized officer of the court will then mark the book or account for purposes of identification, examine and compare the copy with the original, and, if it is found correct, certify it to be so, and then return the book or account to the plaintiff and cause the copy to be filed in court (O.7., r.17 C.P.C.).

It must also be borne in mind that a document which ought to be produced in court by the plaintiff when the plaint is presented, or which ought to be entered in the list to be annexed to the plaint, and which is not so produced or entered, will not, without the leave of the court, be received in the evidence on his behalf at the hearing of the suit. (O.7, r.18(1) C.P.C.). But documents produced for cross-examination of the defendant's witness, or in answer to any case set up by the defendant or handed to a witness merely to refresh his memory are not covered by this rule (O.7. r.18(12) C.P.C.)

The object of these rules, of course, is to prevent false documents being used after the suit has been filed. Unscrupulous or over-zealous plaintiffs may make false documents to back up the contents in their plaints already filed in court. In commentaries on r.14 and r.18 of O.7 of the Indian Code of Civil Procedure, which are identical with r.14 and r.18 of O.7 of the Tanzania Civil Procedure Code, it is stated in Mulla's *Code of Civil Procedure,* at page 762:

The object of r.14 and r.18 is to provide against false documents being set up after the institution of a suit. In those cases, therefore, where there is no doubt of the existence of a document at the date of the suit, the Court should, as a general rule, admit the document in evidence though it was not produced with the plaint or entered in the list of documents annexed to the plaint as required by r.14 (13ᵗʰ Edn). (But the Court may even in such a case refuse to receive it in evidence if it is produced at a very late stage of the proceedings.)

That passage was quoted with approval by the Uganda High Court in the case of *Dattani v. Ahmad* (1959) E.A. 218. In that case, the plaintiff sued for damages on the ground that distress had been wrongfully levied against his property for non-payment of rent for property held under a lease. The lease was not pleaded in the plaint nor produced to the court when the plaint was presented. When he sought it to be admitted, the trial magistrate refused to allow the plaintiff's counsel to put to the respondent in cross-examination the written tenancy agreement signed by both the parties in 1947. On appeal, the High Court held that leave should have been granted because it was obviously a genuine document admissible under r.18(2), and that in any case it could have been put to the defendant in cross-examination because a defendant was as much a defence witness as any other witness who is called to support his case.

Return of a Plaint

The court may, at any stage of a suit, return a plaint to be filed or presented to the court in which the suit should have been filed. If the court should so return a plaint, the Judge or magistrate returning such plaint must endorse on the plaint the date of its presentation, the date it was returned, the name of the party who presented it, and a brief statement of the reasons for returning it O.7, r.10 C.P.C.). One case in which a plaint may be returned is where the suit is not triable by such court but another court. It may also be proper to return a plaint where the suit, although triable by such court, should have been filed in the court of the lowest grade competent to try it within the provisions of section13 of the Civil Procedure Code.

For instance, suppose that a plaintiff in Tanzania were to present his plaint for filing in a District Court in a suit, say, to have the register of business names amended. In such a case, it would be proper for the magistrate to return the plaint to be filed in or presented to the court in which it can properly be tried, that is, the High Court, because under section 6 of the Business Names Registration Ordinance, Cap. 213, the amendment of the register of business names is a matter purely within the province of the High Court.

Similarly, if a plaint were to be presented to the High Court in Tanzania in an action relating to immovable property under customary law, such plaint may be returned by the High Court to be filed in a primary court of competent territorial jurisdiction because such proceeding must, under the provisions of the Magistrates' Court Act (Sixth Schedule) and section 1(3) of the Contract Ordinance in the absence of leave by the High Court, be instituted in no other court than in a Primary Court (*see Joseph Constantine v. Losilale Ndaskoi,* (1968) H.C.D., n.381).

Rejection of Plaint

If a plaint (1) does not disclose a cause of action, or (2) if the relief claimed is undervalued, and the plaintiff, on being required by the court to correct the valuation within a time to be fixed by the court, fails to do so, or (3) if the suit appears from the statement in the plaint to be barred by any law, the plaint must be rejected (O.7, r. 11 C.P.C.).

However, where a plaint does not disclose a cause of action, or where the suit appears from the statement in the plaint to be barred by any law and the court is satisfied that if the plaintiff is permitted to amend the plaint, the plaint will disclose a cause of action, or as the case may be, the suit will cease to appear to be barred by any law, the court may allow the plaintiff to amend the claim subject to such conditions as to costs or otherwise as the court may deem fit to impose (O.7, r.11 as amended by the Civil Procedure Code (Amendment of the First Schedule) Rules, G.N. 228 of 1971).

Where It Does Not Disclose a Cause of Action

As we have seen earlier, "a cause of action" is a bundle of essential facts which it is necessary for the plaintiff to prove before he can succeed in the suit. If not pleaded, the plaint is said to disclose no cause of action. For instance, if, in a suit for damages arising out of a motor accident, negligence on the part of the defendant is not pleaded in the plaint, such plaint will be said to disclose no cause of action and so may be rejected.

What, then, is to be looked at in deciding the question whether a particular plaint does or does not disclose a cause of action? In order to determine that question, a Judge or magistrate will look at the plaint as it is and assume the facts alleged to be true and that they were done or omitted to be done, as the case may be, by the other party, or admitted by the other party. The plaint, of course, includes all the annextures properly annexed to the plaint, for, as a general rule, a reference in a document to an annexture has the effect of incorporating the contents of the annexture in the document (*see Castelino v. Rodrigues* (1972) E.A. 223, 225); or, in the words of Windham, J.A. in the *case of Jeraj Shariff & Co. v. Chotai Fancy Store,* (1960) E.A. 374 at page 375:

> The question whether a plaint discloses a cause of action must be determined upon a perusal of the plaint alone, together with anything attached so as to form part of it, and upon the assumption that any express or implied allegations of fact in it are true.

In the case of *Akber Meral Alibhai v. M/S Union Magazine* (1972), Court of Appeal Tanzania Civil Appeal No. 3 of 1979 – as yet unreported) the appellant alleged in his plaint that he was at all material times a partner of the respondent firm and as such entitled to benefits and income accruing from the respondent firm's operation and that nominal payments were made to him by the respondent, although the respondent had failed to furnish a profit and income account despite demand. The appellant also alleged that a member of the respondent firm had purported to exclude the appellant as a partner of the respondent firm and so prayed, *inter alia*, for a declaration that he was still a partner of the respondent firm.

The defence raised a preliminary point, under O.7, r.11 of the Civil Procedure Code, that the suit was not maintainable in law and denied that the appellant had at any time been a partner of the respondent firm or entitled to any profit from it or to any account; and in a counter-claim alleged that the sum of money of T.shs. 200,300/= remitted by it to the appellant was in respect of advances made to the appellant at his request and instance and prayed for an order for repayment of that sum. The learned judge proceeded to deal with the preliminary objection and heard addresses of both counsel and reserved his ruling. He then delivered what he called "judgment." In that "judgment." the learned Judge went into an analysis of the contents of the plaint and its annextures, the defence and the reply and came to the conclusion that on the "established facts" the appellant had not proved that at all times he had been a partner of the respondent and payments to the appellant were not towards the appellant's profits in the firm. He then concluded that the Court could not force the respondent to take the appellant as a partner and "dismissed" the suit as not "maintainable at law."

On appeal, after observing that the learned Judge ought to have "rejected" the plaint, and not "dismissed" the suit, Mustafa, J.A. said:

> I think that a trial Judge in dealing with such an application (under O.7, r.2) should only look at the plaint and if necessary its annextures to see if there is a cause of action. The appellant has alleged in the plaint that he was a partner of the respondent firm and that he has received payment as such partner from it. For the purposes of O.7, r..2, these allegations are to be taken as true; see for example *Jeraj Shariff & Co. v. Chotai Fancy Stores*, (1960) E.A. 374 at 375. However, the trial Judge instead went on to analyse the allegations and counter-allegations in the plaint, the annextures and the defence, made inferences and deductions and came to the conclusion that the appellant was not a partner of the respondent firm nor had he received money from it as his share of the profits, and I think that the trial Judge erred in doing so. He had only to look at the allegations in the plaint, and if they disclosed a cause or action, then he could not reject it. He cannot look at the defence or decide issues of fact.

His Lordship went on to emphasize:

> The Judge took into account extraneous and irrelevant matters and decided issues of fact in coming to the conclusion that the plaint was not maintainable at law. He should only have looked at the plaint filed and should not have decided matters in controversy between the parties in arriving at his finding as to whether or not to reject a plaint under the provisions of O.7 r..2 of the Civil Procedure Rules.

The Court accordingly allowed the appeal holding that the plaint did disclose a cause of action, and so ordered that the matter be remitted to the High Court for trial on its merits.

The court need not, therefore, look at the defence that may be or has been raised. All it has to do is to look at the plaint and assume that those facts are true and that they have been admitted by the other party.

When the judge or magistrate has looked at the plaint in that light and forms the opinion that on the face of it the plaint does not disclose a cause of action, he will then proceed to consider whether or not it should be rejected. His next step, then, will be to consider whether, if the plaintiff is allowed to amend the plaint, such plaint will disclose a cause of action. Should he be satisfied that such is the case, then he may allow the plaintiff to amend the plaint so as to disclose a cause of action instead of rejecting it.

In other words, a plaint must not be rejected merely because, on the face of it, it does not disclose a cause of action unless it is plain that no amount of amendment would make it disclose a cause of action. As was stated in the case of *Arbon v. Anderson and Others* (1942) 1 All E.R. 264, at page 266, in interpreting the English R.S.C.25, r. 4, which is equivalent to O.7, r.11 of the Tanzania Civil Procedure Code:

> It is well-settled that it is only in plain and obvious cases that recourse should be had to the summary process of dismissing an action under R.S.C. Ord. 25, r.4, and that an action will not be dismissed under it unless the case is beyond doubt. The fact that the case is weak and not likely to succeed is no ground for dismissal of the action under R.S.C. O.25. A pleading will not be struck out under either order unless it is not only demurrable but something worse than demurrable, i.e., such that no legitimate amendment can save it from being demurrable, or it is embarrassing (see also *Byombalirwa's case – supra; and Tanzania Olympic Committee v. A. Simbaulanga*, (1997) T.L.R 184).

It is, therefore, the duty of every judge or magistrate to examine a plaint and its annextures carefully and to ascertain whether or not such plaint discloses a cause of action, and to determine whether, if it does not disclose any cause of action, it can be amended to disclose a cause of action.

In the case of *S.M. Hirji v. Sadrudin*, (1974) LRT n.13, the appellant, who was a court broker, alleged in his plaint that consequent upon the respondent's advocate's written instructions, he towed an attached motor vehicle from the judgement debtor's house to Tukuyu Police Station and incurred expenses in doing so. By virtue of the promise the appellant claimed against the respondent (I) T.shs. 557/= being charges due to him as court broker according to the fees prescribed in the Attachment and Sale (Broker and Fees) Rules 1964; (ii) T.shs. 226/= of which T.shs 200/=

was the agreed and/or reasonable charges for towing the said motor vehicle and 26/= being damages paid by him to one Francis for damage to his property which occurred while the motor vehicle was being towed to the police station.

When the case came up for hearing, one of two preliminary objections was that the plaint disclosed no cause of action because r.11(2) of the Attachment and Sale (Brokers and Fees) Rules provide that "the fees charges and allowances payable under this rule shall be collected by the court and ... paid to the executing officer." The second submission was based on a Rule which provides that after making an attachment of movable property the executing officer shall immediately forward to the court which issued the attachment warrant "an inventory" in the form of an itemized list with values, showing the items attached and the requirement was a precondition to the appellant's cause of action and as the appellant had not complied with it, the suit was not maintainable.

The learned magistrate upheld both submissions and rejected the suit. On appeal to the High Court, the High Court held that since the estimated value of the property attached was the basis of fees or charges, it was not correct to argue that since the decretal amount was far less than that of the motor vehicle, there was no reason to comply with rule 5. The Court (Onyiuke, J.), however, quoted r.11 of O.7 and said, at page 49:

> I can however see no unsurmountable difficulty in the appellant placing an estimated value on the motor vehicle. I should think that this is a case where the magistrate can exercise his discretion to allow the plaintiff to amend his plaint so that it can disclose a cause of action in view of my earlier decision that the appellant can recover his fees and charges by suit.

In the case of *Auto Garage and Others v. Motokov* (No.3) (1971) E.A 514, the facts were that in an action on bills of exchange the judge ruled that the plaint disclosed no cause of action and the respondent thereupon applied to amend the plaint to claim in the alternative for the goods sold and delivered to the first appellant in respect of which the bills of exchange were given. The appellants opposed the application on the grounds that the court had no power to amend a plaint which disclosed no cause of action and that if there was a power to amend, it should not be exercised so as to introduce a new cause of action after the expiry of the period of limitation. The judge allowed the application holding that the court had power to allow amendment of a plaint disclosing no cause of action and that no new cause of action was introduced. On appeal to the Court of Appeal for East Africa, Spry, V-P.' said, at page 519:

> I would summarize the position as I see it by saying that if a plaint shows that the plaintiff enjoyed a right, that the right has been violated and that the defendant is liable, then in my opinion, a cause of action has been disclosed and any omission or defect may be put right by amendment.

What the court there was saying, in effect, was that if facts do not go the root of the matter, a plaint is not bad for want of cause of action. This appears to be the principle enunciated in the case of *The United Africa Co. v. Manji's Ltd.* (1970) H.C.D. n. 231, in which it was held that one does not have to plead facts to show where a cause of action arose in order to show that one does have a cause of action because, on general principles, the place where a cause of action arose cannot be said to be an essential ingredient of an action, and so an omission to plead it is not one of the reasons for rejection of a plaint, although it may be a reason for returning a plaint for amendment under O.7, r.11 of the Civil Procedure Code.

It has also been held that the provisions of O.7, r.11 were never intended to apply to any pleading which raises a question of general importance, or serious question of law (see *Katikiro of Buganda v. A.G.* (1958) E.A. 765, 767). The rationale of these provisions and authorities is that O.7, rule 11 is intended to ensure that a plaintiff is not denied his remedy merely on grounds of technicality, for the rules of procedure "are intended to serve as the handmaidens of justice, not to defeat it." Indeed, in the *Motokov* (No. 3) case, the court said that where amendment is permissible in the interests of justice, the power to allow amendment will be exercised liberally.

This, however, is no justification for not drawing a plaint in accordance with the rules. A party is duty bound to set out in his plaint all the essential facts with sufficient particulars so as to disclose a cause of action. Where leave to amend is granted, it should be borne in mind that such leave will most likely increase cost against the plaintiff because the proviso to r. 11 of O.7 expressly states that "the court may allow the plaintiff to amend the claim subject to such conditions as to costs or otherwise as the court may deem fit to impose."

There is another reason for being careful in drawing a plaint. Although a court will more often than not allow a plaintiff to amend his plaint if it is satisfied that by such amendment the plaint will disclose a cause of action, strictly speaking, a court is not bound to allow such amendment. This is clear from the use of the word "may" in the proviso. That word suggests that the court has a discretion to allow an amendment or not to do so. But, of course, as this is a judicial discretion, courts have to exercise it judicially.

Where the Suit Appears From the Statement in the Plaint to be Barred by any Law

As we have seen above in the proviso to r.11 of O.7, where the suit appears from the face of the plaint to be barred by any law, and the court is satisfied that if the plaintiff is permitted to amend the plaint the suit will cease to appear to be barred by any law, the court may allow the plaintiff to amend the plaint so that it ceases to appear to be so barred, subject to such conditions as to costs or otherwise as the court may think fit to impose.

The principles that a court should follow with regard to this part of the proviso are the same as those regarding amendment of a plaint which does not disclose a cause of action.

Where Relief Claimed is Undervalued

There are plaintiffs who, in order to bring a suit within the jurisdiction of the court, will undervalue the relief claimed. If such fact be plain on the face of the plaint, a court must reject the plaint or allow the plaintiff to amend it so that the relief claimed is as correct as it can possibly be assessed in the circumstances and nature of the suit.

CHAPTER EIGHT

ISSUE AND SERVICE OF SUMMONS ON DEFENDANTS

When a plaint has been properly drawn in accordance with the provisions of Orders 6 and 7 of the Civil Procedure Code we have discussed in the preceding two chapters, it will be filed in the court which has jurisdiction to try the suit, and the plaintiff will be required to pay the necessary court fees as prescribed by the Court Fees Rules, 1964 (see G.N 308 of 1964), as amended from time to time.

Summons

When a suit has been thus duly filed, the next step is the issuance of a summons to the defendant. This is done at the time when the suit is assigned to a specific judge or magistrate as provided in O.4, r.3 of the Civil Procedure Code.

There are two types of summons in this regard. The first is called a *summons to appear.* This is a summons which informs the defendant that the plaintiff has filed a suit against him and calls upon the defendant to appear and answer the claim on a date to be specified in the summons. Such summons will further direct the defendant to produce on that day all documents in his possession or power upon which he intends to rely and all the witnesses upon whose evidence he intends to rely to support his case (O.5, rr.1. and 4 C.P.C.). The second type is known as a summons to file a defence. This type of summons is issued where the suit is instituted in a court other than the High Court, and where the court so decides. A summons to file a defence informs the defendant that a suit has been filed in court against him and requires him to file what is known as a *written statement of defence* (O.5, r. 1 C.P.C.).

It sometimes happens that a defendant appears before the court at the time the plaint is presented. In such an event, and if the defendant proves his identify to the satisfaction of the court, and admits the plaintiff's claim, no summons will be issued to him and judgement will be entered against him to the extent of his clear admission (O.5, r. 1 C.P.C.).

Contents of a Summons

A summons to a defendant must contain the following: (1) the name of the court in which the suit is filed; (2) the names of the parties to the suit; (3) the full address of the defendant on whom the summons is to be served; (4) where it is a summons to appear, the date and time when the defendant must file his Written Statement of Defence; (5) the date on which the summons is issued; (6) the signature of the Judge, magistrate or other authorized officer of the court; and (7) the court seal (O.5 r. 2.C.P.C.).

The requirement that a summons must be duly signed by the judge or magistrate or other officer appointed by the Chief Justice in that behalf, and that it must be sealed with the seal of the court would appear to be fundamental and not merely one of form. In the case of *Kaur and Others v. City Auction Mart Ltd.* (1967) E.A. 108, the facts, in so far as they are material, were that a notice of motion issued under O.5, r.1 (3) of the Uganda Civil Procedure Code (which is in *pari materia* with O.5, r. 2 of the Tanzania Civil Procedure Code), the summons which was served on the defendant was not duly signed by a judge and merely contained "a squiggle" and a minute to the Judge by the Acting Chief Registrar for "perusal directions." Dealing with the validity of that notice of motion Jones, J., said at page 110:

> This summons was not signed by a Judge and apart from an endorsement on a minute sheet on a chamber summons…, whatever it may mean, there is no certificate of urgency under the vacation rules or any intelligible direction to the Acting Deputy Chief Registrar. If it can be construed as a direction within the meaning of O.5 r. 1 to issue a summons, I cannot say that the provisions of O.5. r. 1(3) have been complied with. The "summons" has not been signed or sealed. There is some mark or hieroglyphic on the summons, which could have been done by anyone. A signature means signature and not initials. This is an official document purporting to be issued from the High Court initiating proceedings and not a departmental minute. The squiggle on the summons is not sufficient and in no way complies with the provisions of O.5 r. 1(3). The law lays down that a

document, such as a summons, should bear the seal of this court, for obvious reasons, such as to show that the fees have been paid, that it is issued under proper authority and out of the proper office.

His Lordship concluded, at page 111:

In my view these proceedings have failed to comply with a fundamental statutory requirement, and are therefore a nullity.

In surbodinate courts, magistrates sign all summonses in suits originating in their courts. In the High Court a Registrar, Deputy Registrar or District Registrar usually signs the summonses. It is therefore the duty of all the authorized officers to see that a summons has been duly signed and not merely initialed and that the same has been duly sealed with the seal of the court before it is sent for service upon a party.

When the summons has been duly signed and sealed, it will be sent out for service upon the defendant. It is important to remember that such a summons must be accompanied by a copy of the plaint. The reason for this, of course, is so as to enable the defendant to know the nature and subject matter of the claim and thus afford him an opportunity of preparing his defence (if he has any) to the claim.

In addition, copies of other documents as may be prescribed by the Chief Justice for the information of the defendant regarding the future conduct of the suit must also be attached. Chief among these is what is called an "Initial Notice" (see O.5, r.3 C.P.C. as amended by Government Notice No. 422 of 1994). This is discussed later in this book.

Service of a Summons Upon Defendant

In the Normal Way

When the summons to a defendant has been duly issued and a copy of the plaint has been attached thereto, the court, in the case where the defendant resides within the jurisdiction of the court in which the suit is instituted or has an agent resident within that jurisdiction empowered to accept service, will deliver or send the summons to a proper officer (usually referred to as a process server) or his surbodinate to be served on the defendant or his agent (O.5. r.9 C.P.C.).

The proper officer must effect service of the summons by delivering or tendering the same to the defendant or his agent. As far as is practicable, the service must be made on the defendant personally or, if he has an agent, on the agent.

Service of the summons, which has been duly sealed and signed by an authorized officer, must be made within twenty-one days after it has been received by the process server (O.5, 10 C.P.C. as amended by Government Notice No. 422 of 1994).

A copy of the summons must be delivered to the defendant together with the copy of the plaint and other documents after the defendant or agent has been made to sign in an appropriate place on the summons as evidence that he has been duly served. The process server will then return the original copy of the summons to the court (O.5, r.16 C.P.C.), and will swear to an affidavit stating how or when he duly effected the service on the defendant or his agent. Such affidavit constitutes sufficient evidence of service (O.5, r. 18 C.P.C.).

The rule that the summons must be delivered to the defendant personally or his agent and that a copy thereof must be delivered or tendered to the defendant so served, would appear to be mandatory. In the case of *Erukana Kavuma v. S.T. Mehta* (1960) E.A 305, the affidavit of a process server who went to serve a summons on the defendant at his shop stated that he did not find the defendant there, thereat he was told that the defendant was in India, and so served the summons on the defendant's wife. The plaintiff obtained an *ex-parte* judgment and decree in default. The defendant then applied to have the same set aside contending that the service of the summons was bad on the grounds, *inter alia*, that no duplicate of the summons was tendered or delivered to the defendant's wife. The Uganda High Court held that in those circumstances, service was bad, and so set aside the *ex-parte* judgement and decree.

The requirement that a defendant must ordinarily sign the summons to acknowledge acceptance of service would similarly appear to be mandatory. In the case of *Mehta & Co. Ltd. v. The Baron Verheyen* (2) T.L.R. (R) 300), the court dealt with the provisions of O.5. r.16 of the Indian Code of Civil Procedure (which is in *pari materia* with O.5, r.16 of the Tanzania Civil Procedure Code) and said, at page 306-307:

> O.5 of r.16 provides that the serving officer "shall require the signature of the person to whom the copy is so delivered or tendered to an acknowledgement of service endorsed on the original...." As 1 read rule 16 it is mandatory and non compliance with it means that service has not been duly made.

If, however, the defendant, his agent or such other person authorized to accept service refuses to sign the acknowledgement, the service officer must leave a copy thereof with him and return the original to the court together with an affidavit stating that the person upon whom he served the summons refused to sign the acknowledgement, that he left a copy of the summons with such person and the name and address of the person (if any) by whom the person on whom the summons was served was identified (see proviso to O.5, r.16 C.P.C.). In such an event, the service will be taken to be effective, and the defendant cannot challenge it on the ground that he did not sign it in acknowledgement.

Should there be more defendants than one, each of them must be served with a summons (O.5, r.11 C.P.C.). Where the suit relates to any business or work against a person who does not reside within the local limits of the jurisdiction of the court from which the summons is issued, service on any manager or agent, who, at the time of service, personally carries on such business or works for such person within such limits, will be deemed to be good service. Under this rule, the master of a ship is deemed to be the agent of the owner or charterer (O.5, r.13(1) and (2) C.P.C.).

In the case of *M.B. Automotive v. Kampala Bus Service,* (1966) E.A. 480, it was held that disclosure of the name and address of the person who identified and witnessed delivery or tender of the summons to the defendant is a statutory duty, and the failure to comply with it renders the service defective. It is important to note that where a summons to appear is to be issued, the date for the defendant's appearance must not be fixed irrespective of the convenience of the court and of the defendant. In fixing the day for the appearance of the defendant, the court must pay due regard to the current business of the court and the place of residence of the defendant and the time necessary for service of the summons. In other words, the court must ensure that the defendant is allowed sufficient time to enable him to appear and answer on such appointed day (O.5, r.6. C.P.C.).

It is for that reason that rule 8 of O.5 of the Civil Procedure Code provides that no party must be ordered to appear in person unless he resides within the local limits of the court's ordinary jurisdiction, or where he resides outside such limits but at a place less than fifty miles or, where there is railway or steamer communication or other established public conveyance for five-sixth of the distance between the place where he resides and the place where the court is situate, less than two hundred miles distance from the court house. In any other case, a summons to file defence be issued, and normally a defendant is given 21 days from the date of service to file his defence. But this period may be extended on application to the court.

Where the court sees reason to require the personal appearance of the defendant, the summons will order him to appear in person in court on the day specified in the summons. So too where the court sees reason to require the defendant's personal appearance, the court may issue a separate summons to that effect (O.5, r.7(1)(2)(3) C.P.C.). In all other cases, where the court requires the personal appearance of the defendant, a defendant may appear either (a) in person; or (b) by an advocate duly instructed and able to answer all material questions relating to the suit or (c) by an advocate accompanied by some person able to answer all such questions.

Service Other Than on the Defendant Personally

If, in a suit to obtain relief respecting, or compensation for wrong to, immovable property, service cannot be made on the defendant in person, and the defendant has no agent empowered to accept the service, the summons may be served on any agent of the defendant who is in charge of the property (O.5, r.14 C.P.C.). If, in any suit, the defendant cannot be found and has no agent who is empowered to accept service of the summons on his behalf, the summons may be served on any adult male member of the family of the defendant who is residing with him, but an adult male member here does not include a servant (see *Erukana v. S.P. Mehta - (supra)*.

There are cases when the defendant cannot be found, and has no agent empowered to accept service, nor any other person on whom service can be made. In such a case, after the process server is satisfied after all due and reasonable diligence that such is the case, such process server must affix a copy of the summons on the outer door or some conspicuous part of the house in which the defendant ordinarily resides or carries on business or personally works for again. Having done so, the process server must, within fourteen days of affixing such copy, return the original to the court which issued the summons with a report endorsed thereon and annexed thereto stating that he has so affixed the copy, the circumstances under which he did so, and the name and address of the person (if any) by whom the house was identified and in whose presence the copy was affixed (O.5, r.17 C.P.C.). This should normally be done by way of an affidavit.

It is important to note that service under these provisions can only be justified and deemed to be good where the process server has in fact used all due and reasonable diligence to find the defendant or his agent or any other person who can accept service. Perfunctory inquiries cannot justify a process server stating that "the defendant cannot be found." The case of *Omuchilo v. Ayub Machiwa*, (1966) E.A. 229, is a good example. In that case, the facts were that the court process server accompanied by an agent of the plaintiff visited a house in which the defendant ordinarily resided to serve a summons on the outer door of the house and swore a brief affidavit of service to that effect. Subsequently judgement was entered ex-parte in default of appearance and after formal proof the defendant applied to set aside the judgement. It was there held that the service was wholly ineffective. Setting aside the *ex-parte* judgement , the court quoted with approval a passage in Mulla's *Code of Civil Procedure* (12ᵗʰ Edn.) at page 566 which states:

> To justify such service, it must be shown that proper efforts were made to find the defendant, e.g., that the serving officer went to the place or places and at the times where and when it was reasonable to expect to find him. Thus, if a serving officer goes to a defendant's house, but does not find him there, and the defendant's adult son, who is in the house, refuses to accept service on behalf of the father, these facts by themselves do not justify the officer in resorting to the mode of service prescribed by this rule; he must, before effecting such service, inquire of the son as to where the defendant is and otherwise exercise due and reasonable diligence in finding the defendant.

Having quoted that passage, the Court, Morris J., said, at page 232:

> The position under O.5, r.14 (of the Civil Procedure Revised rule) in regard to finding the defendant is similar, and as I have already stated, I must hold that the service upon the defendant in the present case was wholly ineffective. I should perhaps add that the affidavit of service is defective for the further reason that it does not aver that the fixing of the copy of the summons to the premises was carried out in the presence of the person by whom the premises were pointed to the serving officer, nor does it state the address

of that person. Further more, although the rules do not perhaps expressly so provide the affidavit clearly should state the town and street or other particulars of the situation of the premises to which the summons was affixed. In the present case the affidavit does not even say that the premises in question are within the jurisdiction of this court.

In the case of *Erukana Kavuma v. Mehta* (supra), which was quoted in *Omuchilo's* case, the court held that same view. In that case, as we have seen, the process server said in his affidavit of service: 'there I did not find the defendant; I was told that the defendant is in India." On those facts, Sir Audley Mackissack, C.J., said, at page 306:

> This seems to me a most inadequate ground for saying that the defendant could not be found. The affidavit does not reveal whether or not any inquiry was made about the defendant's address in India., or whether it was expected that the defendant would return to Uganda from India, and if so, when. The attempt to find the defendant appears to me to have been most perfunctory. I cannot regard absence from Uganda, without any information about the Country to which he has gone, or whether or not he can be found there, and without any information as to the expected length of his absence, or as to when he had left Uganda, as being sufficient grounds for saying that a defendant "cannot be found.") (see also *Waweru v. Kiromo* (1969) E.A. 172,174. *Mohamed Nassoro v. Ally Mohamed*, (1991) T.L.R. 133, *Kulwa Daudi v. Rebecca Stephen*, (1985) T.L.R. 116, and *Amiri v. Rajabu*, (1995) T.L.R. 26).

To ensure that a process server has in fact conducted diligent and reasonable inquiry as to the whereabouts of a defendant and that such inquiry did not yield results before he proceeded to serve the summons in the manner indicated in r.17, the rules further provide that in cases in which a summons is returned as served under r.17, of O.5, the court must, if the return under that rule has not been verified by an affidavit of the process server, and may, if it has been so verified, examine the process server on oath, or cause him to be so examined by another court, touching upon the manner and circumstances in which he conducted his inquiry and affected service, and may make such further inquiry in the matter as it thinks fit. After such examination and inquiry, the court must declare that the summons has been duly served or order such service as it thinks fit (O.5, r.19 C.P.C.).

Where the court is satisfied that there is reason to believe that the defendant is keeping out of the way for the purpose of avoiding service, or that for any other reason, summons cannot be served on him by the ordinary way, the court will order that the summons be served by affixing a copy of it in some conspicuous place in the court-house (usually on the notice board of the court-house), and also on some conspicuous part of the house (if any) in which the defendant is known to have last resided or carried on business or personally worked for again, or in such other manner as the court thinks fit. This is called substituted service, and is as effectual as if it had been made on the defendant personally. In such a case, the court must fix such time for the appearance of the defendant as the case may require (O.5, r.20) C.P.C.). The process server, of course, will swear an affidavit that he affixed the summons in the place as directed by the court.

Another method of serving the summons on such a defendant is to publish the summons in the local press.

Service of Summons in Special Cases

Serving by Post

If the court should be satisfied that to require a summons to be served on a defendant in the ordinary manner or by substituted service may cause undue delay and that the summons may more conveniently be served by post, the court may order that the summons be served by post (O.5, r. 21 C.P.C.).

Under the provisions of r.30 of O.5 of the Civil Procedure Code, service by post may be deemed to have been duly effected if:

a) The summons is returned by the defendant endorsed with an acknowledgment of service; or

b) A letter or other document is received from the defendant acknowledging or indicating that he has received the summons; or,

c) Evidence is produced showing that a postal packet was received by the defendant, supported by a certificate of an officer of the court that the postal packet contained the summons (O.5, r.30 C.P.C.).

That is why postal packets should usually be registered.

Where service had been effected by post and the court is satisfied that it may be deemed to have been duly served under the foregoing provisions, it will deem it to have been so effected, and such service will be as effectual as if the summons had been served on the defendant personally (O.5, r. 21(2) C.P.C.).

Service by Plaintiff or Agent

A plaintiff or his agent may himself serve a summons on a defendant. In such an event, service may be deemed to have been duly effected if an affidavit is filed by the person who effected the service stating that he personally served the summons on the defendant; that the defendant was personally known to him or by exhibiting the summons or a copy of it endorsed by the defendant with an acknowledgment of service or giving reasons why such acknowledgement could not be obtained (O.5, r. 31 C.P.C.).

Service Where Defendant is Confined in Prison

If the defendant is confined in prison, the original and copy of the summons must be delivered or sent to the officer in charge of the prison for service on the defendant (O.5, r.24. C.P.C.). In such a case, the officer in charge must serve the summons, if possible, and return it under his signature, with a written acknowledgment of the defendant or, if there is no such signature, a certificate will be deemed to be evidence of service. If for any reason it is impossible to serve the summons, the summons must be returned to the court with a full statement of such cause and of the steps taken to procure service, and such statement will be deemed to be evidence of non-service (O.5, r. 27 C.P.C.).

Service on Officers of the Government

If the defendant is an officer of he Government or a Local Authority, the court may, if it appears to it that service of the summons may be most conveniently so effected, send the original and copy of the summons for service on the defendant to the head of the office in which the defendant is employed. (O.5, r.25 C.P.C.). If the defendant is a member of the armed forces, the court will send the original and copy of the summons to his commanding officer. Such head or commanding officer, as the case may be, will comply with the provisions of O.5, r.27 discussed above (O.5, rr. 26 and 27 C.P.C.).

Service Where Defendant Resides in Jurisdiction of Another Court

If the defendant resides outside the jurisdiction of the court issuing the summons, the issuing court will send the summons duly signed by a Judge or magistrate or proper officer and sealed with the seal of the court to the court within whose local jurisdiction the defendant resides requesting such court to effect service of the summons on the defendant.

On receipt of the summons, the court within whose local jurisdiction the defendant resides will endorse it for service, and then give it to a process server to serve the same on the defendant. When the summons has been duly served by such court, such court will send the original summons to the issuing court with an affidavit showing the manner in which service was effected (see section 24 and O.5 r.22 (1) and 23 C.P.C.).

Under the provisions of O.5, r. 23 of the Civil Procedure Code, as amended, the court serving the summons must return it to the issuing court within fourteen days after concluding the serving proceedings. (Government Notice No. 422 of 1994).

Because normally the distance between the two courts may be considerable, a summons for service on a defendant who resides outside the local jurisdiction of the issuing court, should be summons for orders or a summons to file defence, and not a summons to appear and answer or a summons for disposal of suit.

If the court which is requested to serve the summons on the defendant cannot for any reason effect service, it will endorse on the summons the reasons for its failure to effect service and then return it to the issuing court "unserved."

A summons may be returned unserved by the court requested to do so for several reasons. Among these are: inadequacy of the defendant's address shown on the summons, absence of signature and seal of the issuing court, and lack of an endorsement on the summons by the issuing court to the effect that service fees have been paid by the plaintiff.

Service of Summons Outside Tanzania

If the defendant is not resident in Tanzania and is believed to reside in Kenya, Uganda, Malawi, or Zambia and has no agent in Tanzania to accept service, then service can be effected, where the plaintiff has furnished the postal address of the defendant, by post; in any other case, through the courts of the country in which the defendant is believed to reside; or, by leave of the court, by the plaintiff himself or his agent (O.5, r.28 C.P.C.).

If, on the other hand, the defendant is believed to reside outside Tanzania and elsewhere than in Uganda, Kenya, Malawi or Zambia, he may be served (a) by post; (b) by the plaintiff himself or his agent; or (c) through the courts of the country in which the defendant is believed to reside (O.5, r.29 C.P.C.).

Where the court of the Resident Magistrate or District Court has ordered service of a summons to be effected through the court of any other country other than Kenya, Uganda, Malawi or Zambia, it must remit to the Registrar of the High Court at Dar es Salaam, and where the High Court has so ordered, the Registrar will issue a summons, together with two copies thereof and two copies of translation of it in the language of the country in which the summons is to be served, if that language is other than English, and the Registrar will thereupon send those documents together with a certificate as to the sum of money deposited or secured to cover the expenses of service, to the Principal Secretary of the Ministry for the time being responsible for legal affairs:

a) Where leave has been given for service to be effected in a country with which a convention has been made by the United Republic concerning the service of Civil Processes, for transmission to the representative of the United Republic in the country or as the convention may otherwise provide; or

b) For transmission to the Government of the country in which leave has been given for service to be effected through the courts of that country (O.5, r.33(3) C.P.C.).

But where the defendant is believed to reside in Kenya, Uganda, Malawi or Zambia, the court which issues the summons may send the original and copy of the summons for service direct to any court having civil jurisdiction in the place where the defendant is believed to reside (O.5, r. 33(2) C.P.C.).

Service through the courts of the country in which defendant is believed to reside may be deemed to have been duly effected if the summons is returned by any such court with an endorsement that it has been served (O.5, r.32 C.P.C.).

CHAPTER NINE

WRITTEN STATEMENT, SET-OFF AND COUNTER-CLAIM

Having dealt with the service of summons on a defendant, let us now move on to the position of a defendant who has been duly served with a summons.

If a defendant feels that the manner in which the service of the summons has been served on him renders such service ineffectual, then, as we have seen earlier, he may move the court which issued the summons to set aside the service (see *Donnebaum v. Mikolaschek, (*1964) E.A. 645; and *Omuchilo v. Ayub Machiwa* (supra).

Where the defendant has been duly and properly served and there is nothing on which the service can be challenged, then, if it is a summons to appear, the defendant may, and if so required by the court, must, within seven days before the first hearing, present to the court what is called a written statement of defence. If the summons is a summons to file a defence and the defendant wishes to defend the suit, he must within twenty one days from the date of service of the summons upon him present to the court a written statement of his defence.

But the Court may, within twenty one days of expiration of the prescribed period, grant an extension of time for presenting the written statement of defence on application by the defendant (see O.8, r.1(2) proviso-as amended by Government Notice No. 422 of 1994).

If, on the other hand, a defendant on whom a summons to appear or a summons for disposal of suit has been duly served admits the claim as a whole, he may make such admission verbally when he appears before the court in answer to the summons. In such an event, he need not file a written statement of defence. On his admission of the whole claim the court will ordinarily enter judgment for the plaintiff against him as prayed.

WRITTEN STATEMENT OF DEFENCE

Definition

A written statement of defence as we have seen, means a written statement by a defendant formally denying the facts on which the plaintiff's claim is based and the material facts on which the defendant intends to rely in his defence to the suit.

Contents of a Written Statement of Defence

A properly drawn written statement of defence must contain the following things:

1) The name of the court in which the suit has been filed;
2) The name of the parties;
3) A statement in concise form of the material facts on which the defendant relies for his defence but not the evidence by which he intends to prove those facts;
4) A prayer that the suit be dismissed, struck out etc., as the case may be; and
5) Verification.

Drawing a written statement of defence can be a tricky business. Before preparing a written statement of defence, therefore, the defendant must peruse the plaint and all annextures thereto very carefully. He must be certain that he has clearly understood the content and form of the plaint, the nature of the claim and the legal basis of it. Having fully understood the plaint and all its aspects, the defendant must then consider whether it is possible, and reasonable, to attack the plaint on preliminary points, e.g. that the plaint discloses on cause of action; that there has been misjoinder or non-joinder of parties and/or causes of action; that the suit is bad for being frivolous, vexatious and/or embarrassing; that it is barred by any law, such as the law of limitation or *res judicata,* and so on.

In addition to such preliminary points he decides to raise, the defendant should next consider the substantial grounds of his defence – just in case the preliminary points should be resolved against him. In considering this he must be sure that all documents he will need to answer the plaintiff's claim are available, and whether he should proceed in the ordinary way or institute third party proceeding under rules 14 to 22 (inclusive) of Order 1 of the Civil Procedure Code (ante).

Denial Must be Specific

It is an important rule that a defendant's denial of any fact alleged in the plaint must be specific. It is not sufficient for him in his written statement of defence to deny generally the grounds alleged by the plaintiff. The denial must deal specifically with each allegation of fact the truth of which he does not admit. The only exception to this is damages (O.8 r. 3 C.P.C.). A defendant must take each fact that is alleged against him separately and say that he admits it, or denies it, or does not admit it.

If an allegation of fact in a plaint is to be denied specifically or by necessary implication, or if it is not stated to be not admitted in the written statement of defence, it will be taken to have been admitted except as against a person under disability (O.8, r. 5 C.P.C.).

In the case of *Yusuf Alimohamed Osman v. D.T. Dobie & Co.* (1963) E.A. 288, the defendants generally denied their indebtedness to the plaintiff. It was submitted by the appellant that the written statement of defence was defective under Rule 3 of Order 8. Biron J., stated at page 290:

> It cannot be disputed that the written statement of defence fails to comply with the rule and is in fact defective. But is such defect necessarily fatal? To my mind it is saved by r. 5 of the same Order....

His Lordship quoted r. 5 of the Order and continued:

> To my mind, para 1 of the written statement of defence that: "The defendant denies he is indebted to the plaintiff company in the sum of Shs. 6,321/96 as alleged in para 2 and 3 of the plaintiff or at all", not only by implication but expressly denies the company's claim as laid in para 2 of the plaint which sets out the work done and materials supplied, and as laid in para 3 of the plaint which avers, inter alia, that the work was done at the plaintiff's request. To my mind, although the pleading is defective, it traverses the averment in the appellant's request, at lowest, sufficiently to exclude the possibility of any such admission being implied.

These provisions were also discussed in the case of *E.A. Posts and Telecommunications Corp. v. M/S Terrazzo Paviors* (1973) L.R.T. n. 58. In that case, the plaintiff took exception to paragraph 4 of the written statement of defence which read as follows:

> Save as herein before expressly admitted the defendant denies each and every allegation of facts contained in the plaint as if the same were set forth and specifically traversed.

Onyiuke, J. stated, at pages 256 - 257

> A general or comprehensive traverse of the nature of paragraph (4) of the Written Statement of Defence in this case in hallowed by usage and appears in practically every written statement of defence. The courts sometimes frown on it but it continues to appear all the same. The effect of this form of traverse is to put the plaintiff to strict proof (*Warner v. Samson* (1959) 1 All E.R. 120). It shortens the pleading and it is not bad *per se* but where its effect is to make it difficult for the plaintiff or the court to know what defence a defendant is putting forward then it may well be embarrassing and defective (see also *Meyasi v. N.B.C.*, (1977) LRT n.42.)

Judicial wisdom and fairness notwithstanding, every material allegation of fact which goes to the root of the matter must be traversed specifically, although the traverse need not be sentence by sentence.

New Facts Must be Specially Pleaded

As we have already noted, a court will generally not grant relief outside the pleadings. Similarly, a defence which has not been pleaded cannot be argued. The defendant, therefore, must raise in his pleadings all matters which show that the suit is not maintainable, or that the transaction is either void or voidable in point of law, and all such grounds of defence as, if not raised, would be likely to take the opposite party by surprise, or would raise issues of fact not arising out of the plaint, as, for instance, fraud, limitation, release, payment, performance, or facts showing illegality (O.8, r. 2 C.P.C.). If such matters are not specially pleaded in the written statement of defence, they cannot be subsequently raised and argued.

In the case of *G.P. Jani Properties Ltd. v. Dar es Salaam City Council*, (1966) E.A. 281, the defence argued on appeal that a certain planning scheme in the City of Dar es Salaam, on which the plaintiff's suit for recovery of two sums of money was based, was *ultra vires*. This matter, however, had not been pleaded and leave to amend the written statement of defence in order to include such a plea had not been sought at the earliest possible moment. The Court quoted with approval Chitaly and Rao on the *Indian Code Civil Procedure*, (5th edition) wherein it is stated:

It is the duty of a defendant to particularize in his defence all points, either of fact or of law, which he desires to take.

As with most rules regarding pleadings, this rule again is designed to ensure that each party is entitled to know in advance what the case of his opponent will be and thus limit the generality of the allegations in the pleadings so as to clearly define the issues to be tried.

It must be noted, however, that a defendant should not plead matters which are not alleged against him and which are no part of his defence. In other words, he must not plead to irrelevant matters. Besides, he must not plead to matters which are plain and acknowledged or which it is not in his interest to prove or which he cannot prove; nor is it advisable to deny the obvious for to do so may unnecessarily increase costs against such party.

Evasive Denial

In line with the rule that a denial must be specific, where a defendant denies an allegation of fact in the plaint, such denial must not be evasive; it must answer the point of substance alleged in the plaint. So, if it is alleged that the defendant received a certain sum of money, it will not be sufficient to deny that he received that particular amount; he must deny that he received that sum or any part thereof, or else set out how much he received. Similarly, if an allegation refers to diverse circumstances, the denial must not be merely general. The diverse circumstances must be denied O.8 C.P.C.).

In the English case of *Thorp v. Holdsworth*, (1876) 3 Ch. D. 406, the defendant's defence stated:

The terms of the arrangement were never definitely agreed upon as alleged.

It was held that such a denial was evasive denial and that it amounted to an admission that an agreement was in fact made as alleged. Jessel, M.R., had this to say, at page 639.

The whole object of pleadings is to bring the parties to an issue, and the meaning of the rules of this Order (English O.18) is to prevent the issue being enlarged which would prevent either party from knowing, when the cause came on for trial, what the real point to be discussed and decided was.... The defendant is bound to deny that any agreement or any terms of arrangement were ever come to, if that is what he means; if he does not mean that, he should say that there were no terms of arrangement come to, except the following terms, and then state what those terms were.

Now, what are the consequences of an evasive denial? Generally speaking, such a pleading will be amended, for, as we have seen, the purpose of pleadings is to bring the parties to an issue. An application for an amendment of such a pleading will only be refused where it is plain to the court that the party is acting *mala fide*.

A defendant, therefore, may confine himself to merely denying the plaintiff's allegations, or go on and add his own version of the matter. That is within his discretion. But whatever course he chooses, he must bear in mind that the purpose of pleadings is to bring parties to an issue, and so he must specifically deny that which he denies; he must never be evasive; and he must specially plead new facts.

Pleas in Confession and Avoidance

There are cases in which the defendant admits doing acts alleged against him, but at the same time wishes to plead justification or some other excuse of the acts or omissions alleged against him. For instance, in a suit for libel, a defendant may admit the fact that he published the words complained of, but he may then plead justification, privilege or fair comment. That he is allowed to do, and such a plea is sometimes referred to as a plea in confession and avoidance in that it admits the act or omission complained of but at the same time pleads justification or excuse from legal liability.

A defendant is at liberty to plead as many distinct and separate defences as he pleases, even if they are inconsistent, provided that they are not embarrassing. But, as we have seen earlier, a pleading is not embarrassing merely because it contains inconsistent averments. In a suit for damages for breach of contract, for example, the defendant may deny the existence of such an agreement as one defence; performance as another and illegality of the contract as a third, all stated in the alternative. But such defences must be stated separately and distinctly.

One more point. It is true that a defendant is at liberty to raise as many objections on points of law as he wishes or can find in an opponent's pleading. But one has to be very careful in doing so. Such objections must only be raised in your pleadings where the fault is apparent on the face of it and where there is something reasonably substantial to be gained by it. Generally speaking, little is gained by objections to mere omissions or matters of form, for the opposite party may be allowed to amend his pleading. It is only where the objection is one which, if the ruling be in your favour, will dispose of the whole suit or give you substantial gain in the final result that it is advisable to object. As some eminent Judge once observed, the days of the special pleader are gone. The eminent English Judge, Sir Edward Coke, offers the following advice:

> When the matter in fact will clearly serve your client although your opinion is that the plaintiff has no cause of action, yet take heed you do not hazard the matter upon a demurrer, in which, upon the pleading and otherwise, more perhaps will arise than you thought of; but first take advantage of the matters of fact, and leave matters in law, which always arise upon the matters fact and ultimum, and never at first demur at law, when after trial of the matters in law (as in this case it was) will be served to you. (In the Lord Cromwell's case (1581). A Rep. At p. 14 – quoted in *Odgers on Pleadings and Practice* 19th Edn. Pp. 144 –145).

SET – OFF

In often happens that a defendant in a suit for recovery of money claims to set-off, that is, he claims that the plaintiff owes him money too. For instance, in a suit for recovery of money for goods sold and delivered, the defendant may claim that since the filing of the suit by the plaintiff, he (the defendant) has paid a certain sum of money to the plaintiff towards the settlement of the debt which is the subject matter of the suit. That claim is called a *set-off* in that the defendant will plead that the amount be off-set from the sum claimed in the plaint.

For there to be a proper set-off the suit must be one for the recovery of money; the sum which the defendant claims to set-off must be an ascertained sum of money legally recoverable by him from the plaintiff, which sum must not exceed the pecuniary limits of the jurisdiction of the court; and both parties must fill the same character as they fill in the plaintiff's suit. In such a case, the defendant may, within a period of twenty-one days of being served with the summons, present a written statement containing the particulars of the debt sought to be set-off (O.8, r. 6(1) C.P.C.).

In such a case, the written statement assumes the same effect as a plaint in a cross-suit and so enables the court to pronounce a final judgement in respect of both the original claim and the claim of the set-off, (O.8, r.6(2) C.P.C.). For the same reason, the rules relating to a written statement of defence apply to a written statement to a claim of set-off by a plaintiff (O.8, r.6 (3) C.P.C.)

The essential points to remember with regard to set-off, therefore, we may repeat, are four: (1) that the suit must be one for the recovery of money; (2) that the set-off must be for an ascertained sum of money which is legally recoverable by him from the plaintiff; (3) that the amount of the set-off does not exceed the pecuniary jurisdiction of the court; and (4) that both parties fill the same character as they fill in the plaintiff's suit.

Of the four requirements, only the last one requires explanation. "The same character" here means that the set-off, like the main claim itself, must be in respect of the same parties, and they must not be totally unconnected claims. For instance, A sues B for T.shs. 5,000,000/= being the price for goods sold and delivered. B claims set-off of the sum of T.shs. 250,000/= paid to A towards the satisfaction of the debt which is the subject matter of the suit which A has omitted to credit B's account. That would be a proper set-off to be pleaded. But where C owes D T.shs. 100,000/= and D is a Managing Director of a company which owes C T.shs. 50,000/=, then in a suit by D for T.shs. 100,000/=, C cannot claim set-off of T.shs. 50,000/= because the character of the parties is not the same. (See *Nelson v. Roberts* (1893) L.T. 352).

If the defendant relies on several distinct grounds of defence or set-off founded upon separate and distinct facts, they must be stated, as far as possible, separately and distinctly (O.8, r. 7 C.P.C.), and any ground of defence which has arisen after the institution of the suit or after a written statement claiming counter-claim has been presented, it may be raised by the defendant or plaintiff, as the case may be, in his written statement (O.8, r. 8 C.P.C.)

COUNTER - CLAIM

Definition

If a defendant has a claim against a plaintiff, which he might have asserted by bringing a separate action, he may raise it in an existing action by adding to his statement of defence a statement of the facts on which he bases his claim and of the relief which he claims against the plaintiff. Such a claim is called a *counterclaim*: It is in fact a cross-suit.

So where in any suit the defendant alleges that he has any claim or is entitled to any relief or remedy against the plaintiff in respect of a cause of action accruing to him before presenting his written statement of defence, such defendant may, in his written statement of defence, state particulars of the claim made or relief or remedy sought by him (O.8, r. 9(2) C.P.C.).

Since a counterclaim is a cross-suit, the written statement of defence containing a counterclaim will have the same effect as a plaint in a cross-suit. A counterclaim, therefore, must comply with the rules governing the drawing of plaints (O.8, r. 9(2) C.P.C.P.

Differences Between Set-off and Counterclaim

The difference between a set-off and a counterclaim is that a set-off is in the nature of a defence to the whole or part of the plaintiff's suit, while a counterclaim is in the nature of an independent suit within the original suit.

In Odgers on *Pleadings and Practice*, the distinction between the two is neatly put as follows:

> Speaking generally, a set-off may be described as a shield which operates only as a defence to the plaintiff's action, and a counterclaim as a sword with which the plaintiff may be attacked (page 210, 18th Edition).

Besides, while a set-off must be in a suit for money and for ascertained sum where both parties fill the same character as in the plaintiff's suit, a counterclaim may, generally speaking, be brought in respect of any claim that could be the subject of an independent action, and it need not be for an ascertained sum, nor need it relate to or be connected with the subject – matter of the plaintiff's suit.

In *Halsbury's Laws of England*, a counterclaim is described as follows:

A counterclaim can in general be brought in respect of any claim that could be the subject of an independent action. It is not confined to money claims, or to causes of action of the same nature as the original action; and except where a person other than the plaintiff is also made a defendant to it, it need not relate to or be connected with the original subject of the cause or matter..... The defendant by his counterclaim may ask for any form of relief (see Vol. 34, page 411 3rd Edition).

Pleading a Counter-claim

Before a counterclaim can be pleaded, it is essential that the plaintiff must be a party to such counterclaim. However, where a defendant, by his written statement, sets up any counterclaim which raises questions between himself and the Plaintiff along with another person (whether or not a party to the suit), he may join that person as a party against whom the counterclaim is made (O.8, r.10(1) C.P.C.), but he cannot join third parties to a counterclaim if the plaintiff is not made a party to it.

Since a counterclaim is in the nature of a cross-suit, the fact that the plaintiff's suit has been dismissed, say, for want of prosecution or as being frivolous or vexacious, or if it is stayed, will not, *per se*, affect the counterclaim: the defendant may nevertheless proceed with his counterclaim and obtain judgement thereon which he can execute in the ordinary way.

From the wording of Rule 9 of Order 8, it is clear that the cause of action of the counterclaim must have arisen or accrued to the defendant before the presentation of his written statement of defence. So, it need not have arisen at the same time as that of the plaintiff. It can even be pleaded where it arises after the plaint has been filed but before the written statement is presented. In fact, under the liberal rule of amendment of pleadings, a counterclaim could, in a proper case, be pleaded by way of amendment after the written statement has been presented, unless to do so would violate the rules of joinder of actions.

As to the amount to be pleaded in a counterclaim, it is irrelevant that such amount exceeds that claimed in the plaint, so long as it does not exceed the pecuniary jurisdiction of the court. It is, however, important to note that since a counterclaim is in the nature of an independent suit, a defendant is not bound to counterclaim. He is at liberty to bring an independent suit. The rule as to counterclaims are to save the defendant the trouble of filing an independent suit in that both the main suit and the counterclaim can be disposed of in a single trial (see *Karshe v. Uganda Transport* Co. (1967) E.A. 774, at page 782).

As pointed our earlier, in drawing a counterclaim, the defendant must do so in accordance with the rules governing the drawing of plaints. Where the defendant joins a person as a party against the counterclaim, he must add to the title of the written statement of defence a further title similar to the title in a plaint setting forth the name of such other party so joined and a copy of such written statement of defence together with a notice requiring such person, should he wish to defend the defendant's counterclaim, to file his written reply in answer to the claim within 21 days from service of the notice or within such period as the court may fix on application by such person in the same way as if the notice were a summons and such counterclaim were a plaint (O.8, r. 10 (2) C.P.C.).

Reply to Counterclaim

Since a plaintiff is in the position of a defendant with regard to a counterclaim, his reply thereto will take the form of a written statement of defence and must, therefore, comply with the rules governing the drawing of Written Statement of Defence. So where the defendant sets up a counterclaim, the plaintiff and the person, if any, who is joined as a party against whom the counterclaim is made, must each, if they wish to dispute the counterclaim, present to the court a written reply containing statement of defence in answer to the counterclaim within 21 days from the date of the service upon him/them of the counterclaim (O.8, r.11 C.P.C.).

Power of the Court to Order Separate Trial of Counterclaim

Where a defendant has set up a counterclaim, the court may, if it is of the opinion that the subject matter of the counterclaim ought for any reason to be disposed of by a separate suit, strike it out or order it to be tried separately or make such other order as may be expedient (O.8, r. 12 C.P.C.). That, however, is a matter of judicial discretion which a court must exercise judicially (see *General Trading v. Patel* (1985) E.A 702; *and Chibinza Kulwa v. Amosi Kibushi and Others,* (1990 T.L.R.36.).

OTHER PROVISIONS

Reply to Written Statement of Defence

Generally speaking, no pleading subsequent to the presentation of a written statement of a defendant other than by way of defence to set-off or counterclaim must be presented except by leave of the court and upon such terms as the court thinks fit, but the court may, at a pre-trial conference, require a written statement or an additional written statement from any of the parties and fix a time for presenting the same (O.8, v. 13 C.P.C.) as amended by G.N. No. 422 of 1994).

The exception to this rule, however, is that where a defendant has presented a written statement of defence in accordance with a summons to file a defence, the plaintiff may, without obtaining leave of the court, present a reply to the written statement of defence within seven days after the written statement of defence, or, where there are two or more defendants, within seven days after the last of the written statements of defence is served on him (see proviso to O.8, r. 13 C.P.C.). The reply referred to here is not to be confused with a plaintiff's reply to counterclaim or set-off. It is a reply or answer to the facts pleaded in the written statement of the defendant other than those in set-off or counterclaim. As explained in *Odgers on Pleading and Practice*.

> In (reply) main function is to raise in answer to the defence any matters which must be pleaded by way of confession and avoidance…, or to make any admission which you may be disposed to make.

If you merely deny the facts alleged in the written statement of defence, a reply is not necessary because where no reply is filed, all averments in the written statement of defence are deemed to be in issue. As was stated by Georges, C.J., in *William Murray v. Fatehali H.L. Murji* 1968 H.C.D. n. 390:

> A plaintiff is presumed to put in issue every fact alleged in the defence, unless it is admitted, and a reply is only necessary when it is desired to confess and avoid.

In other words, the main function of a reply is to raise in answer to the defence any matters which must be pleaded to meet such pleas as self-defence in a suit for assault, privilege and justification in a suit for defamation, and such other pleas of confession and avoidance. In such cases, the plaintiff may file a reply setting out the facts on which he relies to answer the defence.

As soon as the written statement of defence, or the last written statement of defence (if there are more defendants than one), and the reply (if any) thereto, or the last reply (if there are more plaintiff's than one) or other pleadings have been presented, the case is deemed to be ready for hearing, and a day will then be fixed by the court for hearing unless the provisions of O.8A and O.8B apply to the case (O.8, r.15 C.P.C.).

Consequences of Failure to Present a Written Statement of Defence

If any party who has been required to file or present a written statement of defence in answer to a plaint or a reply to a counterclaim has failed to do so within the time fixed by the court, the court must pronounce judgement against him or make such order in relation to the suit or counterclaim, as the case may be, as it considers fit; and in any case in which a defendant who is required under sub-rule (2) of rule 1 of Order 8 to present his written statement of defence fails to do so within the period specified in the summons, or, where such period has been extended, within the period of such extension, the court may, where the claim is for a liquidated sum not exceeding one thousand shillings, upon proof by affidavit or oral evidence of service of summons, enter judgment in favour of plaintiff without requiring him to prove his claim, and in any other case, fix a day for *ex-parte* proof and may pronounce judgement in favour of the plaintiff upon such proof of his claim. In any other case, on application in writing by the plaintiff, the court may fix a day for *ex- parte* proof and may pronounce judgment on such proof of the claim (O.8., r.14 C.P.C.).

So a defendant who fails to file his written statement of defence to a plaint, or plaintiff who fails to file his reply to a counterclaim, is at the mercy of the court in that once the court is satisfied that the summons was duly served and that the defendant or the plaintiff has been given ample time and opportunity to file his written statement or reply (as the case may be), it may enter judgement against him (see *Joe Rugarabamu v. Tanzania Tea Blenders* (1990) T.L.R. 24).

Sub-rule (3) of rule 14 of Order 8, provides that notwithstanding rule 14 of the Order, where the Attorney General is required to present a written statement of defence or a reply and fails to present the same within the time fixed by the court or within the time specified in the summons or, where the period has been extended by the court, within the period of such extension, the plaintiff or the defendant, as the may be, may apply in writing to adduce *ex-parte* proof of his claim or counter claim and the court will thereupon fix a day for the hearing of the application and will direct that notice of the application and the day of the hearing be given to the Attorney General. Should the Attorney General appear at the hearing of such an application and gives good cause for his failure to present the written statement of defence or the reply, the court must extend or further extend the period within which the written statement of defence or reply should be presented, on such terms as to costs, or otherwise as the court may direct. If the Attorney General does not appear, or appears but fails to show such good cause, the court may pronounce judgment upon *ex-parte* proof of the claim, as the case may be, as it thinks fit (O.8, r.14(3) and (4) C.P.C. as amended by Government Notice No. 376 of 1968).

CHAPTER TEN

APPEARANCE OF PARTIES AND CONSEQUENCE OF NON-APPEARANCE

When a summons to appear has been duly issued and served or where a summons to file defence has been duly issued and served and a day for the hearing of the suit is fixed in accordance with r.15 of O.8 of the Civil Procedure Code, then on the day so fixed for the defendant's appearance or for hearing (as the case may be) the parties must be in attendance at the court – house in person or by their recognized agent or advocates, and the suit will then be heard unless the hearing is adjourned for some reason to a future date to be fixed by the court (O.9, r.1 C.P.C.) (see *William Andrea Shangarai v. Farm Vehicles* (1969), H.C.D. n. 16.).

Meaning of "Appearance"

The question that sometimes presents some difficulty is the meaning of the term "appearance." "Appearance" here means attendance in person or by advocate in Court on the date stated in the summons which is also the date for the hearing of the suit. So once a party is present either in person or by his advocate when the suit is called up for hearing, that is sufficient appearance.

In the case of *E.A. Posts and Telecommunications Corp. v. M/S Terrazzo* (1973) L.R.T. n.58 (supra), the High Court of Tanzania (Onyiuke, J.) considered the meaning of the phrase "entering an appearance." After quoting O.9, r.1 of the Civil Procedure Code, His Lordship stated, at p. 249:

'Appearance' under the Code means attendance in person or by advocate in Court on the date stated in the summons which is also the date for hearing of the suit. Once the defendant is present either in person or by advocate when the case is called up that is sufficient appearance.

His Lordship went on, at page 250:

> appearance is the process by which a person against whom a suit has been commenced shows his intention to defend the suit and submits to the jurisdiction of the Court.

In the case of *Moshi Textile Mills v. De Voest* (1975) L.R.T. n. 17, the same court (Makame, J. – as he then was) had this to say on the meaning of the term "appearance," at page 71:

> There is no appearance if the party has neither filed a Written Statement of Defence nor appeared personally or by his advocate.

In the case of *Shah Kachra Merag v. Chandhi & Company* (1957) E.A. 466, the appellant's advocate did not appear, but the appellant attended the court and asked for an adjournment which the judge refused to grant. Thereupon the appellant declined to go on with the case adding. "I elect not to appear." The judge, on application by the respondent's advocate, dismissed the suit for "non-appearance." On appeal to the Court of Appeal for Eastern Africa, it was held that the appellant did, in fact and in law, appear. In dismissing the appeal, the court quoted with approval (at page 468) the following passage in Mulla's *Code of Civil Procedure* (12th Edition) Vol. 1 at page 643:

> The mere presence of a party in court at the hearing is sufficient to constitute "appearance" within the meaning of this Order. It does not matter for what purpose he appears or what action he takes on the appearance. A plaintiff appearing and applying for an adjournment on the ground that his witnesses are not present will be deemed to have 'appeared' ... Similarly, a defendant appearing and applying for an adjournment on the ground that he had no time to prepare his case, will be deemed to have 'appeared.' (see also *Kenya Poultry Dev. Ltd. v. S.J. Hunt* (1975) L.R.T. n. 61.)

In the case of *Opa Pharmacy Ltd. v. Howse & Mcgeorge Ltd.* (1972) E.A. 233, the Uganda High Court (Oteng, J.) defined the term as meaning:

> to take a step showing an intention to defend a suit and submit to jurisdiction.

In the case of an advocate, where he has been duly instructed and actually appears at the hearing but withdraws on failing to obtain an adjournment, he is deemed to have appeared (see *Din Mohamed v. Lalji Visran & Co.* (1937) 4 E.A.C.A, 1,2).

What is the position where an agent appears on behalf of a party on the date of the hearing of the suit? In the case of *The Land Officer v. Abdulrasul Jiveraj* (1 T.L.R. (R) 410, on the day the case was fixed for hearing, the Land Officer, who was the plaintiff, was represented by his attorney while the respondent was represented by his advocate. The respondent's advocate contended that there was no legal appearance on the part of the plaintiff. Thereupon the district court dismissed the suit for "non-appearance." On application to the High Court for revision, the Court stated at page 420:

.... Where a recognised agent is present in court when a suit is called on for hearing, the question is whether he intended to appear and did in fact appear for his principal, by virtue of the provisions of section 36 of the 1882 Code (now O.3, r.1).

The court quoted with approval a leading Indian case of *Soonderlal and Another v. Georprasad and Another* and *Georpraasad and Another v. Soonderlal and Another* (23 Bombay 414) in which Strachy, J., said:

... section 37 (now O.3, r.2) only defines the recognised agents by when appearance may be made. If the recognised agent personally applied for an adjournment, that would, under section 36 (now O.3, r.1) be an application by the party, and such an application would include an appearance, as to which it is unnecessary to decide whether it would or would not constitute an appearance of the party within Chapter VII. But if the recognised agent neither made any application, nor did any act, the question would be not merely whether he was present in court when the application for adjournment was made, but whether he intended to appear and in fact appeared for the party in the exercise of his power under section36 (now O.3, r.1). If, at the time, he stated, either in answer to Court or otherwise that he appeared or that he did not appear for his principal, the question of the party's appearance would be definitely determined. If he made no such statement, the question of the party's appearance would be definitely determined. If he made no such statement, the question might be difficult to determine; but in the absence of all evidence on the point, his presence at the time of the application should not, I think, be assumed to constitute an appearance by the party.

These authorities appear to suggest that the test to be applied with regard to appearance by recognised agents is whether such agent intends to appear for the party when the suit is called on for hearing and if he does so, then his appearance constitutes "appearance" by the party.

Dismissal of Suit for Non-Service of Summons

When on the day fixed for appearance in answer to a summons to appear or on the day fixed for hearing the suit it is found that the summons has not been served upon the defendant as a result of the failure by the plaintiff to pay the court-fees or postal charges (if any) chargeable for such service, the court may dismiss the suit. But no such order of dismissal of the suit must be made if on the day for him to appear the defendant attends in person or by agent (O.9, r.2 C.P.C.).

It often happens that a summons for service upon a defendant is returned unserved for one reason or another. Among these may be inadequacy of the address for service, change of address of the defendant, and temporary absence of the defendant from his address of service. In such an event, it is the duty of the plaintiff to apply to the court for issue of a fresh summons and re-service.

The court will usually grant this on payment of fees for re-service. If the plaintiff fails to apply for a fresh summons within twenty-one days from the date of the return of the summons as certified by the serving officer, the court must order that the suit be dismissed as against that defendant. However, if the plaintiff can, within that period, show: (1) that he has failed after using his best endeavours to discover the residence of the defendant; or (2) that such defendant is avoiding service of process; or (3) that there is any other sufficient cause for not dismissing the suit, the court will not dismiss it. It may, instead, extend the time for making such application for such period as it thinks fit (O.9, r.5(1) C.P.C. as amended by G.N. No. 422 of 1994).

A plaintiff, therefore, must be careful. As soon as he has been informed of the non-service of the summons upon the defendant, he must apply for the issue of a fresh summons.

What, then, is the consequence of dismissal of a suit on the failure by the plaintiff to pay the court fees for service? In such an event, the plaintiff may, if not barred from so doing by the law of limitation, bring a fresh suit, or apply for the order of dismissal to be set aside. In the latter case the court will make an order setting aside the order of dismissal if it is satisfied that there was sufficient cause for his failure to pay the court-fees or postal charges within the prescribed time, and will then appoint a day for proceeding with the suit (O.9, r.4 C.P.C.).

In the case of a suit dismissed for the plaintiff's failure to apply for a fresh summons to be issued within the prescribed period of six weeks the plaintiff's remedy lies in bringing a fresh suit, if it is not barred by the law of limitation (O.9, r.5(2) C.P.C. as amended by G.N. No. 422 of 1994).

Dismissal of Suit Where Neither Party Appears

A third situation in which a suit may be dismissed is where neither party appears when the suit is called on for hearing (O.9, r.3 C.P.C.). If a suit is so dismissed, the plaintiff has three possible remedies. He may, if the suit is not barred by the law of limitation, file a fresh suit, or he may apply to the court to have the order of dismissal set aside, and the court, if satisfied that he had sufficient cause for his non-appearance, will set aside such order of dismissal and appoint a day for proceeding with the suit (O.9, r.4 C.P.C.); or, it has been held, he could refer the matter to the High Court for review.

The application of these provisions was discussed in the case of *Jehangir Emporium v. Teema Garments* (1970) H.C.D. n.184, In that case, an interlocutory proceeding involving the question whether a third party should be joined in the suit was fixed for hearing before a Senior Resident Magistrate. On that day, the applicant had another matter before a Judge in Chambers. The applicant, following a well known practice that the High Court takes precedence over a lower court, attended the Judge in Chambers. Meanwhile his case was called up in court before the Senior Resident Magistrate. Both parties were absent, and so the court dismissed the entire suit for non-appearance of the parties. The applicant then referred the matter to the High Court for revision. The High Court held that the applicant could have applied under r.4 of O.9 to set aside the dismissal order; or he could have applied for review to the High Court. Commencing on the court's powers of dismissal under r.3 of O.9, the Court (Seaton, J.) said:

O.9 r.3 allows a court to dismiss the suit where neither party appears when the suit is called for hearing. This power is discretionary and that is why the legislature found it safe to use the word "may" rather than "shall.".In the present situation there were a number of reasons which would have forced a cautious magistrate not to proceed under this Order. In the first place the hearing was not for a suit but for a third party proceeding ... the application which was to be heard before the learned Senior Resident Magistrate was not a suit for the purpose of O.9, r.3.

In other words, the power to order dismissal for non-appearance of both parties is discretional and not mandatory and it being a judicial discretion, it must be exercised judicially. A court must first inquire, so far as it can, say, into the possible causes of non-appearance of the parties, the manner in which the parties have so far conducted themselves with regard to the case the distance between the court-house and their residence, the means of transport available to them, and any other material factor.

Consequences of Non-appearance of Defendant

If, when the suit is called on for hearing, the plaintiff appears but the defendant does not appear, then, if the suit is before the High Court and it is proved that the summons was duly served, the court may proceed *ex-parte*; if it is before any other court than the High Court, and the summons issued was summons to file defence and it is proved that the summons was duly served, the court may proceed *ex-parte*; and if the summons was a summons to appear and it is proved that the summons was duly served, the court may enter judgement for the plaintiff (O.9, r.6(1) C.P.C.).

Before a court can exercise its discretion to proceed *ex-parte* or to enter judgement for the plaintiff (as the case may be), it must be satisfied that the summons was duly served, in sufficient time and that the defendant is absent (see *Ester David Mmari v. Emmanuel Makaidi* (1967) H.C.D. n. 178).

If it is not proved that the summons was duly served on the defendant, then of course, the court cannot proceed *ex-parte* or enter judgment, but it will direct that a second summons be issued and served on the defendant; and if it is proved that the summons was duly served but not in sufficient time to enable him to appear and answer on the day fixed in the summons, the court must adjourn the hearing of the suit to a future day to be fixed by the court, and must direct that notice of such day be given to the defendant (O.9, r.6(1) C.P.C).

If it is shown that the summons was not duly served or was served in in-sufficient time as a result of the plaintiff's default, then the court must order the plaintiff to pay the costs occasioned by the adjournment (O.9, r.6(2) C.P.C.).

As we have seen earlier, in considering whether service has been duly effected, the court will normally look for an affidavit of service. This is why there is the requirement that the officer or person effecting service of a summons must file an affidavit of service. As the Court of Appeal for Eastern Africa pointed out in the case of *Kanji Naran v. Velji Ramji*, (21 E.A.C.A. 20), as a general practice, the court should require an affidavit of service of summons in every case before entering judgement in default of appearance.

The question again arises: does the word "appearance" here refer to personal appearance of the defendant? As we have seen earlier, in the case of *William Andrea Shangarai v. Farm Vehicles Ltd.* (1969) H.C.D. n. 16, the plaintiff sued the defendant for Shs. 319/15, being the balance of an account due for goods sold and delivered and work done. On the date set for hearing, the defendant was personally absent but was represented by his advocate who stated that he had been fully instructed and was prepared to proceed with the case. The trial court gave judgement for the plaintiff on the ground that O.17, r.2 and O.9, r.6 (1) (a) (ii) B of the Civil Procedure Code required the personal attendance of the defendant and not merely by his advocate. On appeal to the High Court, it was held that the provisions of O.9, r.6 (1) and O.7, r.2 (infra) must be read together with the provisions of O.3, r.1 and O.5, r.5(b) which stated that appearance of a party may be made by an advocate, and so the trial court erred in giving judgement for the plaintiff as though the defendant were absent.

From the wording of r.6 of O.9, it is clear that it is not mandatory upon a court to proceed *ex-parte* with a matter if a defendant fails to appear. The Rule is permissive. It gives a discretion to the court. So even where it is shown that a summons has been duly served upon the defendant and in sufficient time and the defendant has failed to appear on the day of the hearing of the suit, the court may refuse to proceed with the suit *ex-parte* and may adjourn the hearing to another date to be fixed by it if, in the court's opinion, it would be in the interest of justice to do so, or it may adjourn the suit to another date for *ex-parte* hearing.

If the defendant has not appeared and the court has adjourned the hearing of the suit *ex-parte*, and the defendant, at or before such ex-parte hearing gives good cause for his previous non-appearance, he may, on such terms as to costs or otherwise, be heard in answer to the suit as if he had appeared on the day fixed for his appearance. (O.9, r.7 C.P.C.). All he has to do is to appear at or before the day to which the hearing is adjourned, and show good cause for his previous non-appearance.

What amounts to "good cause," of course, will depend on the circumstances of each case. Illness, lack of means of transport, or appearance before a superior court on the day fixed for the hearing of the suit, may all amount to "good cause" in proper cases.

Where, however, it is clear to the court that non-appearance of the defendant is being used as a delaying tactic that will not constitute "sufficient cause." As was pointed out in *Watson Seafood and Poultry Co. v. H.H. Shariff,* (1967) H.C.D. n.56:

> A party's failure to give proper instruction to his advocate does not justify non-appearance at a hearing. A party cannot claim "sufficient cause" where his non-appearance seems to have been another episode in a long line of delaying tactics.

Consequences of Non-Appearance of the Plaintiff

If the defendant appears but the plaintiff does not appear on the day the suit is called on for hearing, the court must dismiss the suit unless the defendant admits the claim, or part thereof, in which event it will pass a decree against the defendant on such admission, and where the defendant admits only part of the claim, the court will dismiss the suit so far as it relates to the remainder (O.9, r.8 C.P.C.). If the suit is wholly or partly dismissed under the provisions of rule 8 (supra), the plaintiff will be precluded from bringing a fresh suit in respect of the same cause of action. The court, however, on his application, will set aside the dismissal order if it is satisfied that there was sufficient cause for the plaintiff's non-appearance when the suit was called on for hearing, on such terms as to costs or otherwise as the court may think fit, and will then appoint a day for proceeding with the suit. But no order must be made unless notice of the plaintiff's application for the same has been served on the defendant (O.9, r.9 C.P.C.).

These provisions, it must be noted, do not cover every non-appearance by a plaintiff. If, for instance, a plaintiff has given his evidence and made out his case and the case is adjourned to another date for hearing the defence case, non-appearance of the plaintiff on such other hearing date will not justify dismissal of the suit. In such an event, the proper course is to hear the evidence of the defendant and then decide the case on the merits (see *Gamaha v. Lwavu* (1970) H.C.D. n. 257).

If there are more plaintiffs than one, and one or more of them appear and the others do not appear, the court may, at the instance of the plaintiff or plaintiffs who have appeared, permit the suit to proceed, in the same way as if all the plaintiffs had appeared, or it may make such order as it thinks fit (O.9, r.10., C.P.C.). But where there are more defendants than one, and one or more of them appear, and the others do not appear, the suit must proceed and at the time of pronouncing judgement, the court will make such order as it thinks fit *vis-a vis* the defendant or defendants who do not appear (O.9, r.11, C.P.C.).

If a party who has been ordered to appear in person does not do so, or fails to show good cause for his non-appearance, such party, be he a plaintiff or defendant, is at the mercy of the court in that he will be treated in the manner described above for non-appearance of parties.

Setting Aside Decree Passed Ex-Parte

In any case in which a decree is passed *ex-parte* against a defendant, such defendant, if dissatisfied, may apply to the court by which the decree was passed for an order to set aside such *ex-parte* decree. If he satisfies the court that the summons was not duly served, or that he was prevented by any sufficient cause from appearing when the suit was called on for hearing, the court must make an order setting aside the decree against him on such terms as to costs, payment into court or otherwise as it thinks fit, and will fix a day for proceeding with the suit. If the suit is of such a nature that it cannot be set aside as against such defendant only, it may be set aside as against all or any of the other defendants also (O.9, r.12, C.P.C.).

If judgement has been entered by a court pursuant to paragraph (a) (ii) (B) of sub-rule 6 of O.9 or sub-rule (2) of rule 4 of Order VIII, it is lawful for the court, on application made by an aggrieved party within twenty-one days from the date of the judgement, to set aside or vary such judgement upon such terms as may be considered by the court to be just. But where a decree has been issued prior to such application being made, the provisions of the Law of Limitation Act will apply (O.9, r.13 C.P.C. as amended by G.N. No. 422 of 1994.).

As we have seen earlier, a decree can only properly be said to be *ex-parte* if the defendant did not appear when the suit was called on for hearing. A judgement entered where a defendant has made an appearance is not *ex-parte*. In the words of Haris, J., in *Kimani v. McConnelll* (1966) E.A. 547, at page 549:

> I am of the opinion that, generally speaking, an order which, in proceedings that are themselves inter partes, is made on the application and in the presence of one party but in the absence of the other may be correctly termed *ex-parte* notwithstanding that the other party had notice of the application and chose not to appear.

And Makame, J., had this to say in the case of *Moshi Textile Mills v. De Voest* (supra) at page 71:

> I am of the opinion that, an *ex-parte* judgement is a judgment given when there is no appearance by the party against whom it is given.

It is for the defendant to satisfy the court that there was "sufficient cause" for his non-appearance when the suit was called on for hearing. What, then, will constitute 'sufficient cause?" That will depend on the circumstances of each case, for no two cases are exactly the same. But decided cases offer a good guide from which general principles can be drawn. To these we must now turn.

In the case of *Eksteen v. Kutosi s/o Bukua* (1951) 24 (2) K.L.R. 90, the Kenya Supreme Court held that to constitute "sufficient cause" it must be shown that there was "some element of an intervening cause which the suitor was unable reasonably to prevent or overcome," and that the mere fact that an advocate forgot the date on which the suit came up for hearing does not constitute "sufficient cause."

The Uganda High Court has held that failure by a party to give proper instructions to an advocate cannot possibly constitute "sufficient cause" (see *Zirahamuzale v. Corrett* (1962) E.A. 694).

In the case of *Otanga v. Nabunjo* (1965) 384) the same court held that where a defendant fails to appear and is not represented by an advocate and if such non-appearance was due to his ignorance of the rules of procedure, that does not amount to "sufficient cause."

The case of *Shabir Din v. Ram Parkash Anand*, (1955) 22 E.A.C.A. 48, would appear to override the decision in *Aksteen's* case, In *Shabir Din's* case, it was held that a mistake or misunderstanding by a plaintiff's advocate, though negligent, may be accepted as "sufficient cause," but that each case must be decided on the basis of its own peculiar facts. Referring to *Eksteen's* case, Briggs, J.A. said, at page 50:

> According to the headnote, which I think correctly summarises the judgement on this point, "mere oversight on the part of an advocate or clerk cannot of itself be held to constitute "sufficient causes" to set aside a judgement under O.9, r.24." I think the learned Judge and the learned magistrate whom he upheld both took a wrong view of the law in this respect. I think such an oversight can be "sufficient cause." Whether it is so or not is a question depending on the facts of each case.

The phrase "prevented by any sufficient cause" was also considered in the case of *Shamsudin Mitha v. Abdulaziz Ladak,* (1960) E.A.1054, In that case, the defendant who had given a power of attorney to his brother appeared at the trial by his advocate A. on March,15, but his attorney withdrew A's instructions and applied for an adjournment to March, 16 when he appeared by another advocate T.T. who applied for and was granted a postponement of the trial on condition that the defendant paid T.shs. 2,000/= into court by March 17 failing which the trial was to take place on March 19. The condition was not complied with, the attorney withdrew instruction from T. and on March 19 again asked for a postponement; this was refused and the attorney took no further part in the day's proceedings, which resulted in an *ex-parte* decree in favour of the plaintiff. The defendant by another advocate R. later applied to another magistrate for the decree to be set aside under O.9, r.13. The application was refused. On appeal, the High Court dismissed the appeal. Citing the case of *Land Officer v. Abdulrasul Jivraji* (supra) with approval, the Court, (Simmons, J.) stated, at page 1056:

> It will be observed that the question is not solely whether the appellant did appear...; he must show also that he was prevented from appearing, and so prevented by "sufficient cause." This appellant has failed to satisfy me on any of the three elements necessary to bring him within the rule. First, I find that he did appear... I take it, and hold that if a defendant comes and asks for an adjournment to give him time to prepare the case, he has

appeared and has no remedy under the rule. Even an agent who may have no right of audience can appear for the purpose of O.9.

The Court went on, at page 1057:

> Even if it were held that this did not amount to an appearance, the defendant was not "prevented" from appearing... If a party deliberately withdraws instructions from his advocate he is not "prevented" from appearing, he prevents himself; however, if he is regarded as being prevented I hold that he is not in these circumstances prevented by "sufficient cause." The cause was of his own making and not sufficient to give him the benefit of O.9, r.13.

What emerges from the foregoing authorities, then, is that an application under O.9, r.13 can only succeed if it establishes (1) that the applicant did not in fact appear, (2) that his non-appearance was owing to the fact that he was prevented from appearing; and (3) that he was so prevented by any sufficient cause. Once the applicant has satisfied the court on those three elements of the rule, then the court must set aside the *ex-parte* decree and fix a day for the suit to be proceeded with, on such terms as to costs or otherwise as the court may deem fit. But the power to order payment of costs or to require the defendant to deposit with the court a sum of money is discretional, and it has been held that an order for costs should not exceed those thrown away by the opposite party (See *Patel v. The Star Mineral Water* (1961) E.A. 454).

The principle in *Mitha's* case (supra) that the court must confine itself to the three elements and not the merits of the case has been questioned on at least two occasions. In the case of *Kimani v. McConnell* (1966) E.A. 547, the High Court of Kenya considered the application of O.9 r. 10 of the Civil Procedure (revised) Rules, 1948, which is the equivalent of O.9, r. 13(2) of the Tanzania Civil Procedure Code, 1966. Haris, J., there said, at page 555:

> It would not perhaps be easy to define with exactitude the several considerations to which the court may properly have regard in dealing with an application under O.9, r.10... r.10 makes reference to the defendant having been so prevented and confers upon the court what would appear to be an absolute discretion to be exercised judicially in the light of the facts circumstances and merits of the particular case.

Looking at O.9 as a whole, and attempting to comprehend the purpose of rr. 10 and 24, it seems to me that a reasonable approach to the application of these rules to any particular case would be... to determine whether, in the light of all the facts and circumstances both prior and subsequent and of the respective merits, it would be just and reasonable to set aside or vary the judgement, if necessary, upon terms to be imposed.

In the case of *Mbogo v. Shah* (1968) E.A. 93, the latter part of the above quotation was quoted with approval by the Court of Appeal for East Africa (per Sir Charles Newbold, P., at page 95).

The High Court of Tanzania has adopted that view. This was in the case of *Paul S. Albert v. (1) Theresia Andrea* and (2) *Hon. The Attorney – General* (Mwanza Registry Civil Case No. 9 of 1978 – as yet unreported) in which the Court considered the provisions of O.9, r.13(2) of the Tanzania Civil Procedure code.

After referring to the principle in *Mitha's* case the Court stated:

But even in this case the authorities are not entirely in harmony and contrary positions have been taken as in *Sorabji v. Ramjilal* (1924) Bom. L.R. 321, a decision of the High Court of Bombay. Leaving that aside, there is in fact authority for the proposition that in an application under r.13(2) the court may, among other things, address itself to merits of the case.

His Lordship then quoted the above passage from *Kimani's* case and continued:

The latter part of the above statement was quoted with approval by the Court of Appeal in *Mbogo v. Shah* 1968) E.A. 93, at p.95, per Sir Charles Newbold, P. It follows that I uphold the submission of Mr. Mlewa that the merits of the case may be taken into consideration.

The better view, therefore, would seen to be that in an application under sub-rule (2) of r.13, the court may take into consideration, among other things, the merits of the case.

From these authorities, it would appear that courts have wide powers to set aside decrees which have been passed *ex-parte*. The principle seems to be that if the opposite party can be compensated by costs, and there is no evidence that the conduct of the party was a deliberate abuse of the process of the court, parties to suits must as far as possible be given fair hearing and suits decided on merits, and that there is really no yard-stick for measuring what amounts to sufficient cause. Each case must be decided on its own peculiar facts.

It sometimes happens that a defendant against whom an *ex-parte* judgment has been passed seeks remedy by way of an appeal. This is wrong. The remedy for such defendant is to file an application in the same court seeking to set aside the *ex-parte* judgement. In the case of *Mandi s/o Mtaturu v. Ntinangi* 1972) H.C.D. n. 150, the appellant originally sued the respondent for recovery of brideprice and obtained judgement *ex-parte* in Merya Primary Court. When it was being executed, the respondent went to Singida District Court requesting leave to appeal out of time, and the District Court proceeded to decide the appeal on its merits in favour of the respondent. On appeal to the High Court, the Court stated:

> ...the application was brought prematurely since the only way to seek to avoid a judgement *ex-parte* is to apply to the very court which made the order. In this case if the respondent was aggrieved by the *ex-parte* judgement against him, he had to approach the Merya Primary Court and convince it that he had sufficient cause to be absent at the trial and if he succeeded, then the matter would be determined in the same court without resorting to a court of appeal.

The court accordingly held that the *ex-parte* judgement of the Primary Court would hold until the said primary court had decided whether or not to set it aside and hear the parties afresh (see also *Mtondoo v. Janmohamed* (1970) H.C.D. n. 326).

Where judgement has been entered by a court pursuant to O.9, r.6(1) (a) (ii) (B) or O.8. r.14(2) of the Civil Procedure Code, the court, on application by the aggrieved party within twenty-one days from the date of judgement, may set aside or vary such judgement on such terms as may be considered by the court to be just. But where a decree has been issued prior to such application being made, the provisions of the Law of Limitation Act, 1971, will apply (see O.9, r.13(2) C.P.C. as amended by G.N. No. 422 of 1994.).

For purposes of the law of limitation, it has been held that the period for an application to set aside an *ex-parte* judgement is computed from the date the decree became known to the applicant, and that knowledge of decree means knowledge not merely that a decree has been passed by some court but that a particular decree has been passed in a particular court in favour of a particular person for a particular sum. (see *Attilia Mosea v. Hassanali Kassam Damji* (1967) H.C.D. n. 176; *Surjit Singh Toor t/ a Frank Sistito & Co. v. Babla & Gaijar Auto Garage* (1968) H.C.D. n. 292; and *Dr. M. Daya, Administrator of H.H. The Aga Khan Hospital Dar es Salaam v. T. Sanga* (1968) H.C.D. n. 53).

Once an application to set aside an *ex-parte* judgement is out of time, it must fail. In *Ntare v. Shinganya*, (1971) H.C.D. n. 255, an *ex-parte* decree was passed. An application to set it aside was out of time, but the Judge who heard the application allowed it "exercising" powers in the interests of justice. On appeal to the Court of Appeal for East Africa; the Court stated:

> We think it must succeed. Section 3 of the Indian Limitation Act, which applied at the relevant time is mandatory and it is not suggested that section 5 has been extended to application under O.9, r.13. We held in *Osman v. United India Fire and General Insurance Co. Ltd.*, (1968) E.A. 102, that the inherent powers of the court cannot be invoked to override the express provisions of the Limitation Act and we can see no reason to depart from that decision... the law is clear and we have no discretion.

If an application to set aside an *ex-parte* judgement has been rejected, the unsuccessful party may appeal against such rejection, if it is a case open to appeal (see O.40, r.1 (d) C.P.C.).

As noted above, where the decree is of such a nature that it cannot be set aside as against such defendant only, it may be set aside as against all or any of the other defendants also. This refers to suits in which several defendants are involved and the application to set aside the *ex-parte* decree is made by one or some only of such defendants.

What, then, is the nature of decrees contemplated here? Mulla's *Code of Civil Procedure* gives four categories of decrees which fall within the proviso. The learned author states, at page 819:

> The object is to provide for cases where it may be necessary in the ends of justice to set aside the decree not only against the applicant but also against the other defendants. This would as a general rule be so:
>
> 1) Where the decree is one and indivisible;
> 2) Where the suit would result in inconsistent decrees, if the decree were not set aside as against the other defendants also;

3) Where the relief to which the applicant is entitled in the suit could not effectively be given otherwise than by setting aside the decree as against the other defendants also;
4) Where the decree proceeds on a ground common to all the defendants.

Let us take a couple of examples. X sues A and B for goods sold and delivered to A and B who own a partnership. Both A and B do not appear on the day the suit is called on for hearing and so an *ex-parte* decree is passed against them in favour of X. Subsequently B applies for an order to set aside the *ex-parte* decree and succeeds, but A does not make an application. If the *ex-parte* decree is not set aside as against A also, and on a trial of the case against B, B proves that the goods were paid for, there would be two inconsistent decrees: one holding A liable and another declaring that X is not entitled to recover. Such a situation would defeat the ends of justice. In such a case, therefore, the court would set aside the degree as against both. A sues B, C and D jointly for an order to restrain each of the defendants from using a path which passes through his vineyard from a house in which all the defendants are tenants. Both are served with notice of hearing. On the day the case is called on for hearing, none of the three defendants appears; whereupon an *ex-parte* judgement is entered against each of them. C and D apply for an order to set aside the *ex-parte* judgement, but B, who had no sufficient cause for his non-appearance does not do so. Since the relief cannot usefully be given otherwise than by setting aside the decree as against B also, and since the decree proceeds on a ground common to all the three defendants, the court may in such a case set aside the *ex-parte* judgement not only as against the applicants C and D but also as against B.

Finally, what is the meaning of the phrase "called on for hearing?" The High Court of Tanzania has held that a suit is said to be "called for hearing" under O.9, r.13 (1) when it is to be heard for the first time (see *Moshi Textile Mills v B.J. De Voest, - (supra)*.

In all cases, however, no order to set aside an ex-parte judgement must be made without notice being served on the opposite party. In other words, when an application for an order to set aside an *ex-parte* judgement has been filed, the court must issue a notice and cause it to be served on the opposite party so that he may be heard if he so wishes (O.9, r.14 C.P.C.).

Other useful authorities on this sub-topic include *Patel v. E.A. Cargo Handling,* (1974) E.A. 75; *Jacobs v. Booths* (1960) E.A. 1054; and *Shaban v. Karadha,* (1973) E.A. 497; and (1975) L.R.T. n.13.

EXAMINATION OF PARTIES, DISCOVERY, INSPECTION AND INTERROGATORIES

EXAMINATION OF PARTIES

The purpose of pleadings, we have already noted, is to bring the parties to an issue, that is, to ensure that matters which are in dispute are clearly ascertained before the hearing of the suit starts and on what matters the parties are agreed. Those facts on which the parties do not agree and on which the court is called upon to adjudicate are called *issues*.

To that end, therefore, and at the first hearing of the suit, the court must ascertain from each party or his advocate whether he admits or denies such allegations of facts as are made in the plaint or written statement (if any) of the opposite party, and as are not expressly or by necessary implication admitted or denied by the party against whom they are made. The court must then record all such admissions and denials (O.10, r.1 C.P.C.).

So, at the first hearing of the suit, or at any subsequent hearing, any party appearing in person able to answer any material questions relating to the suit by whom such party or his advocate is accompanied, may be examined orally by the court; and if the court thinks fit, it may put in the course of such examination questions suggested by either party. This is called examination of the parties by the court, and the substance of all the answers must be recorded by the court and form part of the record (O.10, r.3 C.P.C.).

If the advocate of any party who appears by an advocate or such person accompanying an advocate as is referred to in r.2 of O.10, refuses or is unable to answer any material questions relating to the suit which the court is of the opinion that the party whom he represents ought to answer, and is likely to answer if interrogated in person, the court may postpone the hearing of the suit to a future day and direct that such party must appear in person on such day (O.10, r.4(1) C.P.C.). For instance, if during the examination a defendant requests the court that the plaintiff be asked by the court whether there has been payment of the whole or part of the amount claimed by the plaintiff subsequent to the filing of the suit, and the advocate of the plaintiff is unable to answer that question, the court may adjourn the hearing to another day and order that the plaintiff shall appear in person on such future day for the purpose of answering that question.

If, when directed to appear in person, such party fails without lawful excuse to appear in person on the day so appointed, the court may pronounce judgment against him, or make such order relating to the suit as it thinks fit (O.10, r.4(2) C.P.C.).

INTERROGATORIES

Definitions

The term "discovery" is defined in *Halsbury's Laws of England* as a term used to describe "certain processes by which a party to a civil cause or matter is enabled to obtain from the opposite party answers on oath to questions as to the facts in dispute between them and to obtain information as to, and production of, the documents relevant to the dispute, for the purpose of preparing for the trial of the cause and of obtaining a final judgment" (see Volume 12, Page 2, 3rd Edition).

The purpose of "discovery," therefore, is to make the other party disclose the existence of documents and the inspection of documents by the party applying for such discovery. The term "inspection" here simply means inspection of documents which have been disclosed by the opposite party at the instance of the other party for discovery.

Closely connected with the terms "discovery" and "inspection," is the term "interrogatories." The term "interrogatories" refers to questions formed by a party to require his opponent to answer on oath such questions relating to the matter in question in the suit between the parties "as may be necessary for disclosing fairly of the cause or matter for saving costs, regard being had to any offer by the party sought to be interrogated to deliver particulars or make admission or produce documents" (see *Halsbury's Laws of England* Vol. 12, pp 63 – 64, 3rd Edition).

Interrogatories

R.1 of O.11 of the Civil Procedure Code provides that in every suit the plaintiff or defendant, with the leave of the court, may deliver interrogatories in writing for the examination of the opposite party or parties. When such interrogatories have been prepared they must have a note at the foot thereof stating which of such interrogatories each of such parties is required to answer. But no party should deliver more than one set of interrogatories to the same party unless there is a court order to that effect. Besides, interrogatories which do not relate to any matters is question in the suit, that is, irrelevant matters, will be ignored even if they might be admissible in oral cross-examination. The reason for this is that interrogatories must be to the point.

The purpose of delivering of interrogatories is to discover from the other party what matters are admitted or denied by the opposite party. In a sense, therefore, interrogatories serve the same purpose as examination of parties by the court. As stated in *"Odgers on Pleading and Practice"*

> The object of interrogating is twofold; first, to obtain admissions to facilitate the proof of your own case; secondly, to ascertain, so far as you may, the case of your opponent. There is therefore some art required in drawing interrogatories. Think rather of the answer the defendant will probably give you than of the answer which you are instructed he ought to give. The defendant's version of the matter must differ from the plaintiff's version, and your object is to discover precisely where and to what extent they differ (page 275, 19th Edition).

Delivery of interrogatories, however, is not always a necessity, and most suits these days proceed to full trial without such interrogatories, especially when the pleadings are so clear as to leave no doubt as to what are the issues between the parties. Besides, as the language of r.2 of O.2 suggests, delivery of interrogatories is not a matter of course. The court has the discretion whether or not to grant or refuse to grant leave to deliver interrogatories. In determining whether to grant leave to a party to deliver interrogatories, the court will have to be satisfied that the interrogatories sought to be delivered are necessary and not unreasonable. In the case of *D'souza v. Ferrao* (1969) E.A. 1000, the Court of Appeal for East Africa dealt with the considerations which a court must bear in mind in granting or refusing to grant leave to deliver interrogatories. Gould, J.A., there stated, at page 1003:

> As I read r. 2, however, a judge, even though he takes the view that the proposed interrogatories would not save costs, should allow them if he considers them necessary for disposing fairly of the suit. The use of the words "either .... or" in the rule makes it clear, though the element of cost may also be one of the factors to be considered in deciding the question of fair disposal.

His Lordship added:

> Interrogatories must be necessary and not unreasonable. I am satisfied on the ordinary meaning of language that the concepts of necessity and reasonableness extend to the number of persons who are required to answer particular interrogatories as well as to the material sought to be included (see also *Knapp v. Harvey*, (1911) 2 K.B. 725, 726).

D'ouza's case is also authority for the proposition that when interrogatories have been delivered, it is mandatory that they must have a note at the foot of them stating which parties are required to answer which interrogatories, and that such note must always appear on the draft to be submitted to the court.

In the case of *Aggarwal v. Official Receiver* (1967) E.A. 585, the same Court considered the application of the provisions of O.11, r. 2 of the Tanzania Civil Procedure Code. Duffus, J.A., stated, at page 588:

> The general principle followed is to allow such interrogatories as may be necessary either for disposing fairly or more expeditiously of the case or for the purpose of saving costs and this is a matter in the discretion of the judge.

Sir Charles Newbold, P., in the same case, stated, at page 589:

> The Civil Procedure Code of Tanzania provides that a party to a suit may only administer interrogatories with the leave of the court; and then in his application he has to submit the precise interrogatories in respect of which leave is sought. There is therefore no right to administer interrogatories.

Furthermore the terms of O.11 of the Civil Procedure Code make it quite clear that in certain cases the application for leave to administer interrogatories should be refused. Those cases include, but are not restricted to, cases where the interrogatories are sought to be administered to persons who are not parties to the proceedings and where they are sought to be administered in respect of matters irrelevant to the issue in the suit. Further, in exercising his discretion a judge, and it is so specifically stated in the rules, may refuse to grant leave to administer the particular interrogatories if they are prolix, oppressive or unnecessary. By "unnecessary" the rule means that the interrogatories will serve no useful purpose.

His Lordship added, at page 590:

I may say here that certainly the main reason for granting leave to issue any particular interrogatory in respect of which leave is sought is if the judge is satisfied that the answer to this interrogatory would bring the suit to an earlier close and result in a saving of costs. Interrogatories are not intended to provide a substitute for evidence in a suit.

If a party chooses to seek leave to deliver interrogatories, he must take particular care to see that such interrogatories are reasonably bona fide and at reasonable length because, at the time of adjusting the costs of the suit, say, during taxation of the bills of costs, inquiry will be made, at the instance of any party, into the propriety of exhibiting such interrogatories, and if it is the opinion of the court, either with or without an application for inquiry, that such interrogatories have been exhibited unreasonably, vaxaciously, or at improper length, the costs occasioned by the said interrogatories and the answer thereto will have to be paid in any event by the party at fault (O.11, r.3, C.P.C.).

Where any party to a suit is a corporation or a body of persons, whether incorporate or not, which is allowed by law to sue or be sued, whether in its own name or in the name of any officer or other person, any opposite party may apply for an order allowing him to deliver interrogatories to any member or officer of such corporation or body, and an order may be made accordingly (O.11, r.4, C.P.C.). Where interrogatories have been duly delivered, the party to whom they have been delivered may object to answering them on the ground that they are scandalous or irrelevant or not exhibited bona fide for the purpose of the suit, or that the matters inquired into are not sufficiently material at that stage; or he may object on any other ground. Such objection, however, should be taken by affidavit in answer within seven days from the service of the interrogatories (O.11, r.5. C.P.C.).

On application by a party to whom the interrogatories have been delivered, the court may, as we have seen, set them aside or strike them out if it is of the opinion that they have been exhibited unreasonably or vexaciously, or are prolix, oppressive, unnecessary or scandalous. As with filing an affidavit in answer, such application must be made within seven days after service of the interrogatories (O.11, r.6, C.P.C.).

Affidavits in answer to interrogatories must be filed within ten days, or within such other time as the court may allow (O.11, r.7 C.P.C.). Should such affidavit in answer be objected to as being insufficient, the question of such insufficiency will be determined by the court (O.11, r.8 C.P.C.). Should the person interrogated be found to have omitted to answer, or to have answered insufficiently, the party interrogating may apply to the court for an order requiring him to answer, or to answer further, as the case may be, and the court may make such order requiring him to answer or answer further, either by way of an affidavit or by viva voce examination, as the court may direct (O.11, r.9 C.P.C.)

DISCOVERY AND INSPECTION

Discovery and Objections to Discovery

Any party may, without filing an affidavit, apply to the court for an order directing any other party to any suit to make discovery, that is, to disclose, on oath, any of the documents which are or have been in his position or power, relating to any matter in question in such suit. During the hearing of such application the court may, if satisfied that such discovery is not necessary, or not necessary at that stage, refuse the application or adjourn it, or it may make such order, either generally or limited to certain classes of documents, as it may, in its discretion, think fit. In any event, the court must refuse to make an order for discovery if it is of the opinion that it is not necessary either for disposing fairly of the suit or for saving costs (O.11, r.10 C.P.C.).

Should a party who has been ordered to make discovery object to making such discovery, he must file an affidavit stating which documents mentioned in the order he objects to produce (O.11, r.11 C.P.C.).

R.12 of O.11 of the Tanzania Civil Procedure Code provides

that it is lawful for the court, at any time while the suit is pending, to order the production by any party to such suit upon oath, of such of the documents in his possession or power relating to any matter in question in such suit, as the court thinks right; and that the court may deal with such documents, when produced, in such manner as it shall appear just.

On what grounds, then, may a party object to disclose documents or any of them? There are three main grounds, namely: (1) where the document in question is a public document and whose disclosure would be injurious to State interests; (2) where the document in question is a communication between a party and his advocate; and (3) where the document in question consists exclusively of the party's own case or title.

A party resisting disclosure or discovery on any of these grounds must do so in the affidavit of documents and must state the ground or grounds of the objection.

Discovery may also be prohibited or excluded by statute either impliedly or expressly. One example of such statutory prohibition is section 132 of the Tanzania Evidence Act, 1967. That section prohibits the production in evidence of the contents of any document forming part of any unpublished official records or communications received by a public officer in the course of his duty where the Minister has certified that he has examined the contents of such document and that he is of the opinion that the production of it would be prejudicial to the public interest, either by reason of the contents of it or of the fact that it belongs to a class which, on grounds of public policy, should be withheld from such production.

Inspection of Documents

Once a party has made discovery of documents in accordance with the provisions discussed above he must allow that other party to inspect such documents and take copies of such of them as the inspecting party may desire. The inspecting party will peruse the documents in question and take note of any material which he thinks will assist him at the trial.

Notice to Produce

In addition to the provisions regarding the discovery of documents, every party to a suit is entitled, at any time, to give notice to any other party in whose pleadings or affidavits reference has been made to any document, to produce such document for inspection by the party who has given such notice, or of his advocate, and to allow him or them to take copies of them. This is known as *"notice to produce."*

If, after receiving such notice, the party fails to produce the documents in question, then he will be precluded afterwards from putting any such documents in evidence on his own behalf in such suit unless he satisfies the court, where he is a defendant, that such document relates only to his own title, or that he had some other cause or excuse which, in the opinion of the court, is sufficient for not complying with such notice, in which event the court may allow the same to be put in evidence on such terms as to costs or otherwise as the court thinks fit (O.11, r.13 C.P.C.).

The party to whom notice to produce has been given must, within ten days of receipt of it, produce to the party giving the notice, notice stating a time within three days from the delivery of such notice at which the documents, or such of them as he does not object to produce, may be inspected. Such inspection may be at the office of his advocate, or, in the case of banker's books or other books of account or books in constant use for the purpose of any trade or business, at their usual place of custody. But he must clearly state in such notice which (if any) of the documents he objects to produce, and why (O.11, r.14 C.P.C.).

If the party served with a "notice to produce" omits to give the notice of a time for inspection or objects to give inspection, or offers inspection elsewhere than at the office of his advocate, the party desiring the inspection of the documents may apply to the court for an order for inspection, and the court may make such order for inspection in such place and in such manner as it may think fit. The court, however, will not order inspection where it is of the opinion that it is not necessary, either for disposing fairly of the suit or for saving costs (O.11, r. 15 C.P.C.).

Should privilege be claimed on an order of inspection for any documents, the court may inspect the document for the purpose of deciding whether or not the claim of privilege is valid (O.11, r. 16 C.P.C.).

The provision that a court may examine the document in respect to which privilege is claimed would appear to include all types of privilege. If that be so, the law in Tanzania would appear to differ from that in England. The English law would appear to make exception of privilege on the ground that the production or disclosure of a document would not be in the interest of the community. In the case of *Gain v. Gain*, (1962) 1 ALL E.R. 63, the question was whether official records kept by the Admiralty relating to the husband could be produced in a suit for divorce, whether if not, questions relating to them could be answered by a witness, and whether or not a court could inspect the documents in order to satisfy itself that the privilege is validly claimed. Quoting with approval the decision of the House of Lords in *Duncan v. Cammel Leid & Co. Ltd* (1942) 1 All E.R. 587, Wrangham, J., said, at page 64:

> It is clear from *Duncan v. Cammel Leid & Co. Ltd.* that such a certificate is conclusive of the matters which it purports to certify, if it is signed by the political head of the department of the public service involved…That being so, I am precluded from inquiring whether or not the document in question, the medical records and reports relating to the husband, ought to be withheld from production. It is clear also from *Duncan v. Cammel Leid & Co. Ltd.* that I ought not to inspect the documents in order to satisfy myself that the Permanent Under-Secretary is right.

In Tanzania, however, from the wording of r.16 (2) of O.11 of the Civil Procedure Code, it is quite apparent that the law permits a court to examine the document to which privilege is claimed for the purpose of deciding whether or not the claim of privilege is valid. This applies to all types of public policy or public interest. This is clear from the use of the words *"any document"* in the sub – rule.

On the application of any party to a suit at any time, and whether an affidavit of documents has or has not been already ordered or made, the court may make an order requiring any other party to state by affidavit whether anyone or more specific documents, to be specified in the application, is or are, or has or have at any time been, in his possession or power; and, if not then in his possession, when he parted with the same and what has happened to them.

Such an application, however, must be made on an affidavit which must state that in the belief of the deponent the party against whom the application is made has, or has at some time had, in his possession or power, the document or documents specified in the application and that they relate to the matters in question in the suit or to some of them (O.11, r.16 (3) C.P.C.).

Three requirements must be satisfied for the sub-rule to apply: (1) the application must be by affidavit; (2) the affidavit must state the deponent's belief as to the opposite party's possession of the documents; and (3) particular documents are applied for.

In the case of *Motor Mart v. The Standard Gen. Insurance*, (1960) E.A. 616 the plaintiff, in a suit for damages, applied for an order for discovery of documents under O.10, r.19 (3) of the Uganda Civil Procedure Rules, which is in *pari materia* with O. 11, r. 16(3) of the Tanzania Civil Procedure Code. The affidavit supporting the application did not contain any specific description of the documents sought to be discovered but merely referred to "any document or documents relating to" some question in the suit. Dismissing the application, Sir Audley Mackisack, C.J., said, at page 617:

> In my view, however, the application is defective in three respects. Firstly, specific documents... have not been "specified" in the application or affidavit, as O.10, r. 19 (3) requires. Secondly, the affidavit contravenes that rule by failing to state the deponents belief as to the defendant's possession of the documents. And thirdly, the decision on White v. Stafford (1901) 2 K.B. 241 shows that an affidavit is not sufficient if it merely established on a prior reasoning that certain classes of documents must be (or have been) in the opponent's possession.

In some cases, where the party from whom discovery of any kind or inspection is sought objects to the same or any part of it, and the court is satisfied that the right to the discovery or inspection sought depends on the determination of any issue or question in dispute in the suit, or that for any reason it is desirable that any issue or question in dispute in the suit should be determined before deciding upon the right to the discovery or inspection, it may order that such issue or question be determined first, and reserve its decision on an objection to discovery if it is satisfied that the application can best be dealt with after disposing of an issue or question in dispute on which the disposal of the application depends (O.11, r. 17, C.P.C.).

If a court has made an order of discovery or inspection of documents, or to answer interrogatories, and such party fails to comply with such order, then, if he be the plaintiff, he will be liable to have the suit dismissed for want of prosecution; and if he be the defendant, he will be liable to have his defence, if any, struck out, and to be placed in the same position as if he had not defended the suit, and the party interrogating or seeking discovery or inspection may apply to the court for any order to that effect, upon which the court may order accordingly (O.11, r. 18, C.P.C.).

The rule, it will be re-called, is similar to sub-rule (2) of rule 4 of O.10. As in cases falling under O.10, r. 4 (2), a suit should only be dismissed under this rule where the default is wilful. In other words, this rule should only be invoked where it is plain that the party in default does not intend to comply with the order of the court in respect thereto. As was pointed out by Sir Charles Newbold P., in the case of *Eastern Radio Service v. Tiny Tots* (1967) E.A. 392, at page 395:

> It is not, I think, in dispute that a litigant who has failed to comply with an order for discovery should not be precluded from pursuing his claim or setting up his defence unless his failure to comply was due to a wilful disregard of the order of the Court. Nor is it, I think, in dispute that wilful means intentional as opposed to accidental.

As earlier noted, interrogatories may be used for cross-examination. During a trial, any party may use in evidence any one or more of the answers or any part of an answer of the opposite party to interrogatories without putting in the matters or the whole of such answer. However, if in such a case the court is of the opinion that any others of such answers are so connected with those put in that those put in ought not to be used without those omitted, it may direct that those omitted be also put in (O.11, r. 19, C.P.C.). This discretion of the court is so as to ensure that the true picture is brought out and so avoid distortion of the effect of the answer by taking them out of context.

The provisions regarding discovery and inspection apply equally to minor plaintiff and defendants, to next friends and guardians for suits of persons under disability (O.11, r. 20, C.P.C.).

CHAPTER TWELVE

ADMISSIONS

The purpose of the rules of *Civil Procedure*, as we have noted earlier, is to bring out matters in issue so that real questions of controversy between the parties can be determined at minimal cost. One way of ensuring that this is achieved is to give a party an opportunity of admitting matters which he does not dispute in a particular suit, and so do away with the necessity of adducing evidence to prove such matters, for that which is clearly admitted requires no proof.

On the basis of that principle, any party to a suit may give notice, by his pleading or otherwise is writing, that he admits the truth of the whole or any part of the case of any other party (O.12, r. 1, C.P.C.)

In addition either party may call upon the other party to admit any document, saving all just exceptions. Should such party refuse or neglect to make such admissions after such notice, then the costs of proving such document will be paid by the party so neglecting or refusing, whatever the result of the suit may be, unless the court otherwise directs, but no costs of proving any document must be allowed unless such notice is given, except where the omission to give the notice is, in the opinion of the court, a saving of expense (O.12, r. 2 C.P.C.).

Similarly, where neither party has voluntarily made admissions under r.1 of O.12, either party may, by notice is writing, at any time not later than nine days before the day fixed for the hearing of the suit, call upon any other party to admit, for the purposes of the suit only, any specific fact or facts mentioned in such notice. Should the party on whom such notice has been served refuse or neglect to admit such facts within that period or within such further time as may be allowed by the court, the costs of proving such fact or facts must be paid by the party so refusing or neglecting, in any event, unless the court should otherwise direct. But any admission made as a result of such notice will be deemed to be made only for the purposes of the particular suit, and not as an admission to be used against the party on any other occasion or in favour of any person other than the party giving the notice.

A party making such admission, however, may, with the leave of the court, and on such terms as the court may think just, amend or withdraw any admission so made (O.12, r. 3 C.P.C.). But generally speaking, a party will not be allowed to resile from any admission which he has pleaded, unless such admission was made under a genuine mistake of fact (See *Hollis v. Burton* (1892 3 Ch. 226)

If admissions of a fact or facts have been made by any party, either on the pleadings or otherwise, the other party may apply to the court for such judgment or order as he may be entitled to upon such admission, without waiting for determination of any other question between the parties. On such application, the court may make such order, or give such judgment as it may think just (O.12, r. 4 C.P.C.).

It should be noted, however, and this is plain from the language of the rule, that a judgment on admission is not a matter of right for the party in whose favour the admissions have been made. It is a matter within the discretion of the court. The court may refuse an application for judgment on admission if it appears to it that the question in the suit is such that it ought not to do so. For instance, it has been held that where there is a counterclaim, judgment on admission ought not to be given unless it in plain that the counterclaim is frivolous or unsubstantial. In the case of *Mohamed Damji v. Lulu & Co.* (1960) E.A. 541, the defendant was sued for the sum of Shs. 3,871/70 being the balance of a running account. The defendant set up a counterclaim but admitted liability to the extent claimed by the plaintiff. Before hearing evidence, the learned magistrate, on the application of the plaintiff under Rule 6 of Order 12, and though it was opposed by the defendant, gave judgement for the respondents for the amount claimed by them with costs, and then proceeded to hear issues on the counterclaim. On appeal, Crawshaw, J., said, at page 544:

> With respect, I do not think that the learned magistrate was correct in first giving judgment on the respondents' claim before hearing the counterclaim.

His Lordship then quoted the case of *Mercy Steamship Co. v. Shuttleworth &*
Co., (1833) Q.B.D. 468, (1883) 11 Q.B.D. 531 and continued:

> In the court of first instance (1883) 10 Q.B.D. 488), Watking Williams, J.,
> observed that if the right to judgment was applied in all cases where the
> claim is admitted but there is a counterclaim for damages of equal or
> superior amount, it would take away in effect the right to set up a
> counterclaim, but that if the counterclaim was apparently frivolous or
> unsubstantial, judgment on the claim might be justified. It has not been
> suggested that the counterclaim in the instant case was frivolous or
> unsubstantial nor have any special reasons been given by the learned
> magistrate for awarding judgment.

Where a defendant clearly admits part of a claim, the court may enter
judgment for the plaintiff for the part admitted by the defendant, and
then proceed to hear evidence on that part of the claim which has not
been admitted. For example, if in a suit for arrears of rent, mesne profits
and vacant possession, the defendant clearly admits the claims for arrears
of rent and mesne profits but resists vacant possession, the court may, on
application by the plaintiff, enter judgment against the defendant in respect
of arrears of rent and mesne profits, and then proceed to try the issue of
vacant possession.

The words "or otherwise" in the rule, it has been held, must be taken
in a wide sense. The admissions of matters of fact may be by the admitting
party's pleadings, in answer to interrogatories or examination by the court,
by letter or even verbally, for, in the words of Mellin L.J., *in Gilbert v.*
Smith (1876) 2 C.D. 686, at page 689, the rule:

> ... was framed for the express purpose that if there was no dispute between
> the parties, and if there was on the pleadings such an admission as to make
> it plain that the plaintiff was entitled to a particular order, he should be
> able to obtain that order at once upon motion. It must, however, be such
> an admission of facts as would show that the plaintiff is clearly entitled to
> the order asked for, whether it be in the nature of a decree, or a judgment,
> or anything else. The rule was not meant to apply when there is any serious
> question of law to be argued. But if there is an admission on the pleadings
> which clearly entitles the plaintiff to an order, then the intention was that he
> should not have to wait, but might at once obtain any order which could
> have been made on an original hearing of the action.

Should evidence of the due service of any admissions made in pursuance of any notice to admit documents or facts be required, an affidavit of the advocate or his clerk to that effect will be sufficient evidence of such admission (O.12, r.5. C.P.C.). Similarly, an affidavit of the advocate or clerk of the service of the notice to produce, and of the time when it was served, with a copy of the notice to produce, will in all cases be sufficient evidence of the service of the notice, and of the time when it was served (O.12, r. 6 C.P.C.).

It is worth noting that while a party refusing or neglecting to admit documents will bear the costs of proving such documents, the costs occasioned by a notice to admit or produce specified documents which are not necessary will be borne by the party giving such notice (O.12, r. 7 C.P.C.) The warning here is that you must not issue notice to admit or produce unnecessary matters. As is pointed out in *Odgers on 'Pleading and Practice."*

The process should not be abused by calling on the other side to admit matters which, from the nature of the action, must obviously be seriously in issue (Page 266, 19th Edition).

CHAPTER THIRTEEN

PRODUCTION, IMPOUNDING AND RETURN
OF DOCUMENTS

PRODUCTION OF DOCUMENTS

At the first hearing of the suit, the parties or their advocates must produce all the documentary evidence of every description in their possession or power on which they intend to rely and which have already been filed in court, and documents which the court has ordered to be produced. Such documents must be accompanied by an accurate list in such form as the High Court directs, and when so listed, the court will receive them (O.13, r. 1 C.P.C.)

The High Court does not appear to have formulated the form in which such documents are to be listed. But it is preferable that the list should list the documents, be it in chronological form or in the order in which the particular subjects of the suit are to be dealt with.

The word "produce" here does not mean that the documents must be filed in court. It simply means that they should be with the parties in court. No documentary evidence in the possession or power of any party which should have been but has not been produced at the first hearing of the suit must be received at any subsequent stage of the proceedings unless the same were not produced earlier. If the court decides to receive the same, then it must record its reasons for doing so (O.13, r. 2, C.P.C.)

The purpose of this rule would appear to be to prevent fraud by the late admission of suspicious documents while at the same time allow the courts some discretion to admit such documents where it would be in the interests of justice so to do.

What amounts to "sufficient cause," of course, will depend on the nature of the suit, the nature of the documents, the conduct of the party so defaulting and other circumstances of the particular case.

If a document is irrelevant or inadmissible, the court may at any stage of the suit reject it. If it does reject it, however, it must give its reasons for doing so (O.13, r. 3 C.P.C.).

Once a document has been admitted in evidence in a suit, it must be endorsed with the following particulars: (1) number and title of the suit; (2) name of the person producing the document; (3) the date on which it is produced; and (4) a statement to the effect that it has been so admitted. Such endorsement must be signed or initialled by a judge or magistrate. So too where the document is a copy of an entry in a book, account or record (O.13,r.4,C.P.C.).

The question that arises is: that would be the consequence of failure to comply with these provisions? In the case of *Sadik Hassan Khan v. Hashim Ali Khan,* (1916) 38 Allahabad 627, a case that originated in India, the Privy Council had this to say, at page 644:

> Their Lordships, with a view of insisting on the observance of the wholesome provisions of these statutes will, in order to prevent injustice, be obliged in future on the hearing of Indian appeals to refuse to read or permit to be used any document not endorsed in the manner required.

In the case of *Secretary of State v. Shrimati,* (A.I.R.) (1928) Lahore, the Lahore High Court was of the same view. It there said:

> A reference to the entire documentary evidence for both sides in this case discloses the fact that the provisions of Order 14 rule 4, have been completely ignored by the court below, with the result that the documentary evidence for the Secretary of State, as well as for the objector, can not be regarded as having been legally before us. In these circumstances, in order to avoid failure of justice, it would be necessary for us to direct a re-trial.

The *ratio decidendi* in these two decisions would appear to be that Indian courts view these provisions as mandatory.

The position appears to be different in East African. In the case of *Alwi A. Saggar v. Abed A. Algeredi,* (1961) E.A. 767, the Court of Appeal for East Africa referred to the Privy Council's opinion in the *Sadik Khan's case* (supra) and stated (per Forbes, V-P), at page 783:

The Privy Council then proceeded to lay down the rule of practice referred to in order to prevent injustice in respect of future cases. It is to be noted that the rule is a rule of practice and not a rule of law. I find it difficult to suppose that their Lordships of the Privy Council would adhere rigidly to it where to do so would cause manifest injustice, for instance in a case where there was no dispute as to the identity of the exhibits and previous appeals had proceeded without question on the basis of the genuineness of such exhibits. The position, of course, would be very different where the identity of the exhibit was in question.

The position in East Africa, then, would appear to be that the rule that exhibits not duly endorsed will not be looked at is a rule of practice only and will be relaxed where no injustice would result by admitting them.

Except as otherwise provided by the Evidence Act, 1967, where a document admitted in evidence in the suit is an entry in a letter-book or a shop-book or other account in current use, the party on whose behalf such book or account is produced may furnish a copy of the entry; and where such a document is an entry in public record produced from a public office or by a public officer, or an entry in a book or document belonging to a person other than a party on whose behalf the book or account is produced, the court may require a copy of the entry to be furnished, if the record, book or account is produced on behalf of a party, then by that party, or if the record, book or account is produced in obedience to an order of the court acting of its own motion, then by either or any party. In such an event, the court, after causing the copy to be examined, compared and certified as required by Rule 17 of Order 7 (*ante*), the court must make the entry and cause the book, account or record in question to be returned to the person producing it (O. 13, r. 5 C.P.C.).

This rule is designed to ensure that parties to the suit or those that are not parties to the suit are not unduly inconvenienced as a result of the production in court of their books, record or accounts which are currently in use in their day to day dealings.

In addition to documents produced by the parties, the court may, on its own motion, and may, in its discretion, on the application of any of the parties to a suit, send for, either from its own records or from any other court, the record of any other suit or proceeding, and inspect the same (O.13, r. 10 (1) C.P.C.). For example, if in a suit the question is whether a certain issue is *res judicata*, the court may call for the record of the alleged suit or proceeding in which that issue is alleged to have been decided.

Should a party wish to apply for production of a record under the foregoing rule, his application must be supported by an affidavit which must state in what way the record is material to the suit in which the application is made, and that the applicant cannot, without unreasonable delay or expense, obtain a duly authenticated copy of the record or of such portion thereof as the applicant requires, or the production of the original is necessary for the purposes of justice (O.13, r. 10 (3) C.P.C.). In other words, these provisions cannot be used for admitting in evidence documents which are not admissible.

The term *"documents"* in Order 13 also applies to real evidence, that is, material objects producible as evidence (O.13, r. 11, C.P.C.). Documents which have been ruled by the court as being inadmissible must also be endorsed by the Judge or Magistrate with a statement to the effect that they have been so rejected. Obviously such documents do not form part of the record. But those admitted and endorsed form part of the record (O.13, rr. 6 and 7 C.P.C.).

IMPOUNDING AND RETURN OF DOCUMENTS

Impounding Documents

As a general rule, documents which have not been admitted in evidence and so do not form part of the record must be returned to the person who produced or sought to produce them (O.13, r. 7 (2) C.P.C.). However, notwithstanding this rule and rules 5 or 7 of Order 13 or rule 17 of Order 7 of the Civil Procedure Code, the court may, if it sees sufficient cause for doing so, direct any document/or book produced before it in any suit to be impounded and kept in the custody of an officer of the court for such period and subject to such conditions as the court thinks fit (O. 13, r. 8, C.P.C.)

Return of Documents

Unless a document is impounded by the court under the foregoing provisions, any person, whether a party to the suit or not, who desires to receive back any document produced by him in the suit and placed on record, is entitled to receive back the same, where the suit is one in which an appeal does not lie, when the suit has been disposed of, and, where the suit is one in which an appeal lies or is allowed, when the appeal has been disposed of, or when the court is satisfied that the time for preferring an appeal has elapsed and no appeal has been preferred.

In some cases, however, a document may be returned at any time earlier than the disposal of the suit or appeal if the person applying for it delivers to the proper officer a certified copy in substitution for the original and undertakes to produce the original if and when required to do so. But no document will be returned which has become wholly void or useless by force of the decree. For instance, if a party were to sue another for breach of a written contract, and the contract were to be found to be void for illegality, then the contract document may be impounded because by the nature of the decree that document is wholly void or useless (O.13, r. 9 C.P.C.).

CHAPTER FOURTEEN

ALTERNATIVE DISPUTE RESOLUTION (A.D.R.)

Introduction

The expression "Alternative Dispute Resolution" is used to refer to all modes of dispute resolution other than the traditional mode of settlement of disputes by way of trials in courts of law. As we have seen, these include arbitration, reconciliation, mediation and early neutral case evaluation.

In Tanzania, apart from arbitration and reconciliation, Alternative Dispute Resolution has taken the form of mediation.

This mode of dispute settlement was introduced in Tanzania by Government Notice No. 422 of 1994 which amended the First Schedule to the Civil Procedure Code Act, 1966. Those amendments introduced certain stages between the completion of pleadings and a trial in given cases.

Those amendments introduced into the Code three new Orders, namely, O.8A, 8B and 8C in addition to amending several other Orders. The amendments came into effect on 1st November, 1994. However, by Government Notice No. 196 of 1995 the provisions of O.8A and 8B were made applicable only to Mwanza, Arusha and Dar es Salaam Regions. The rest of the Registries of the High Court, resident and district magistrates were exempted from applying those provisions for one year. In other words, mediation was permitted only in those three areas loosely referred to as the "Pilot Areas." Although more than one year has passed, mediation, as of early 2002, is not practiced in the other areas; but technically, mediation can be practised in the rest of the country.

The reason for the restriction was that at the time Mediation was introduced at the end of 1994, very few judges, resident and district magistrates had been trained as mediators. At the moment, virtually all of them have been trained as mediators.

Initial Notice

This is a document which is sent to the parties, together with the summons and the plaint (in the case of a defendant) after the suit has been assigned to a judge or magistrate under O.4, r.3 of the Code as amended by Government Notice No. 422 of 1994. It is issued in pursuance of the provisions of Os. 4, 5, 8A, 8B and 8C of the Civil Procedure Code as amended.

This Notice informs the parties as to which judge or magistrate the case has been assigned under the individual calendar system. It also informs them as to future activities in the case, such as the period within which the process server must file an affidavit in proof of service of process; when the defendant should file his written statement of defence or other responsive pleading; and the consequences of failure to do so. Finally, it informs the parties that a date for the First Pre-trial Settlement and Scheduling Conference will be fixed within twenty – one days of conclusion of pleadings (see *infra*).

First Pre-trial Settlement and Scheduling Conference

O.8A of the Civil Procedure Code Act, 1966, introduced new steps in the civil procedure law. Those steps are Settlement and Scheduling Conferences, Scheduling Orders, Speed Tracks of cases and Mediation. To those let us now turn.

First Pre-trial Settlement and Scheduling Conference

This is a conference presided overby the judge or magistrate to whom the particular case has been assigned under O.4, r.3 of the Code. The Conference must be attended by the parties or their recognized agents or advocates. It must be held within twenty-one days after conclusion of the pleadings.

At this Conference, the judge or magistrate consults with the parties or their agents or advocates and then determines the Speed Track of the case. Thereafter he makes or prepares what is called a Scheduling Order.

Speed Tracks of Cases

This expression, usually used to refer to traffic lanes, is used in our law to categorize civil cases in accordance with their relative complexity and within what period cases in a particular category should be finalized.

By the provisions of O.8A, rule 3(3) of the Code, there are four Speed Tracks. Speed Track One is reserved for cases which the assigned judge or magistrate considers, after consulting with the parties, to be relatively simple and should, in the interests of justice, be disposed of fast. Cases within this Track should be completed within a period not exceeding ten months from the commencement of the suit.

Speed Track two is reserved for cases considered by the assigned judge or magistrate to be normal cases capable of being or are required, in the interests of justice, to be concluded within a period not exceeding twelve months; while Speed Track Three is reserved for cases considered by the court to be complex cases capable of being or are required, in the interests of justice, to be finalized within a period not exceeding fourteen months.

Speed Track four is reserved for cases considered by the court to be special or very complex cases which do not fall within the three foregoing Track categories but which nevertheless need to be concluded within a period not exceeding twenty four months.

These are the Speed Tracks which the court determines during the First Pre-trial Settlement and Scheduling Conference after consulting with the parties.

What these provisions mean, it is obvious, is that no civil case must be pending in the courts for more than twenty four months.

Scheduling Order

At that Conference, after fixing the Speed Track of the case, the judge or magistrate proceeds to make what is called a Scheduling Order. A Scheduling Order is an order which sets out future events in the case from the date of that Conference. It fixes dates and times for dealing with future events such as disposal of preliminary applications, the filing of affidavits, counter affidavits, and notices, and for the use of alternative dispute resolution. For example, if all pleadings in a case have been completed by the time the Conference is held, which is usually the case, but there is a pending application, the Scheduling Order will specify by what date the pending application must be determined. The Scheduling

Order will also specify whether the case will proceed by way of arbitration, mediation or trial, and by what dates those steps must be completed having regard to the Speed Track of the case.

When such a Scheduling Order has been made, such Order will not be departed from or amended unless the court is satisfied that such departure or amendment is necessary in the interests of justice. Should the court be so satisfied, it will depart from or amend the Order. But in such a case, unless the court should direct otherwise, the party in whose favour the departure or amendment is made must pay the costs of such departure or amendment (see O.8A, r. 4 C.P.C.).

Failure to Appear at Conference or Failure to Comply with Scheduling Order

Where parties or their agents or advocates have been duly served to appear at the Conference, a party or his agent or advocate fails without good cause to appear at the Conference or appears but is substantially unprepared to participate in the consultations at such Conference, the court must make such orders against the defaulting or unprepared party, agent or advocate as it deems fit, including an order for costs, unless there are exceptional circumstances for not making such orders. Similar sanctions will be imposed on a party who, without good cause, fails to comply with a Scheduling Order (see O.8A, r. 5 C.P.C.).

It is further provided, by r.6 of O.8A of the Code, that a Conference convened under r.3 of that Order must not be adjourned except for reasons beyond the control of the parties or the court. However, that notwithstanding, r.7 of the Order provides that the court may hold more than one session of the Pre-trial Conference for the purpose of dealing with all matters required to be dealt with at such a Conference.

Procedure at Mediation Sessions

Mediation session procedures are not, at least for the time being, to be found in the Civil Procedure Code Act, 1966. They have been designed and formulated by six local experts in Alternative Dispute Resolution mechanisms. These are contained in a Manual entitled "Manual For Mediation Training In Tanzania" (*ante*). Let us now examine those procedures.

Notice of Mediation Sessions

When, in accordance with the Scheduling Order made at the first Pre-trial Settlement and Scheduling Conference or in accordance with an amended Scheduling Order, the case is ready to proceed to mediation, a date for mediation will be fixed, and a Notice of Mediation is sent to the parties or their advocates. The Notice informs them of the date, time and place of mediation, and before whom such mediation will take place. It also informs the parties or their advocates that those people who are to attend the Mediation Session (especially in cases involving firms or corporations) must be people with authority to make a final decision in the case; that they must bring with them relevant documents; that the principle of confidentiality regarding the proceedings and anything to be produced during the mediation sessions will be respected; and that failure to attend at the Mediation session will attract sanctions – including dismissal of a suit or a default judgment.

b) **Mediator's Introductory Remarks**

On the appointed day, after welcoming the parties in his Chambers (or courtroom), the mediator and the parties introduce themselves. After ascertaining that the parties present have the authority to make a final decision in the case, the mediator makes a brief but comprehensive introductory statement, also called a Mediator's Initial Remarks. In that Statement, the mediator will tell the parties what mediation process is all about, what his role as a mediator and that of the parties is going to be, how the parties should conduct themselves during the mediation sessions, the confidentiality of the process, the advantages of mediation over other modes of dispute settlement, and the consequences of success or failure of the mediation process in the case.

The *"Manual for Mediation Training in Tanzania"* contains two samples of a mediator's introductory statement. A reader of this book would do well to familiarize himself with them.

Statement of Understanding

After ascertaining that the parties and their advocates have clearly understood the privileged confidential nature of the process as well as the consequences of success or failure of he mediation process, the mediator will ask the parties to sign what is called a Statement of Understanding which contains the information mentioned above.

Mediation Sessions

A mediator conducts mediation by holding what are called Joint and Separate Sessions. Joint Sessions are those in which all the parties appear before the mediator and the discussions begin or continue. Separate (or private) Sessions are those in which the mediator, in turns, conducts discussions with one of the parties and his advocate in the absence of the opposite party.

Invariably, a mediator starts with a First Joint Session. In this Session, each party gives a brief statement of his case, the mediator gets a general picture of the case of each party and starts noting the sticky points in the whole dispute. He may then try, using his skills and experience, to see if an agreement can be reached in that Joint Session. But that is not often the case.

When the mediator realizes that no progress is being made in that First Joint Session, or if tempers flare up, he will break into Separate Sessions to calm frayed tempers, investigate more about areas of disagreement, solicit suggestions for a possible settlement, and generally try to break stalemates.

There can be as many joint and/or separate sessions as the mediator may decide. It all depends on the progress he/she is making at each stage. But it should be pointed out that it would be wrong for a mediator to decide that mediation has failed simply because the parties are, sometimes seemingly, too far apart after the First Joint Session. Infinite patience is one of the virtues of a good mediator, for few people will readily admit that they are to blame.

Final Joint Sessions

Final Joint Sessions are those held at the conclusion of the mediation process in any given case, whether the Mediation has failed or ended in a mutual agreement. In a case where an agreement to a settlement has been reached, the agreement must be carefully drafted and all aspects of the agreement must be carefully tested with each party in separate sessions. Only when the whole agreement has been accepted by both sides should a Final Joint Session be convened. Similarly, only when all avenues for an amicable settlement have been explored without success should a Final Joint Session be convened at which the mediator will announce failure of the mediation process to resolve the dispute.

Where the mediation results in an amicable settlement of all matters in controversy between the parties, the mediator will fill in a form known as a Consent Settlement Order form. This form will contain the following particulars: (1) name of the court; (2) Number of the case; (3) names of the parties, and (4) the full terms of the agreement. The same will then be signed by all the parties as well as the mediator. But the mediator signs it in his capacity as a judge or magistrate.

Effect of Settlement Agreement

When the case has been settled through mediation and the Consent Settlement Order has been duly signed, that Order has the same legal force as an ordinary court decree, and so it can be executed as such should any of the parties default to discharge his obligations as particularized in the Consent Settlement Order.

Since such order is in the nature of a judgment by consent, it is normally not appealable. However, it may be subject to review on grounds such as fraud or misrepresentation.

The case of *Guru Engineering Works Limited v. Coast Region Co-operative Union* (Dar es Salaam District Registry Civil Case No. 320 of 1996 (unreported) affords a good example. The brief facts of the case were that on 12th August, 1999, a Consent Settlement Order was recorded and signed following a successful mediation between the plaintiff and his advocate on the one hand, and the alleged representatives of the respondent (who did not come with their advocate) on the other. When the plaintiff sought to execute the decree, the judgment-debtor filed two applications: one was for setting aside the Consent Settlement Order, and the second was for stay of execution. The earlier application was made under section 95 of the Civil Procedure Code Act, 1966.

The applicant filed two affidavits, namely, one by their learned advocate who deposed that the applicant's stand was that the applicant owed nothing to the plaintiff. On mediation day, unknown to the learned advocate who was waiting for his clients within the court premises, representatives of the applicant appeared before a mediator and settled the case on terms contrary the applicant's stand. The second affidavit was that of the applicant's Chairman who deposed that those who appeared before the mediator had no authority to represent the applicant.

For their part, neither the respondent nor those who purported to have authority during the mediation filed any counter affidavit.

The respondents argued that there was no provision in the Code permitting setting aside a consent decree. Learned counsel for the applicant submitted that the court could use its inherent power under section 95 of the Code.

The court held that where there were no provisions governing a given situation, the court would be entitled to exercise its inherent powers so that substantial justice is done. On the evidence before it, the court was satisfied that those persons who appeared at the mediation had no authority to act for the applicant. The court added:

> In my view, where a person purports to have authority of his principal in affairs affecting his principal when in fact he has no such authority, that is no less than a misrepresentation; and if such act results in adversely affecting the rights of his principal, then it becomes the duty of the court to move in and rectify the situation so that real and substantial justice is done.

The Court added:

> To put it differently, it is contrary to our sense of justice to allow to stand a judgment obtained through misrepresentation even if it suggests that it was by consent.

The court accordingly set aside the purported consent settlement order and ordered mediation to proceed afresh.

Partial Settlement

It sometimes happens that during mediation, the parties agree on the most important issues in the case but may disagree on minor issues. In such a case, it is permissible for a mediator to draw up a consent settlement order on matters agreed upon. The same will be signed by the parties and the Mediator-as judge or magistrate. The minor matters on which the parties fail to agree may then be referred to trial. Such would be the case, for instance, if the parties agree on the principal sum owed to the plaintiff by the defendant, but they disagree on the rate of interest to be charged on the principal sum agreed to be payable. This is in line with the provisions of r.4 of O.14 of the Civil Procedure Code.

Effect of Non-Settlement by Mediation

If the case does not settle at all by way of Mediation, it will be assigned to another judge or magistrate for next steps as described hereunder.

Final Pre-trial Settlement and Scheduling Conference

If, after compliance with the provisions of O.8A, rule 3(2) of the Code, that is, if, in the case that went to mediation, that case remains unresolved, the judge or magistrate to whom the case has been re-assigned will convene what is called a Final Pre-trial Settlement and Scheduling Conference. At this Conference, the parties are given a last chance to resolve the dispute by an amicable settlement. If that fails, the court will make another Scheduling Order at that Conference for future events and steps which are likely to arise in the conduct of the case, including the date or dates of trial. In making such Scheduling Order, of course, the court will be guided by the Speed Track to which the case was allocated under O.8A, rule 3(2) and (3) of the Code (see O.8B, r.3(1) and (2) C.P.C.). Sub-rule 3 of r. 3 of O.8B of the Code provides that the Final Pre-trial Settlement and Scheduling Conference must be held within a period not exceeding thirty, forty or sixty days from the time of full compliance with the First Pre-trial Settlement and Scheduling Order in respect of cases allocated to Speed Tracks One, Two or Three respectively. So, in cases which went to mediation and no settlement agreement was reached, it means from the time mediation failed to settle the case amicably.

If, at the Final Pre-trail Settlement and Scheduling Conference an amicable settlement is not reached, the court will make a final Scheduling Order as pointed out above. In addition to setting dates and time for future events, the court must also, after consultation with the parties or their advocates or agents, frame the issues according to O.14 of the Code and generally provide for matters necessary for the expeditious trial of the case depending on the relevant Speed Track of the case (see O. 8B, r. 3(4) C.P.C.).

CHAPTER FIFTEEN

SETTLEMENT OF ISSUES AND DETERMINATION OF SUIT ON ISSUE OF LAW OR ISSUES AGREED UPON

To repeat, the functions of pleadings is to ensure that the questions which are in controversy between the parties should be clearly ascertained so that each party is aware of what the other party contends and also to enable the court to know what questions it has to decide in the particular suit. As we have already noted, those questions on which the parties are not agreed and which the court is called upon to decide are called "issues."

An issue, therefore, arises when a material proposition of fact or law is asserted or affirmed by one party but denied by the other party, and "material propositions" are defined as those propositions of law or fact which the plaintiff must allege in order to show a right to sue, or which a defendant must allege in order to constitute a defence. So, each material proposition affirmed by one party and denied by the other will form the subject of a distinct issue. Issues, therefore, may be of fact or of law (O.14, r. 1(1) (2) (3) (4) and (5) C.P.C.).

For instance, if, in a suit for damages resulting from a motor accident, the plaintiff alleges that the defendant was negligent in his driving, and the defendant alleges that he was driving carefully, the question at issue in this respect will be: whether the defendant was guilty of negligent driving. That will form the subject of a distinct issue.

For obvious reasons, there can be no issues to frame and record if the defendant a t the first hearing of the suit makes no defence, for an issue only arises where one party makes a material proposition of fact or law which proposition is denied by the other party (O.14, 4.1(6) C.P.C.).

It sometimes occurs that in a suit there are issues of both fact and law, and the court is of the opinion that the suit or any part of it may be disposed of on the issues of law only. In such an event, the court must try those issues first. In which case, it may, if it thinks fit, postpone the framing and recording of the issues of fact until after it has disposed of those issues of law (O.14, r.2.C.P.C.).

For instance, if A sues the Tanzania Posts Corporation for damages arising from the negligence of the Corporation in the wording of a telegram, and the Corporation alleges that the suit in not maintainable because the Corporation is not liable under the statute that creates the Corporation, in such a case there will be issues of both fact and law. But since the issue of law goes to the root of the matter and may dispose of the entire suit, the court must first determine the issue of law, namely, whether the suit is legally maintainable.

Such a situation arose in the case of *Singida Regional Trading Company v. Tanzania Post and Telecommunications Corporation* (1979) LRT no. 11. In that case the facts, as revealed by the pleadings, were that the plaintiffs dispatched a telegram at Singida Post Office, which was owned by the defendants, to a company called GALCO at Dar es Salaam. The said telegram asked the said GALCO to dispatch to the plaintiff four thousand corrupted iron sheets to the plaintiffs at Singida. Owing to the negligence of the defendants, either at Singida Post Office or at one of their post Offices at Dar es Salaam, "four thousand" was written as "forty thousand." Upon receipt of the wrongly worded telegram, GALCO dispatched 12,000 corrugated iron sheets to the plaintiffs as a first consignment. So the plaintiffs had to transport back to GALCO the excess number of the corrugated iron sheets at a cost of Shs. 39,200/=, which was the amount claimed in the suit by the plaintiffs.

The defendant denied negligence and further pleaded that the suit was not maintainable because the applicable legislation, namely, the Tanzania Posts and Telecommunications Act, 1977, expressly exempted them from any liability.

In that case, since the issue of law went to the root of the suit, the court had first to determine that issue of law. As it turned out, the court ruled in favour of the defendants, and so the suit was disposed of even before issues of fact were settled.

It is thus clear that in order to frame issues the court examines the allegations made on oath by the parties, or by persons present on behalf of the parties. It will also examine allegations in the suit, and the contents of documents produced by either party. It is from these that the court will frame the issues in the particular suit (O.14,r.3 C.P.C.).

Apart from that, where the court is of the opinion that the issues cannot be correctly framed without the examination of some person not before the court or without the inspection of some document not produced in the suit, it may adjourn the framing of the issues to another day, and may (subject to any law to the contrary) compel the attendance of any person or the production of any document by the person in whose possession or power it is, by summons or other process (O.14 r. 4 C.P.C.).

These provisions make it plain that it is the duty of the court to frame the issues in a suit. Framing of issues is desirable and sometimes necessary in that it enables each party to know exactly what questions are in contest, what facts each of the parties must prove at the trial and so avoid adducing evidence on matters which are not at all in dispute or which are immaterial or irrelevant. Issues also enable the court to decide the questions in dispute to a finality so that the parties or their successors do not fight over the same matters again.

Now, what is the consequence of failure by the court to frame issues in a suit? In the case of *Janmohamed Umerdin v. Hussein Amarshi and Others*, (1953) 20 E.A.C.A. 41, the Court of Appeal for Eastern Africa held that the framing of issues is a rule that governs the conduct of a civil proceeding which neither the court nor counsel is entitled to leave out of account. In the case of *Norman v. Overseas Motor Transport (Tanganyika Ltd.*, (1959) E.A. 131, however, the same Court held that failure to frame issues is an irregularity which is not fatal as long as the parties at the trial knew what is the real question between them, and evidence is taken on it and the court considers it. The Court quoted with approval Mulla's *Code of Civil Procedure* where it is stated:

> If, though no issue is framed on the fact, the parties adduce evidence on the fact and discuss it before the court, and the court decides the point, as if there was an issue framed on it, the decision will not be set aside on appeal on the ground merely that no issue was framed (See also *Tuungane v. Kamala* (1978) LRT n. 21; *Tanzania Sand v. Omoni Ebi*, (1972) H.C.D. n. 219; and *Marco v. Rweyemamu*, (1977) LRT n. 59.).

As the language of the Court in the above passage suggests, there are cases in which it is sometimes necessary to frame issues. In *Umerdin's case (supra)* neither counsel asked the court to frame issues, and none were framed although the suit was a complicated one. Sir Barclay Niheli, P., there stated, at pages 41 – 42:

> The first observation I have to make is that the suit, which on the pleadings was clearly a complicated one, was made much more difficult for the learned trial Judge by the fact that no issues were framed at the commencement of the hearing. It is not clear from the record why they were not. In consequence, the hearing of the suit started in a fog which has never lifted. It may be as well, therefore, to remind Judges in Courts of First Instance in Kenya that Order 14, rules 5 and 6, requires the court at the hearing of a suit to ascertain upon what material propositions of fact or law the parties are at variance and to proceed to frame and record the issues, unless the defendant at the hearing of the suit makes no defence or where the issue has been joined upon the pleadings ....

> It may be that where, as here, neither party asked for issues, the validity of the trial could not be successfully attacked on the ground that the court should have framed issues, nevertheless, in my view neither the court nor counsel are entitled to leave out the requirements of Order 14, rule 5, this being a rule governing the conduct of a civil proceeding.

Although it is the duty of the court to frame and record issues, where the parties are represented, the court will invariably ask the advocates as to what are the agreed issues. Usually advocates will agree on the issues to be framed, and so will tell the court what issues should be framed and recorded. If, however, they do not agree, it will then be up to the court to frame and record the issues from the material before it.

Generally speaking, a party is bound by his pleadings, and so the issues must be so framed as to ensure that no party is precluded from obtaining relief to which he is entitled. The Kenya Supreme Court, however, has held that from the wording of Order 14, r. 1 (5) of the Kenya Civil Procedure (Revised) Rules, 1948, the court may go beyond issues raised by the pleadings. In *Darcy v. Jones* (1959) E.A. 121, Mayers, J., said, at page 124:

> That issues framed by the court may go beyond issues raised by he pleadings is apparent from the provisions of sub-rule (5) of r. 1 of O.14. Those provisions can conveniently be paraphrased as follows: The court shall

frame "the issues:" on which the right decision of the case appears to depend, after reading the pleadings, and after such examination of the parties as may appear necessary to ascertain about what material propositions of fact or law the parties are at variance.

If the court could not go beyond the pleadings in determining what issues ought to be framed it would be useless to confer upon the court the power to examine the parties or their advocates for the purpose of determining in what respects they were at variance. In view of the provisions of O.14, r.14, r.1 (5) it seems to me therefore quite clear that the court not merely has a right but is under a duty when framing issues so to frame them as to ensure that no party is precluded from obtaining relief to which he is entitled by reason of some technical error in his pleadings.

In the case of *Odd Jobs v. Mubia*, (1970) E.A. 476, it was held that a court may base its decision on an unpleaded issue if it appears from the course followed at the trial that the issue has been left to the court, especially where a party leads evidence and addresses the court on it (See also *Nkalubo v. Kibirige*, (1973) E.A. 102, 105).

It is submitted that the same construction should be put on Order 14, rules 1 and 4 of the Tanzania Civil Procedure Code. Having framed and recorded the issues, a court is generally bound to resolve those issues and no others. However, a court may at any time before passing a decree, amend the issues or frame additional issues on such terms as it thinks fit. It has the further power, at any time before passing a decree, to strike out any issues which appear to it to be wrongly framed or introduced (O.14, r.5 C.P.C.).

A good example of the application of these provisions is the case of *Haji M. Durvesh v. Villain*, (1957) E.A. 91. In that case, the appellant, as holder of certain bills of lading, sued the respondents who were the ship owners, for failure to deliver the goods in the bills. The goods were originally the property of an Italian Company and the bills were in the possession of one Rabie, who appeared at one time to have been sole director and administrator of the Italian Company. He, purporting to act on behalf of the company, endorsed the bills for value to the appellant. The shippers refused delivery alleging that Rabie had stolen the bills from the Company, that before the endorsement the company had been declared bankrupt by an Italian court and that Rabie thereafter had no authority to act for the company and that the same court had declared the bills null and void. Issues were framed, the first being whether the plaintiff proved that the company sold the bills of lading to the plaintiff and received the value thereof. After the plaintiff had given evidence the respondents' counsel submitted "no case." The case was adjourned for judgment but when it was called the court asked for further argument on the question whether the onus had been wrongly laid on the plaintiff, he decided that it had and that the issue should have been whether the defendants proved that although the plaintiff had produced the bills, they were nevertheless not obliged to deliver the goods to him. The court ordered that, in view of this amendment, the hearing be continued and gave leave to both parties to adduce further evidence.

The appellant appealed against that order contending that, since the respondents had submitted that there was no case they were now precluded from giving evidence and that the issue should not have been amended.

It was held that it was clearly right that on the view which the court took of the case, it should amend the issues before ruling on the plea of *"no case"* or even after.

Another pertinent example is the case of *Tanzania Tea Packers Limited v. Commissioner of Income Tax and Another* (High Court of Tanzania (Commercial Division) commercial case No. 5 of 1999 – as yet unreported), in which one of the matters in dispute, indeed the crucial one, was whether the plaintiff was entitled to the benefits of corporation tax on the basis of a Certificate of Approval issued to the plaintiff under the National Investment (Promotion and Protection) Act, 1990 (sometimes referred to by its acronym NIPPA). This first issue framed read as follows:

Did the plaintiff fulfill the investment conditions as stipulated in the Certificate of Approval?

At the time of framing this issue, it was not known as to which was the valid Certificate of Approval as there were two such Certificates, namely, one dated 24/3/95 (Exhibit A, on which the defendants relied as the valid one) and one dated 9/11/98 which the plaintiffs claimed to be the valid one. It was at the time of preparing his judgment that the learned trial Judge realized that there were the two certificates. On the evidence on record, the court found that the valid one was that dated 24/3/95 – Exhibit A. Realizing the incorrectness of the issue, the Court stated:

The first issue was framed in the form of a question. "Did the plaintiff fulfill the investment conditions as stipulated in the Certificate of Approval?" At the time of framing this issue, it was not known which was the Valid Certificate of Approval, the one dated 24/3/95 or 9/11/98. The formulation of the first issue is certainly not correct.

Amending or replacing that issue, the learned Judge stated:

> It is my considered view that the bone of contention, and on this the parties are poles apart, is what consequences should follow from non-compliance of the matter specified in Exhibit A.

In this case, no additional evidence would have been required because the issue as amended or replaced still fell squarely within the evidence already adduced by both sides.

The power to amend, add or strike out issues, however, must not be abused. The power should only be exercised where to do so would meet the ends of justice.

As pointed out above, parties may agree as to the questions of fact or of law to be decided between them. Where that is so, they may state them in the form of an issue or issues, and enter into an agreement in writing that, upon the finding of the court in the affirmative or the negative, of such issue, a sum of money specified in the agreement or to be ascertained by the court or in such manner as the court may direct, will be paid by one of the parties to the other of them or that one of them be declared entitled to some right or subject to some liability specified in the agreement; or that some property specified in the agreement and in dispute in the suit must be delivered by one of the parties to the other of them, or as that other may direct; or that one or more of the parties will do or abstain from doing some particular act specified in the agreement and relating to the matter in dispute (O.14, r.6 C.P.C.).

On receipt of such agreement, and where the court, after making such inquiry as it thinks proper, is satisfied that the agreement was duly executed by the parties, that the parties have a substantial interest in the decision of such question which they have framed as an issue, and that the question is fit to be tried and decided, it will proceed to record and try the issue and come to and state its finding or decision on such issue in the same way as if the issue had been framed by the court. It will then, on making a finding or decision on the issue, pronounce judgment according to the terms of the agreement, and a decree will follow (O. 14, r. 7 C.P.C.).

Where parties wish to submit issue for decision by the court under the foregoing provisions, therefore, they must enter into a formal written agreement. In the case of *Khimji and Others v. Bakari and Others,* (1968) E.A. 685, the parties produced an agreed statement of issues for the decision of the court under O.14, r.6 of the Kenya Civil Procedure (Revised) Rules 1948: but they did not sign a formal agreement under rule 7 of the Order. On that point, Harris, J., stated, at pages 686 – 687:

> The rules are in identical terms with the corresponding rules of O.14 of the Indian Civil Procedure Code... but the Indian Code sets out in an appendix the form of the agreement into which the parties are required to enter, making it clear that the rules are intended to mean what in fact they say, namely, that the parties, in addition to stating the issue, must enter into and sign a formal agreement to appropriate action following the court's decision.... Not without some doubt in my mind, I allowed the hearing to continue but a I subsequently had an opportunity to consider provisions of the Indian Code and was satisfied that this statement does not in itself comprise the required agreement, I caused the case to be mentioned in Chambers when I informed the respective counsel that in my opinion a formal agreement was necessary.

CHAPTER SIXTEEN

DISPOSAL OF SUIT AT FIRST HEARING

It sometimes happens that at the first hearing it becomes clear on the pleadings and other material that the parties are not at issue on any question of law or fact, that is, that the assertions of one party are not disputed or are in fact admitted by the other party. In such an event the court may at once pronounce judgment (O.15. R.1, C.P.C.).

In other cases, one of several defendants may not be at issue with the plaintiff on any question of law or fact. In such a case the court may at once pronounce judgment, and the suit will proceed only against the other defendants who are at issue with the plaintiff (O.15, r. 2 C.P.C.).

A judgment entered by a court where the parties are not at issue is often referred to as a judgment "*on admission*" or "*by consent.*" From the wording of the rule, however, it would appear that such a course is not automatic. The rule is merely permissive and not mandatory. The Court could, therefore, in a proper case, refuse to enter such judgment. For instance, a court could refuse to enter such judgment against or for one of several defendants where to do so might result in inconsistent decrees.

Let us take a simple example. A jointly sues B, C and D as partners for arrears of rent and mesne profits in respect of the premises in which the three partners are running their business. D is not at issue with A in that he admits liability. B and C, however, are at issue with A, the issue being whether A is the owner or authorized agent of the owner of the suit premises and so entitled to receive rent from the three partners for the suit premises. Judgment is then entered in favour of A against B. Upon trying the suit, the court finds that the suit premises in fact belong to X and not A and so A has no cause of action against B, D and C. In such a case, the court will end up with two inconsistent decrees in the same suit. So where it is apparent from the pleadings that such could be the result, a court may refuse to pronounce judgment against or for the defendant who is not at issue with the plaintiff, and will proceed to hear the suit as if all the defendants were at issue with the plaintiff.

In yet other cases, the parties may be at issue on some questions of law or fact. In such a case, the court will proceed to frame and record those issues at the first hearing of the suit. If after that the court is satisfied that no further argument or evidence that the parties can at once adduce is required on such of the issue as may be sufficient for the decision of the suit, and that no injustice will result from proceeding with the suit forthwith, the court may proceed to determine such issues, and if the finding thereon is sufficient for the decision, the court will postpone the further hearing of the suit and will fix a day for the production of such further evidence, or for such further argument as the case requires (O.15, r.3, C.P.C.).

In a suit in which a summons to appear has been issued by a subordinate court and either party fails, without sufficient cause, to produce the evidence on which he relies, the court has two options: it may at once pronounce judgment against the defaulting party, or if it thinks fit, it may frame and record issues and then adjourn the suit for the production of such evidence as may be necessary for its decision on such issues (O.15, r. 4, C.P.C.).

It should be noted that where a plaintiff's suit has been dismissed on the ground that the affected party has failed, without sufficient cause, to produce the evidence on which he relies, such a dismissal amounts to a judgment on the merits. In other words, unless reversed on appeal or otherwise by a superior court, such a judgment operates as *res judicata*, and so the plaintiff cannot re-litigate that same cause of action against the defendant. In the case of *Salem A.H. Zaidi v. Faud H. Himeidan* (1960) E.A. 92, the Court of Appeal for Eastern Africa considered, *inter alia*, the provisions of O.15 r.4 of the Indian Code of Civil Procedure, which is identical with the corresponding rule of Order 15 of Tanzania Civil Procedure Code, and stated, at pages 98 – 99, (per Forbes, V-P.):

Similarly in terms of O.15, r.4, of the Indian rules, if a plaintiff fails to produce evidence the court can pronounce judgment.

It does not dismiss the suit for non-prosecution.

His Lordship then went on:

> It is well settled in India that the dismissal of a claim under O.15, 17, r. 3, on account of the plaintiff's default in producing evidence to substantiate his case 'has the same effect as a dismissal founded upon evidence, and that the subject matter of such a claim will be *res judicata*.... Since the decision is deemed to be a decision on the merits, this is a logical conclusion. And it seems to me that a judgment against a party under O.15, r. 4, may, on the same principle, operate as *res judicata*.

As indicated in the passage quoted above, the dismissal of a suit under this rule must be distinguished from dismissal of a suit for non appearance of the plaintiff at an adjourned hearing. The former is a judgment, while the latter is an order and not a judgment (see *Camile v. Merali and Another* (1968) E.A. 314, 316 and 317).

CHAPTER SEVENTEEN

SUMMONING AND ATTENDANCE
OF WITNESSES

The trial of a suit requires adducing oral and/or documentary evidence before the court by the parties and/or their witnesses. So when the pleadings, examination, discovery and inspection and interrogatories, etc., have been completed, the court will fix a date for the hearing of the suit, in a case not involving mediation or where mediation did not result in an amicable settlement of the dispute.

When the hearing date has been fixed, the parties may obtain, on application to the court or to such officer as the court appoints in this behalf, summonses to persons whose attendance is required either to give evidence or to produce documents (O.16, r. 2 C.P.C.).

ISSUING OF SUMMONSES

An application for a witness summons must contain the name of the person to be summoned, and his full address for service of the summons. The party applying for a summons, however, must, before the summons is granted and within a period to be fixed by the court, pay into court such a sum of money as appears to court to be sufficient to defray travelling and other expenses of the person summoned in going to and from the court in which he is required to attend, and for one day's allowance (O.16, r.2 (1) C.P.C.). If the person to be summoned is an expert, say a doctor, in determining the amount payable under these provisions, the court may allow reasonable remuneration for the time occupied in giving evidence and in performing any work of an expert nature necessary for the case (O.16, r. 2 C.P.C.). In the case of a court which is subordinate to the

High Court, it must pay due regard, in fixing the scale of such expenses, to any rules made in that behalf.

So far, no rules have been made in respect of these provisions, and in practice parties in subordinate courts make their own arrangements for expenses of their respective witnesses. When the question arises as to the amount to be paid to witnesses, subordinate courts use scales laid down in Government or Parastatal Staff circulars. In other cases, they are guided by the Criminal Proceedings (Expenses of Assessors and Witnesses) Rules 1964 (G.N. No. 352 of 1964 as amended from time to time.

Once an application for witness summons has been duly filed, the court can not refuse to issue the summons. As is stated in Mulla's *Code of Civil Procedure*:

> A party is entitled as of right to summonses to witnesses. So long as the application is made after the institution of the suit, the court is bound to issue the summons. It does not matter that the party had himself undertaken to bring his witnesses and has failed to do so. Nor does it matter that the application is made at such a late stage of the proceedings that the witnesses can not be present in court before the final disposal of the suit. The court may on either of these cases refuse to adjourn the hearing for the attendance of the witnesses, but it has no power to refuse to issue summonses. The only case in which the court has power to refuse to issue summonses is where the application is not made bona fide.... (Thirteenth Edition, page 875 to 876).
>
> But it is the duty of a party to ensure the attendance of his witnesses (see *Hilarius Karario v. Sabaya Kirahi* (1968) H.C.D. n. 95).

If the summons can be served personally, and the sum has been paid into the court, the sum so paid must be given to the person so summoned at the time of serving him with the summons (O.16, r. 3 (C.P.C.).

If it should appear to the court or such officer as is appointed by the court in such behalf that the sum paid into court is insufficient to meet such expenses or reasonable remuneration of the person summoned as a witness, such court or officer may direct such further sum as appears to it or to him to be necessary on that account. Should the party so directed default to make such payment, the court may order such sum to be levied by attaching and selling the party's movable property. Alternatively it may discharge the person summoned without requiring him to give evidence, or it may both order such levy and discharge such person without requiring him to give evidence (O.16, r. 4(1) C.P.C.)

Sub-rule (1) of Rule 2 of Order 16 requires expenses to be paid for one day's attendance. But if often does occur that the evidence of the witness is not taken on that day or taken only in part and so it becomes necessary for the court to detain such person for longer than a day. In such an event, the court may, from time to time, order the party at whose request the person was summoned to pay into court such sum as is sufficient to defray the expenses of his detention for such further period. Should such party fail or default to make such payment, the court may levy the amount and or discharge the person summoned as outlined above (O.16, r.4 (2) C.P.C.).

In addition to money to be paid into court for witnesses in respect of whom the issue of summonses has been applied for, the party applying will be required to pay fees for issuing the summonses and, if service is to be effected by an officer of the court, fees for service of the same. The fees payable are laid done in the Schedule to the Rules of Court (see G.N. No. 308 of 1964 made under the Judicature and Application of Laws Ordinance as amended from time to time).

The Contents of a Summons

In addition to the name and address of the person to be summoned, a witness summons must contain the name of the court in which the suit is to be tried, the serial number of the suit, the names of the parties, the time and place at which he is required to attend, a statement as to whether he is required for the purpose of giving evidence or to produce a document or both, the name of the party on whose behalf he is required to give evidence or produce the document, and where it is for the purpose of producing a document, a reasonably accurate description of such document. A summons must also show the date on which it has been issued, must be duly signed by the judge or magistrate or other authorized officer, and duly sealed with the seal of the court issuing it (O. 16, r. 5 C.P.C.). Usually, a copy of it will be sent to the person at whose instance the summons is issued.

If the person summoned is summoned merely to produce a document without giving evidence, he will be deemed to have complied with the summons if he causes such document to be produced instead of attending personally to produce the same (O.16, r.6, C.P.C.).

Apart from witnesses summoned under the foregoing provisions, any person present in court may be required by the court to give evidence or to produce any document which is then and there is his possession or power (O.16, r. 7, C.P.C.). There are, however, no provisions as to how and by whom the expenses or allowances of such a witness are to be paid.

But it is submitted that the court may, in a proper case, order reasonable allowance or expenses to be paid to such witness by the person for whose benefit the witness gives evidence or produces a document

Service of Summons to Witness

The rules that govern service of summonses to witnesses and proof of such service are those that govern service of summonses on defendants, *mutatis mutandis* (O.16, r.8, C.P.C.). Those rules have been discussed in Chapter Seven of this book.

It is important to note that in all cases service must be made in sufficient time so as to allow the person summoned a reasonable time for preparation and for traveling to the place where his attendance is required (O.16, r.9 C.P.C.).

Attendance of Witnesses and Consequence of Non-attendance

Any person who has been duly served with a witness summons must attend at the place and date and time mentioned in the summons; or if he has been summoned merely for the purpose of producing a document, he must appear and produce it or cause it to be produced.

If a witness fails to appear or to produce a document in compliance with the directions in the summons, and there is evidence that the summons was issued, the court must inquire into the question whether the same was served upon the person. To that end, the court must, if the certificate of the process server has not been verified by affidavit and may, if it has been so verified, examine the process server on oath, or cause him to be so examined by another court, on the question whether or not the summons was or was not served on the person, and as to the circumstances in which it was served, or the reasons for non-service (O.16, r.10(1) C.P.C.).

If, after such inquiry, the court is satisfied that the summons was duly served, and it has reason to believe that the evidence to be given by the witness or the document to be produced by him is material, and such person has, without lawful excuse, failed to attend or to produce the document as directed in the summons, or if he has intentionally avoided service, it may issue a proclamation requiring him to attend to give evidence, or produce the document at a time and place to be named in such proclamation, and a copy of such proclamation will be affixed on the outer door or other conspicuous part of the house in which he ordinarily resides (O.16, r.10(2) C.P.C.).

Instead of, or at the time of issuing such proclamation or at any time afterwards, the court may, in its discretion, issue a warrant with or without bail, for the arrest of such person, and may order that his property be attached to such amount as it thinks fit. Such amount, however, must not exceed the amount of costs of the attachment and of any fine which may be imposed under the provisions of r.12 (see below) (O.16, r.10(3), C.P.C.).

A proclamation or warrant of arrest or attachment, therefore, ought not to be made unless it is shown: (1) that the summons was duly served or that the person has intentionally avoided service; (2) that he has failed, without lawful cause to attend or produce the document as directed in the summons; and (3) that the evidence to be given or document to be produced is material. Besides, the discretion to issue a warrant of arrest or attachment must not be lightly exercised. In exercising it, the materiality of the evidence to be given by the witness or document to be produced and the conduct of the witness must be carefully weighed, for the real purpose of these provisions, as stated in Mulla's *Code of Civil Procedure*:

> ... is to enable the court to help the parties to compel the attendance of recalcitrant witnesses, who, even though served, fail to appear without lawful excuse (Thirteenth Edition, page 885).

If at any time after attachment of his property, such person appears and satisfies the court that he did not, without lawful cause, fail to comply with the summons or intentionally avoid service, and, where he has failed to attend as directed in a proclamation in time to attend, the court will direct the release of the property from attachment, and will make such order as to the cost of the attachment as it thinks fit (O.16, r.11 C.P.C.)

If such witness does not appear, or if he appears but fails to satisfy the court as to why he failed to appear or produce a required document or avoided service of the summons, the court may impose on him a fine not exceeding one thousand shillings. In deciding the amount of such fine, the court must pay due regard to the witness's condition in life and all the circumstances of the case, and may order his property or any part of it to be attached and sold or, if already attached under the foregoing rules (r.10), to be sold for the purpose of satisfying all costs of such attachment, together with the amount of the said fine, if any. But if the person pays the fine and the costs, the attachment of the property will be raised (O.16, r.12 C.P.C.).

The mode of attachment and sale of property under these provisions is the same as that applicable to the attachment and sale of property in execution of decrees (O.16, r.13 C.P.C.). That is dealt with later in this book.

We have seen that the court has power to cause any person then and there present to give evidence or produce a document which is in his possession or power. In addition, the court has a discretion, subject to any law to the contrary, at any time and of its own motion, to cause any person other than a party to be summoned as a witness to give evidence, or to produce a document in his possession or power, on a day to be appointed, and may examine him as a witness or require him to produce such document (O.16, r.14 C.P.C.) But the court will use this power only where it is absolutely necessary (see *Zenda v. Zenda*, (1977) LRT. N. 23; and *Salumu v. Saidi* (1970) H.C.D. n. 95).

This being a judicial discretion, it has of course, to be exercised judicially. It must only be exercised where the court is satisfied that it is in the interests of justice to do so. Once a person summoned as a witness attends, he must, unless otherwise directed by the court, continue to attend at each hearing until the suit has been disposed of (O.16, r. 16(i) C.P.C.). Usually, however, once a witness has given evidence, he is allowed by the court to depart, unless either of the parties has indicated that the witness may be required again later in the course of the trial, or unless the court itself is of that opinion.

Sometimes it becomes necessary to ensure that a witness will not in fact depart without the leave of the court. In such a case, the court may, on the application of either party, require such witness to furnish security to attend at the next or any other day to which the hearing may be adjourned or until the suit is disposed of. But the party who makes the application will be asked to pay any necessary expenses. If the witness fails to furnish such security, the court may detain him as a civil prisoner (O.16, r. 17 C.P.C.).

As in the case of a summons to appear on a defendant, no one must be ordered to attend in person to give evidence unless he resides within the local limits of the court's ordinary jurisdiction, or, outside such limits but at a place less than fifty or, where there is railway or steamer communication or other established public conveyance for five sixths of the distance between the place where he resides and the place where the court is situated, less than two hundred miles distance from the court – house (O.16, r.19, C.P.C.).

In practice, however, this rule is not followed. Witnesses from distances longer than these mentioned in this rule are often called in person to give evidence. But if the rule is adhered to, then the alternative of obtaining the evidence of such witnesses is by taking it on commission.

Consequence of Refusal by Party to Give Evidence or Produce Document

If a case has been set done for trial, and on the day of the trial a party to the suit and present in court refuses, without lawful excuse, when required by the court to give evidence or to produce any document then and there in his possession or power, the court may pronounce judgment against him or make such order in relation to the suit as it thinks fit (O.16, r. 20 C.P.C.).

Where a party to the suit is required to give evidence, he will be treated in the same way as an ordinary witness and be subject to the same rules that govern ordinary witnesses, *mutatis mutandis* (O.16, r. 21, C.P.C.).

It is, naturally, the duty of parties to give evidence on their own behalf, for the case of a party is usually based on his own evidence. So, if a party, who is in a position to give evidence, does not go into the box, the court is free to draw an inference against him (see *Pirgonda v. Vishnanath A.I.R.* (1956) Bombay 251).

It is worth noting here that where a witness has been summoned at the instance of the court, such witness becomes a witness of the court and not that of any party (see *Joseph Marco v. Paschal Rweyemamu* (1977) LRT n. 59).

CHAPTER EIGHTEEN

ADJOURNMENTS

It is very rare that the hearing of a suit is completed in one day or at one sitting of the court. Nature has not given man immunity against divers inhibiting forces. The hearing of a suit, therefore, may collapse because some witness may be absent, a party may feel indisposed in the course of or just before the hearing, a document may not be available, the judge or magistrate may feel indisposed or may be called upon to attend to more urgent business, and so on.

To that end, courts are empowered to adjourn the hearing of suits from time to time; and if a party shows sufficient cause, the court may, at any stage of the suit, grant time to such party.

Where the court adjourns the hearing of the suit or grants time to the parties or any of them the court must fix a day for the further hearing of the suit, and may make such order as to costs occasioned by the adjournment as it thinks fit. But where the hearing of the suit has begun, the hearing must be continued from day to day until all the witnesses present have been examined. If, however, the court finds the adjournment of the hearing to beyond the following day to be necessary, it will adjourn the hearing to some other day, but it must record the reasons for so doing (O.17, r. 1, C.P.C.).

These provisions, it will be obvious, are intended to ensure quick completion of trials in order to save costs while at the same time accommodating unforeseen circumstances.

It sometimes happens that circumstances are such that on granting an adjournment, it is not possible to fix another hearing date. In such a case, the court may fix a date for the case to be mentioned before another hearing date is fixed. In other cases, say, where the parties are trying to reach a settlement but anticipate that the negotiations will be difficult and protracted, the court may adjourn the case *sine die*, that it, indefinitely, or without any date being indicated.

The question whether or not to adjourn the hearing of a suit is at the discretion of the court and it being a judicial discretion, it must be exercised judicially. The paramount consideration must be the interests of justice. In the words of Lord Atkin, L.J., in the case of *Maxwell v. Kaun* (1927) All E.R. 335 at pages 338 – 339, and (1928) 1 K.B. 645, at page 653:

> I quite agree the Court of Appeal ought to be very slow indeed to interfere with the discretion of the learned Judge on such a question as an adjournment of a trial, and it very seldom does do so; but on the other hand, if it appears that the result of the order made below is to defeat the rights of the parties altogether, and to do that which the Court of Appeal is satisfied would be an injustice to one or other of the parties, then the Court has power to review such an order, and it is, to my mind, its duty to do so.

That passage was quoted with approval by the Kenya Supreme Court in the case of *Rattan Singh v. Jawala Singh* (1952) 25 K.L.R. 73. In that case, the appellant was defendant in a civil suit before the Magistrate at Kisii and was resident at Mombasa. Appearance was entered and defence was filed. On 29th November on the ex-parte application of the respondent-plaintiff the court fixed the hearing of the suit for 10th December. Notification was served on the defendant at 5.30pm on 4th December. On 7th December, defendant's advocate applied by telegram for an adjournment. The application was refused and on 10th December, the defendant did not attend and his advocate renewed his application for an adjournment. The magistrate rejected the application without assigning any reason. De Lestang, J., (as he then was) stated at page 74:

> In the present case, considering that the train leaves Mombasa daily not later than 5 pm., the appellant was given in effect four days to transport himself from Mombasa to Kisii to defend the suit. Is that sufficient notice to give to a defendant in the circumstances? The answer can only be a most emphatic. "No".... Has the learned magistrate exercised his discretion judicially in the present case?" Again, I say most emphatically "No." He knew that the suit was contested. He knew what would result if he

proceeded to trial in the appellant's absence and yet, judging by the record, he appears not to have seriously considered the appellant's application but dismissed it without assigning any reason.

His Lordship concluded, at page 75:

> In my view the appellant having been given such short notice was, as it were, entitled to an adjournment. He had not been guilty of any conduct as would disentitle him of it and no injustice could possibly have been caused to the respondent by an adjournment. In my judgment the refusal of an adjournment in this case amounted to a denial of justice to the appellant.

In the case of *Mohindra v. Mohindra* (20 E.A.C.A. 56), the facts were that when the suit came on for hearing before the court of first instance the appellant asked for an adjournment on the ground that he wished to engage an advocate. He intimated that he wished to call no other witnesses than himself. Trial Judge refused the application without stating reasons. The court quoted *Maxwell's* case (supra) with approval and held that only on rarest occasions will an appellate court interfere with the discretion of the trial Judge as to adjournment of a trial, and that it will not interfere where the Judge's decision was such that justice did not result from the exercise of his discretion and he failed to see that such would be the effect of his decision. The court dismissed the appeal holding that in the circumstances it was impossible to say that the Judge's refusal to allow an adjournment had resulted in injustice.

In the case of *Manumbai Patel v. Richard Gottfreid,* (20 E.A.C.A. 81), the facts were that the plaintiff/respondent sued the defendant/appellant, in detinue. When the plaintiff's case closed, the defendant's advocate opened his case and produced medical certificate that the defendant was ill and recommended complete rest, and sought adjournment. This was opposed by the plaintiff. Evidence was taken on this point by the trial Judge, who refused the adjournment, whereupon counsel for the defendant withdraw and judgment was entered for the plaintiff. On appeal, Sir Newham Worley V-P., said at page 82:

> It is of course not in doubt that any question of adjournment is a matter within the discretion of the Judge of the court of trial and the manner of its exercise will not be interfered with if it appears to an Appellate Court that all necessary matters have been taken into consideration. I should like

to define my approach to this appeal by respectfully adopting the words of Atkin, L.J., (as he then was) in *Maxwell v. Keun* (1928) I.K.B. 645 at page 653,

where he said:

> I quite agree the Court of Appeal ought to be very slow indeed to interfere with the discretion of the learned Judge on such a question as an adjournment of a trial, and it very seldom does do so; but on the other had, if it appears that the result of the order made below is to defeat the rights of the parties altogether, and to do that which the Court of Appeal is satisfied would be an injustice to one or other of the parties, then the court has power to review such an order, and it is, to my mind, its duty to do so.

His Lordship also quoted with approval a passage in the judgment of Scott, L.J. in *Dick v. Piller*, (1943) 1 All E.R. 627, at page 629, which states:

> If an important witness – a fortiori if he is a party – is prevented by illness from attending the court for an adjourned hearing, at which his evidence is directly and seriously material, what is the legal duty of the judge when an adjournment is asked for? My view, if he is satisfied (i) of the medical fact and (ii) that the evidence is relevant and may be important, it is his duty to give an adjournment – it may be on terms – but he ought to give it unless, on the other hand, he is satisfied that an injustice would thereby be done to the other side which can not be reduced by costs.

The appeal was allowed (see also *Ntagazwa v. Bunyambo*, (1997) T.L.R. 242 and *C.R.D.B. v. Filton*, (1993) T.L.R. 284).

It should be emphasized that the decision whether or not to adjourn a case is for the court to make. It cannot be imposed on the court by the parties, even where the parties "consent" to such an adjournment. In the case of *Shabani Mbega and another v. Karadha Co. Ltd. and Another.* (1975) LRT. n. 13, advocates for the parties filed a *"consent letter"* wanting to remove a case from the hearing list. Onyiuke J., had this to say, at page 58:

> An adjournment can not be granted as of right but can only be granted for a sufficient cause. It involves therefore an exercise of discretion by the

court and this must be exercised judicially. To allow a "consent letter" to have an automatic effect claimed for it cannot be said to be a judicial exercise of discretion. It is an abdication of function. It takes the trial of a case out of the control of the court and makes the advocates for the parties the final arbiters as to when it shall be tried.

His Lordship went on, at page 59:

> For these reasons, I rule that a consent letter, filed by the advocates for the parties can be no more than an application for an adjournment or a notice of an intention to apply for an adjournment of a case. It cannot affect the principle adumbrated in the Civil Procedure Code that an adjournment can only be granted for sufficient cause. It would be wrong for advocates to assume that once a "consent letter" is filed, they are at liberty to advise the parties and their witnesses not to attend on the date fixed for the hearing of the case. It would be equally unwise for advocates to wait till the very last moment to file their "consent letter" (see also, *Damodar v. Jariwala*, (1980) T.L.R. 31; and *Central Asbestos v. Dodd*, (1972) 2 All E.R. 1135, 1153).

This principle was reiterated by the Court of Appeal for East Africa in the case of *A.S. Maskini v. George Mbugus & Another*, (1976) L.R.T. n. 62, in which the court held that although a consent letter might be a factor which may be taken into consideration in an application for adjournment, such consent letter can not almost certainly result in an adjournment being granted.

By the provisions of O.17, r.1(2) of the Civil Procedure Code, where a suit has been adjourned at the request of the plaintiff or by consent of both parties, such suit must be placed last in the list of pending cases. By a proviso to that sub-rule, as stated above, once the hearing of the suit has been commenced, it must be continued from day to day until all the witnesses present have been examined. The proviso adds that the court may adjourn the hearing to beyond the following day only if the court finds that there are exceptional reasons or where the circumstances are beyond the control of the party or parties to the case.

As a sterner measure, the proviso adds that the mere fact that a party's advocate is engaged in another court must not be a ground for an adjournment. It is further provided that where a party applies for an adjournment on the ground that his/her advocate is ill or is unable to conduct the case for any other reason, the court must not grant the application for adjournment unless it is satisfied that the party making the application could not have engaged another advocate in time.

In the same vein, the proviso further states that where a witness is present in court but a party or his/her advocate is not ready to examine such witness, the court may, if it thinks fit, receive the evidence of the witness and make such orders as it thinks fit dispensing with the examination inchief or cross – examination of the witness, as the case may be, by the party or his advocate not present or not so ready.

Rule 4 of O.17 of the Civil Procedure Code, as amended by G.N. No. 508 of 1991 provides that where the hearing of the suit has been adjourned generally, the court must, if no application is made within twelve months of the last adjournment, dismiss the suit.

From these authorities, the position would appear to be that it is for a trial court to decide whether or not to grant an adjournment and upon what terms. Since this is a judicial discretion, the discretion must be exercised judicially. An adjournment must not be refused where to do so would result in injustice being done to the parties. It is however, for the applicant to show good cause for seeking an adjournment, and good cause will depend on the circumstances of each case. In the words of Woodroffe & Ameer Ali, "sufficient cause:"

> ...must depend on the circumstances of each particular case, and precedents are not generally of use. The court, however, should act reasonably and with indulgence towards litigants where there is no ground for imputing a deliberate intention to delay.

If an adjournment has been granted and on the day to which the hearing of the suit is adjourned the parties or any of them fail to appear, the court may proceed to dispose of the suit in one of the modes directed by Order 9, or it may make such other order as it thinks fit (O.17, r.2 C.P.C.). The modes directed under Order 9 of the Civil Procedure Code have been discussed in Chapter Eight of this book.

While Order 9 deals with the disposal of a case in the absence of the parties or either of them at the first hearing, O.17, r.2 applies to adjourned hearing. But the consequences may be the same, and a suit dismissed under r.2 of the O.17 may be restored under the provisions of Order 9.

The provisions of the rule make it clear that the court will not automatically proceed to dispose of the suit if parties or one of them fails to attend at the adjourned hearing. It may, in its discretion, decide against proceeding with the suit and make some other order as it thinks fit. In deciding what order to make, a court will bear in mind what course will best serve the interests of justice.

In some cases, a party to a suit may be granted time, either to produce his evidence, or procure and cause his witnesses to attend, or to do any other act necessary to the further progress of the suit. In such a case the court will allow him time within which to do so. If he fails to do that which he had been told or allowed to do within the specified period, the court may, notwithstanding such default, proceed to decide the suit forthwith (O.17, r. 3 C.P.C.)

The distinction between the application of this rule and rule 2 above would appear to be that an order made under rule 2 can be set aside and the suit proceeded with under the provisions of O.9, r. 9: but where a court gives its decision under r.3 of O.17, such decision is a decision on merits and can only be set aside on appeal or revision. Such a decision, therefore, operates as *res judicata* (see *Saleem A.H. Zaid v. Faud Humeidan*, (1960) E.A. 92 – *supra*).

It would also appear that rule 2 applies to cases where there is no material on the record on which the court can pronounce a decision, while rule 3 presupposes that there is material before the court on which it can proceed to pronounce a decision in the suit.

Another distinction between the two rules is that rule 2 relates to cases in which there has been a general adjournment, while rule 3 refers to cases in which the adjournment has been for the purpose of enabling a party to do a particular act.

The purpose of the rule is obvious. It is intended to enable courts to dispose of cases in which the parties are no longer interested. As was stated by the Supreme Court of Kenya in the case of *Victory Construction Co. v. A.N. Duggal* (1962) E.A. 697, at page 700 (per Edmonds, J.):

> The purpose of r. 6(c.f.r. 5 of the Tanzania Civil Procedure Code, 1966) in my view is to provide the court with administrative machinery to disencumber itself of case records in which the parties appear to have lost interest (see also *Kaijage v. Byarushengo*, (1969) H.C.D. n. 351; and *Fazal v. Gulamali* (No. 1) (1976) L.R.T. n. 35).

As stated by the rule, the court need not serve a notice on the plaintiff in this regard, although it may do so as an act of benevolence in order to give the plaintiff an opportunity of showing cause why an order of dismissal should not be made.

The power of dismissal under these provisions is discretionary. It being a judicial discretion, a court must, therefore, exercise it judicially. A case is not to be dismissed as a matter of course merely because the parties or any of them have taken no step for that period. A court must consider the matter first. As was sated by the court in the *Victory Instruction* case (Supra) at page 700:

> rule 6, unlike r. 2 of O.16, makes no provision for notices to the parties, but in order that a plaintiff may not be entirely shut out of his remedy against a defendant in the event of his suit being dismissed, specific provision is made in r. 6 allowing plaintiff, subject to the law of limitation, to bring a fresh suit. However, where a court does adopt the benevolent procedure of giving a plaintiff an opportunity of showing cause against an order of dismissal, the decision thereon is one which is entirely within the discretion of the court, and, even where a plaintiff has taken no steps of any kind, a court may still decide not to dismiss the action if, in its opinion, the interests of justice so dictate.

In any case not covered by the foregoing provisions in which no application is made or step taken for a period of two years by either party with a view to proceeding with the suit, the court may, without notice, order the suit to be struck out for want of prosecution, and then give notice of the order on the court notice board. In such a case, the remedy available to the plaintiff is to file a fresh suit, if he is not barred from doing so by the law of limitation (O.17, r.5 C.P.C. - as amended by G.N. 508 of 1991).

CHAPTER NINETEEN

HEARING OF SUITS AND EXAMINATION OF WITNESSES

In the proceeding chapters we have discussed the manner in which pleadings must be made, the appearance of parties, the mode and contents of interrogatories and examination of parties, how to compel the attendance of witnesses, and the drawing up and recording of issues in the suit. When all those matters have been dealt with, the suit is ready for hearing. We now move on to the actual hearing of suits.

Who has the Right to Begin?

The order in which parties will be required to produce evidence depends, largely, on the question as to who has the burden of proving a particular issue. In general, the plaintiff, being the person who asserts facts on which his cause or causes of action are founded, has the right to begin. But if the defendant admits the facts alleged or asserted by the plaintiff but contends that either in point of law or on some additional facts alleged by him the plaintiff is not entitled to any part of the relief which he seeks, then the defendant will have the right to begin in that the burden of proving those additional facts lies on him (O. 18, r. 1 C.P.C.).

The question as to who has the right to begin, therefore, must be determined by the rules of evidence. The expression *"burden of proof"* or *"onus probandi"* is defined in many ways depending upon the sense in which it is used. In this context, the expression is used to mean the obligation of proving alleged facts, that is, the obligation to adduce evidence to prove or disprove an alleged fact and the failure to discharge which will mean risk of failure in the case. So the burden of proof in any case lies on him who would fail if no evidence at all were given by either side in the case (see section 111 of the Tanzania Evidence Act, 1967).

Therefore, whoever desires any court to give judgment in his favour as to any legal right or liability of the other party dependent on the existence of facts which he asserts, must prove by evidence that those facts exist. Such person is said to have the burden of proof, and so has the right to begin.

So, if in a suit for damages for injuries arising out of a motor accident, the plaintiff alleges that the defendant was negligent, and the defendant denies that allegation, the plaintiff has the right to begin. If, on he other hand, the defendant raises a preliminary objection that the suit is not maintainable because, say, it is *res judicata* or is time barred, then the defendant has the right to begin on those particular objections.

The Procedure at Hearing

On the day the suit comes up for hearing either for the first time or on any other day to which the hearing is adjourned, the party who has the right to begin will state his case and produce his evidence in support of the issues which he is bound to prove. The other party will then state his own case and produce his evidence (if any) and may then address the court generally on the whole case. Thereafter the party beginning may reply generally on he whole case (O.18, r.2 C.P.C.).

There are cases in which several issues are framed and recorded and the burden of providing some only of which lies on one and that of proving the rest lies on the other party. In such a case, the party beginning may, at his option, either produce evidence on those issues or reserve it by way of an answer to the evidence produced by the other party; and, in the latter case, the party beginning may produce evidence on those issues after the other evidence so produced by the party beginning; but the party beginning will then be entitled to reply on the whole case (O.18, r.3 C.P.C.).

The evidence of the witnesses who are present must be taken on oath and orally in open court in the presence and under the personal direction and superintendence of the presiding judge or magistrate. It should, in general, be in narrative and not in question and answer form, and must be signed by the presiding judge or magistrate (O.18, r.4 and 5 C.P.C.).

If a witness is about to leave the jurisdiction of the court, or if there is sufficient reason why his evidence should be taken immediately, the court may, on the application of any party or of the witness, at any time after the suit has been instituted, take the evidence of such witness. This, of course, must be done in the presence of both or all the parties (O.18, r. 11 C.P.C.).

The rule that the evidence of witnesses should not be in question and answer form is not absolute. There are times when the nature and importance of a question or the importance of an answer to it is such that it is necessary to record both the question and the answer to it. In such an event it is perfectly proper for the presiding judge or magistrate to record or cause to be recorded such question and the answer thereto on application by any party or his advocate if there appears to be a special reason for doing so (O.18, r.6 C.P.C.).

Another occasion when a question may be recorded is when a particular question has been objected to and there appears to be any special reason for recording the question, the objection and the name of the person making the objection, together with the ruling of the court on the objection (O.18, r.7 C.P.C.).

The foregoing rules, it will be noted, do not set out the manner in which witnesses should give evidence. Although this is a subject which belongs to the province of the Law of Evidence, it is sufficiently important to warrant mention here.

As a general rule, all witnesses must be examined in open court and on oath or affirmation, that is, they must swear or affirm (depending on their religious faith) to tell the truth, the whole truth and nothing but the truth. The only exceptions to this rule are children of tender years, who, if the court is satisfied, after due inquiry, that although they are sufficiently intelligent to appreciate the value of telling the truth, they do not know the nature, value and obligations of an oath. Such witnesses may give evidence without being sworn or affirmed.

Generally speaking, there are three stages in the examination of witnesses: in examination-in-chief, the party calling the witness examines him, that is, he asks the witness all questions the answers to which will support his case.

The object of examination-in-chief, therefore, is to let the witness give all the material facts which the witness knows and on which the case of the party calling him wholly or partly depends. It is, therefore, most important that the party calling the witness must extract from the witness as much of the material facts in his favour as the witness knows or remembers.

When examination-in-chief has been completed, the opposite party is given the opportunity to examine the witness. This is called cross-examination. Its purpose is to test the accuracy and truthfulness of the witness, to destroy or weaken his evidence, or show that the witness is unreliable, or to extract from the witness evidence which is favourable to the party cross – examining the witness.

When cross-examination is over, the party calling the witness will, if he so desires, examine the witness again. This is called re-examination. The purpose of re-examination is, so to speak, to mend holes or repair the damage done by cross-examination. It is the last opportunity a witness has of explaining vague statements or apparent contradictions revealed in cross-examination.

Leading Questions

Examination of witnesses must not be done haphazardly. It must follow well-defined rules of evidence. For instance, in examination-in-chief, you may not, generally speaking, ask leading questions and a party may not cross-examine his own witness unless the witness has turned "*hostile*" and the court has given permission to the party to cross-examine the witness.

Remarks on Dameanour of Witnesses

The purpose of a trial is to arrive at the truth, and the truth is usually to be found in the evidence of the witnesses. In deciding whether or not to believe a particular witness, a judge or magistrate is assisted, among other things, by the demeanour of the witness, that is, the manner in which the witness comports himself as he gives evidence. The witness's hesitation, his confidence, calmness or precipitancy, etc., ought to be watched carefully by a trial judge or magistrate for they have a lot to reveal about the witness and his evidence.

It is for this reason that findings of fact by a trial court are not lightly interfered with on appeal. It is appreciated that a trial judge or magistrate has had the advantage of seeing and hearing the witnesses as they gave evidence, and his decision as to which witness to believe and which one not to believe is based as much on the evidence as on the demeanour of the witnesses. As was stated by Lord Shaw, afterwards Lord Dunedin, in the case of *Clark v. Edinburgh Tramway Co.* (1919) S.C. (H.H.) 35:

Witnesses without any conscious bias towards a conclusion may have in their demeanour, in their manner, in their hesitation, in the nuances of their expressions and even the turn of an eyelid, left impression upon the man who saw and heard them which could never be reproduced in a printed page.

It is for this reason that a judge or magistrate is permitted to record or cause to be recorded such remarks as he thinks are material respecting the demeanour of any witness while under examination. It is sufficient if he inserts, in appropriate places in the record, remarks such as *"reluctant," "evasive," "hesitant," "precipitate," "unreasonably refuses to answer questions,"* and so on.

Re-call of Witness

It sometimes occurs that after a witness has given evidence, either of the parties or the court may be of the view that some material facts to which the witness could have testified has been omitted. In such an event, the court may, at any time during the hearing of the suit, re-call such witness and, subject to the rules of evidence, put such questions to him as the court thinks fit (O.18, r.12. C.P.C.).

Record in Shorthand

Invariably, evidence of witnesses is recorded in long hand by the trial Judge or magistrate himself, and as nearly as possible in the words of the witness, but in the language of the court.

However, a judge or magistrate may direct a court stenographer to make a shorthand record of the whole of, or the substance of, the evidence of any witness, or other proceedings.

In such a case, the shorthand record must be transcribed and typewritten as soon as practicable thereafter by the same or any other court stenographer who must certify the resultant transcript to be correct and complete, and thereupon it will form part of the record (O.18, r.9(1) and (2) C.P.C.).

The expression *"court stenographer"* here means any person appointed by the Chief Justice to be court stenographer (O.18, r.9(3) C.P.C.).

But with the never-ending shortage of qualified stenographers, a judge or magistrate would do well to settle for the grim prospect of having to record all the proceedings himself in his own long hand until such time when he is saved by technological advances, which is the hope of all of us.

In the Event of Death, Transfer, etc.

If a judge or magistrate is prevented by death, transfer or other cause from finalizing the trial of a suit, his successor may deal with any evidence or memorandum taken down or made under the rules discussed above as if such evidence or memorandum had been taken down or made by him or under his direction, and may proceed with the suit from the stage at which his predecessor left it. The same procedure applies, *mutatis mutandis*, to evidence taken in a suit transferred under the provisions of section 21 of the Civil Procedure Code (O.18, r.10 C.P.C.).

Where in a suit any question has arisen as regards any property or thing, the court may, at any stage in the suit, inspect such property or thing. (O.18, r.13 C.P.C.). For instance, if, in a suit for vacant possession, a plaintiff claims that he has offered reasonably equivalent alternative accommodation, and that if an order for vacant possession is not made, he will suffer great hardship because his present accommodation is quite inadequate, then the court may, at any time of the hearing of the suit, inspect the two properties in question in order to determine the question of reasonableness of the alternative accommodation and the hardship that would be experienced by the plaintiff if an order for vacant possession is not made.

No Case to Answer

The Civil Procedure Code Act, 1966, does not provide for *"no case to answer"* situation. The expression *"no case to answer"* means a submission by a defendant (as by the defence in criminal proceedings) at the close of the plaintiff's (or prosecution's case) that the evidence adduced does not establish a *prima facie* case on which the court could hold the defendant liable and so the court should dismiss the case without calling upon the defendant (or the accused) to adduce evidence in rebuttal.

In a civil case, as is the case of an accused person in a criminal trial, should the defendant make a submission of no case to answer, and the court rules that there is a case to answer, the court will proceed to hear the evidence of the defence and thereafter pronounce a final decision on the whole case as to the liability or otherwise of any of the parties in the suit on the basis of the issues framed. If the defendant elects to give no evidence after the submission of no case to answer has been turned done, then the court will consider the evidence on record and finally decide the case having regard to such evidence and the burden of proof required to be discharged in the given case.

On the basis of the foregoing, it would be wrong for a court to finally decide the case on a finding that there is a case to answer without receiving the evidence of the defence in rebuttal, unless, of course, the defendant elects to give no evidence in his defence (See *Daikin Air conditioning v. Harvard University*, (1996) T.L.R. 1).

To put it differently, a submission of no case to answer in a civil case should be dealt with in the same manner as it is dealt with in a criminal case.

What, then, is the test to be applied in determining whether or not there is no case to answer. It would seem that the test is more or less similar to the test applicable in criminal cases as reiterated in the case of *R.T. Bhatt v. R.,* (1957) E.A. 332. In civil cases, the test was well restated in the case of *Mhozya v Attorney General* (1996) T.L.R. 229 in which Samatta, J.K. (as he then was) stated, at page 237:

> A submission of no case to answer in a civil case stands on the same footing as a submission of no case to answer in a criminal case, save that there is a difference in the standard of proof. What, then, is the test to be applied when such a submission is made? As I understand the law, when the dismissal of the plaintiff's case on the basis that no case has been made out is prayed for, the court should not ask itself whether the evidence given and/or adduced by the plaintiff establishes what would finally be required to be established, but whether there is evidence upon which a court, applying its mind reasonably to such evidence, could or might (not should or ought to) find for the plaintiff. The submission of no case to answer cannot be upheld if there is sufficient evidence on record on which a court might make a reasonable mistake and enter a judgment for the plaintiff. Whereas the test to be applied at the close of the defendant's case is what ought a reasonable court to do? The one to be applied in determining the validity or otherwise of a submission of no case to answer is what might a reasonable court do?

FINAL SUBMISSIONS

As we have seen, a party who has the right to begin states his case, that is, he sets out in a summary form what he intends to prove in the case. After the evidence of both sides has been given, the defendant will then address the court generally on the whole case, and the plaintiff will also address the court generally on the whole case. These final addresses are usually referred to as *final submissions*.

What, then, is the purpose of final submissions? The purpose of final submissions is to enable the parties or their advocates to point out to the court the material facts which each party has established in his favour, the strength on the party's case both as to the evidence adduced and the applicable law, and to appeal to the court to find for such party. Final submissions are also used for the purpose of pointing out any weaknesses in an opponent's case.

To that end, therefore, in his final submission, a party or his advocate will emphasize the strong points in his case, play down his weak points, dramatize the weaknesses in the opponent's case, invite the court to believe his witnesses and disbelieve those of the opponent, and appeal to the court to hold in his favour.

In order to put final submissions to their effective use, then, parties must not approach them perfunctorily. One needs to master the facts brought out by the evidence, and the principles of law that are applicable. Besides, one must have what is sometimes called the art of persuasion. In other words, one must prepare his speech.

Generally speaking, a speech in final submission consists of a review of he evidence in as much detail as may be necessary depending on the nature and complexity of the case, comments on the highlights of the case, and explanation on the weak points of the party's case, a review of the authorities favourable to the party's case, and, in conclusion, a prayer to the court to find in his favour.

In order to be able to do this effectively, a party or his advocate must have examined or cross-examined the witnesses fairly well, kept a record of the proceedings or the substance of the proceedings, and made thorough research on the law. In short, he must be fully familiar with the facts of the case and the relevant authorities in his favour as well as those against him.

CHAPTER TWENTY

AFFIDAVITS

AFFIDAVITS AS EVIDENCE

As we have seen, as a general rule, evidence in a trial must be orally given, that is, that witnesses must appear before the court which is seized of the matter and testify before it to the matters material to the suit in question.

However, if sufficient reason is shown, the court may at any time order that any particular fact or facts should be proved by affidavit or that the affidavit of any witness should be read at the hearing on such conditions as the court thinks reasonable (O.19, r.1 C.P.C.).

Now, what is an affidavit? In its general sense, an affidavit is a written statement which contains matters which the deponent knows or believes to be true and which statement has been made on oath or affirmation.

An affidavit produced at the hearing of a suit under the foregoing provisions, therefore, becomes a substitute for the oral evidence of such deponent.

An order that an affidavit be produced in place of oral evidence must not, however, be made where it appears to the court that either party bona fide desires the production of a witness for cross-examination and that such witness can be produced. In such a case, the witness must be summoned to give evidence orally so as to enable the party wishing to cross-examine him to do so (O.19, r.1 – Proviso).

In other cases, where evidence has been given by affidavit, the court may, at the instance of either party, order the attendance of the deponent for cross-examination. In such an event, the attendance must be in court, unless the deponent is exempted from personal appearance in court, or unless the court otherwise directs (O.19, r.2 C.P.C.). These provisions, it is apparent, are there because it is generally recognized that cross-examination is a very effective means of testing the truthfulness of a witness.

FORM AND CONTENTS OF AFFIDAVITS

An affidavit must contain those matters to which the deponent would have deposed orally as a witness in court in the case. Affidavits, therefore, must be confined to such facts as the deponent is able of his own knowledge to prove (O.19, r.3(1) C.P.C.).

This rule ensures that the rule of evidence that hearsay evidence is generally not admissible is not circumvented by parties by using affidavits whose contents are not within the deponent's own knowledge to prove.

The only exception to this rule is in the case of interlocutory applications. In such applications, a deponent may depose to matters of his own belief; but even in such a case the deponent must state the grounds upon which such belief in such matter is based. In affidavits in interlocutory applications, then, a deponent must specify which of the matters in his affidavit he knows of his own personal knowledge to be true, and which ones he believes to be true and on what grounds. (O.19, r.3(2) C.P.C.).

In the case of *Thesen-Stahlunion Export v. Kibo Wire Industries* (1975) LRT n. 54), the applicant, in a chamber application, asked for leave to defend a suit under O.35, r.3 and for an order rejecting the plaint under O.7 of the Civil Procedure Code. In his affidavit in support of the application, he stated, *inter alia*:

3(a) As stated in paragraph three of the plaint the said Bills of Exchange were drawn by the plaintiff. They were drawn in Germany and are not stamped.

(b) I am advised and verily believe it to be true that if the said bills required stamp duty and if they are not stamped, and if according to the laws of West Germany they are null and void, then this Honourable court should apply the law of West Germany as the proper law governing the said bills of exchange.

7. The plaintiff is not entitled to sue my company on the bills of exchange.

After quoting O.19, r.3 of the Tanzania Civil Procedure Code, the Court, Onyiuke, J. said, at page 219:

> The present application is an interlocutory application and as such statements of belief may be admitted but the ground thereof should be stated. An affidavit must depose to facts either within the deponent's personal knowledge or obtained on information, the sources of which are set out therein. It should not be used as an occasion to enter into legal discourses or to pose hypothetical arguments. This will defeat the very purpose of an affidavit which is to set out facts on which a party intends to rely either as the basis of a legal submission or the existence of which will found the application sought. Turning to the instant application the assertion that "the plaintiff is not entitled to sue my company on the said bills of exchange" is a conclusion of law and not a statement of fact. No grounds for such an assertion were set out in the affidavit. Paragraph 3(b) of the affidavit... did not contain any statements of fact but was a mere narration of hypothetical situations as embarrassing as they were vague. It did not state that the bills which were drawn in Germany required to be stamped according to that law or that they were null and void if not stamped (see also *Premchand v. Quarry*, (1969) E.A. 514) and *Foum v. Registrar of Coop. Societies*, (1995) T.L.R. 75.).

His Lordship accordingly struck out paragraph 3 and 7 of the affidavit as being "vague and embarrassing." (see also *Assanand & Sons v. East African Records* (1959) E.A. 360, 364).

What form, then, does an affidavit take? To start with it must have a title: that is, the cause or matter in which it is sworn; the name of the court before which such cause or matter is: and the names of the parties to the suit, cause or matter. Next, it should have the name and address of the deponent, and the matter of the affidavit. After that will come the matter or facts which the deponent has to swear to the effect that the deponent swore or affirmed to the contents of the affidavit on a particular day, date and year and before a person who is duly authorized to administer such oaths or affirmations.

In Tanzania, the Oaths (Judicial Proceedings) and Statutory Declarations Act 1966, has the list of persons authorized to administer such oaths.

CHAPTER TWENTY ONE

JUDGEMENT, DECREE AND INTEREST

JUDGMENT

Definition

When a court has heard all the evidence and final submissions, it proceeds to prepare and pronounce a judgment in the case either at once or on some future day. If a judge or magistrate puts off the pronouncement of a judgment to some future day, he is said to have "reserved" such judgment. This a judge or magistrate will usually do, particularly in cases involving complicated questions of fact and/or law. But if he does put off the pronouncement of the judgment to some future day, due notice must be given to the parties or the advocates of such party (O. 20, r. 1 C.P.C.). To state the obvious, a judgment must be based on evidence adduced (see *Nkungu v. Mohamed*, (1984) T.L.R. 46).

What, then, is meant by the term *"judgment?"* In a civil suit, a judgment may be defined as a reasoned account and analysis of the evidence, findings of fact thereon, an exposition of the principles of law applicable to such facts, and the decision as to the rights and liabilities of the parties to the suit. In other words, a judgment is a written document which resolves the issues in a suit and finally determines the rights and liabilities of the parties in the suit. In the language of the Civil Procedure Code, a judgment means the statement given by the judge or the magistrate of the grounds of a decree or order (see S. 3 C.P.C.).

For reasons that are obvious, a judgment must be written by, or reduced to writing under the personal direction and superintendence of, the presiding judge or magistrate in the language of the court, and must be dated and signed by him. The date must be that on which such judgment is pronounced in open court.

The Contents of a Judgment

From the above definition of a judgment, it will be clear as to what a judgment should contain. The Civil Procedure Code provides that a judgment must contain a concise statement of the case, the points for determination, the decision thereon, and the reason for such decision (O. 20, r.4 C.P.C.). It further provides that in suits in which issues have been framed, the court must state its finding or decision, with reasons therefor, on each separate issue, unless the finding on any one or more of the issues is sufficient for the decision of the suit (O.20, r.4 C.P.C.).

There is no rule of thumb as to the exact form a judgment should follow. Different people use different styles. All that really matters is that the judgment should be so formulated as to contain a concise statement of the case, the points in issue, a decision on each of such issues, and reasons for the decision (see *Kasusura v. Kabuye*, (1982) T.L.R. 338).

For what it is worth (and it is by no means immutable), let me describe here my own way of preparing a judgment. The first paragraph, which must be below the title "Judgement," starts with a description of the parties and the subject – matter of the suit. For instance, in a suit for recovery of arrears of rent, mesne profits and vacant possession, the judgment will start with something like this:

> The plaintiff in this suit, A.B., claims from the defendant, C.D., arrears of rent, mesne profits and vacant possession in respect of the suit premises situate on Plot No. 20 Block K. in Z township. The defendant has denied liability.

That gives a reader a clear idea of what the suit is all about.

The next paragraph sets out the issues as framed and recorded by the court. After the issues have been set out, the evidence of the plaintiff and his witnesses is then summarized. Next follows a summary of the evidence for the defence. But care must be taken to ensure that all the evidence material for the determination of the issues in the suit are covered.

When all the evidence has thus been summarized, the judgment goes on to evaluate such evidence. Here, discrepancies and inconsistencies, corroborated account, the value of any documentary evidence, the credibility of witnesses, the probability or improbability of certain facts asserted by the witnesses, etc., are dealt with.

After evaluating the evidence the judge or magistrate points out what facts he finds proved and which ones not proved and why. He must take care to make specific finding on each of the issues and record his reasons for arriving at such findings of fact.

When that has been done the judgment will deal with the principles of law applicable in the case and relate those principles of law to his findings of fact, and thus arrive at conclusions as to the rights and liabilities of the parties. The judge or magistrate will then sign the judgment and date it as of the date of delivery of the judgment.

In preparing a judgment, one of the important things to remember is the burden of proof. In civil cases, the standard of proof is on a balance of probabilities or on a preponderance of probabilities, and the burden of proof on any issue is on the party who asserts a fact on such issue.

A Judgement Must be Pronounced in Open Court

As pointed out above, a judgment must be pronounced in open court. An open court means a place to which the public has free and unhindered access to listen to the court proceedings, and it is usually a court-room. This requirement springs from the principle that justice must not only be done but must also be seen to have been done, and this requirement applies as much to civil as to criminal cases.

A court, however, has discretionary power to try a suit and/or pronounce a judgment *in camera*. In other words, a court may exclude the public. It will do so where it is of the opinion that to do so would be in the interests of justice. This discretion, however, must be sparingly used, and used only for a most compelling reason. This point was made abundantly clear by the Court of Appeal for Eastern African in the case of *Muriu and Others v. R.*, (22 E.A.C. A. 417). In that case, the trial judge had excluded the public and the press from the court when he began to read his long judgment but he readmitted them after he had read about one third of the judgment in the presence of the accused person and their advocates. On appeal, the Court said, at page 420:

... we must emphasize with all the powers at our command that the seemingly wide discretion given to a judge or magistrate under the provision of section 77 should only be exercised for a most compelling reason. Both section 77 and 188 by the very wording used in them indicate that a court of law must ordinarily be open to the public at all times, and in exercising the power to exclude we hope that no judge or magistrate will overlook the general principle that justice must not only be done but must be seen to be done.

That, of course, was a decision in a criminal case, but it applies equally to civil cases. A court may exclude the public in cases where a fair trial or proceeding can not be had owing to possible danger of molestation or intimidation of witnesses or the parties to the suit by restless or violent members of the public, or where the nature of the evidence deposed or to be deposed to is such that its publicity would not be in the interests of national security, or where it is thought desirable that loafers and young persons should not hear the evidence to be adduced, such as in some exceptional circumstances in matrimonial proceedings (c.f. Section 84 of the Law of Marriage Act 1971).

What in practice amounts to an open court will depend on the circumstances of each court. The usual place for conducting court proceedings, is of course, in a court-room. But there are places where, owing to shortage of court rooms or other reasons, cases are heard in chambers of magistrates. In such a situation, such chambers must be open to the public in the sense that the public must have free and unhindered access thereto to listen to court proceedings.

Pronouncement of Judgment by a Succeeding Magistrate

It sometimes happens that by reasons of death, transfer or other sufficient cause, a judge or magistrate ceases to exercise jurisdiction in a particular place before pronouncing a judgment which he has prepared. In such an event, the succeeding judge or magistrate may pronounce the judgment which has been written but not pronounced by his predecessor (O.20, r.2 C.P.C.). Such judge or succeeding magistrate will then sign and date it as of the date the judgment is pronounced.

DECREE

Definition

A decree is defined in Section 3 of the Tanzania Civil Procedure Code
Act, 1966, as meaning the formal expression of an adjudication which so
far as regards the court expressing it, conclusively determines the rights
of the parties with regard to all or any of the matters in controversy in the
suit and may be either preliminary or final. It is deemed to include the
rejection of a plaint and the determination of any question within Section
30 or Section 89 of the Code, but does not include an adjudication from
which an appeal lies as an appeal from an order or any order of dismissal
for default (see *Mansion House v. Wilkinson,* 21 E.A.C.A. 98,102.).

A decree is said to be *"preliminary"* when further proceedings have to
be taken before the suit can be disposed of. It is said to be *"final"* when
the adjudication completely disposes of the suit. But some decrees may
be partly preliminary and partly final.

To constitute a final decree, therefore, there must have been a decision
expressed in a suit on the rights of the parties as regards all or any of the
matters in dispute in the particular suit, which decision conclusively
determines those rights as far as the deciding court is concerned, and the
decision must have been a formal expression as an adjudication. Generally
speaking, a finding on an issue or an order is not a decree, and an appeal
lies from a decree while no appeal lies from an order unless it is one of the
orders listed in Section 74 or Order 40 of the Civil Procedure Code.

To put it succinctly, in general, a decree is a summary of the contents
of a judgment. The person in whose favour a decree has been passed is
called a decree – holder, and he against whom it is passed is called a
judgment – debtor.

Contents of a Decree

A decree, being a formal expression of the contents of a decision or
judgment, must agree with the judgment. It must contain the name of
the court passing it, the number of the suit, the names and descriptions
of the parties to the suit, and the particulars of the claim. It must further
clearly specify the relief granted or other determination of the suit.
Besides, it must state the amount (if any) of costs incurred in the suit,
and by whom or out of what property and in what proportions such costs

are to be paid. It must also show the date of the day on which the judgment from which it is extracted was pronounced.

When a decree has been drawn up, it will be duly signed by the judge or magistrate, sealed with the Court Seal and dated as of the day on which it is extracted (O.20, r.7 C.P.C.).

As with pronouncing judgments, where a judge or magistrate has vacated office or ceased to exercise jurisdiction in a particular court after pronouncing the judgment but before signing the decree, his successor may sign a decree drawn up in accordance with such judgment.

Types of Decrees

Decree for Recovery of Immovable Property

If the subject-matter of the suit is immovable property, say, a building, the decree must contain such description of the property as will sufficiently identify it. If it is property registered under the Land Registration Ordinance (Cap 334 of the Revised Laws), the decree must specify its title number (O.20, r.9, C.P.C.).

For instance, if the property is situate in Dodoma township, and it is registered under the Land Registration Ordinance, it may be described thus:

Building situated on plot No. 15
Block X, Hazina, LD No. 2569
In Dodoma Township.

Decree for Delivery of Movable Property

If the suit is for movable property, and the decree is for delivery of such movable property, the decree must also state the amount of the money to be paid as an alternative if delivery cannot be effected (O.20, r.9 C.P.C.).

So if the decree is for delivery of a motor vehicle, say, a car, the decree must sufficiently describe the car, say, by its make and registration number, and must state the amount of money to be paid if the motor vehicle cannot be delivered for one reason or another.

Decree for Payment of Money

Where the decree is for payment of money, the court may, for sufficient reason, at the time of passing the decree, order that the payment of the decretal amount should be postponed or should be made by instalments, with or without interest, notwithstanding anything contained in the contract under which the money is payable (O.20, r.11(1) C.P.C.).

After such a decree has been passed, the court may, on the application of the judgment-debtor and with the consent of the decree – holder, order that payment of the decretal amount must be postponed or made by instalments on such terms as to the payment of interest, the attachment of the property of the judgment debtor, or the taking of security from him or otherwise as it may think fit (O.20, r.11 (2) C.P.C.).

An order for payment of a decretal amount by instalments must not be made arbitrarily. Such an indulgence ought not to be given where, for instance, it would constitute a virtual denial of the plaintiff's right. In the case of *A. Rajabali Alidina v. Remtula Alidina and Another*, (1961) E.A 565, the facts were that five days before the rest of his goods were attached by creditors, the respondent purchased goods from the appellant which he sold at a profit the same day on ninety day's credit. Subsequently the respondent was duly paid, but he failed to pass on any portion of the money to the appellant, and when the appellant applied for payment the respondent offered him twenty percent of the price in settlement. The appellant rejected this offer and sued for the price. He obtained judgement for 6,669/- including costs, whereupon the respondent sought and obtained from the magistrate an order for payment by instalment of T.shs. 75/= per month. The appellant appealed against the order for payment by instalments complaining, *inter alia*, that the magistrate had given no reasons for making the order. The High Court held that in the circumstances of the case there was virtual denial of the appellant's right. The court quoted with approval the case of *Rati v. Kunji Lal* (1932), 54 All 539 in which Boys, J., said:

> The result of this decree is that it would take the plaintiff more than seven years to recover the amount now due to him.... It is manifest that the amount of the instalments and the period for their repayment is a matter for the discretion of the court; but it is a discretion which is to be exercised within bounds. The exercise of it in the manner of the present suit constitutes a virtual denial of the plaintiff's rights.

Earlier, the Court had this to say, at page 566:

All commentators on the Civil Procedure Code agree that the court's discretion to order payment of the decretal amount in instalments is one which must be exercised in a judicial and not arbitrary manner. The onus is on the defendant to show that he is entitled to indulgence under this rule. It is for the defendant to show "sufficient reason" for indulgence being shown to him.

There has to be a sufficient reason for making an order for payment of the decretal amount by instalments. And what constitutes "*sufficient reason?*" That, of course, will depend on the circumstance of each case. But it has been held that matters which should be taken into consideration by a court in deciding whether or not "*sufficient cause*" exists are these:

a) The circumstances in which he debt was contracted;
b) The conduct of the debtor;
c) His financial position; and
d) His bona-fide in offering to pay a fair proportion of the debt at once (see *Alidina's* case (supra).

In the case of *Keshavji Jethabhai v. Saleh Abdulla*, (1959) E.A. 260, Crawshow, J., had this to say, at page 261.

Whilst the courts must be jealous of the creditor's rights, they must consider each case on its merits and exercise their discretion accordingly, and I apprehend it would be wrong for this court to interfere with the exercise of that discretion unless the magistrate had acted on some wrong principle or had failed to exercise his discretion judicially.

The Court also quoted a passage in *Woodroffe and Ammeer Ali on The Civil Procedure Code* (2nd Edition) at page 869, which states:

"Sufficient reason" – The existence of this will depend upon the facts of the particular case. The court will consider the circumstances under which the debt was contracted, the conduct of the debtor, his financial position, and so forth, and instalments should be directed where the defendant shows his bona fides by offering to pay anything like a fair proportion of his debt at once.

The Court went on and referred to the Indian case of *Binda Prasand v. Medho Prasand and Others*, (1879) 2 All. 129, in which Turner, J., said at page 132:

There are some instances in which debts are contracted without any specific agreements as to the time of payment, and when it is shown that dealings have been conducted on this footing and no injury is done to creditor by ordering payment by instalments, but when a contract is distinctly made for payment on a date certain for the purpose of enabling the credit to obtain punctual payment, the circumstances that the payment is secured by an hypothecation of property ought not to deprive him of that right.

The Court further referred to the case of *Sawatram Ramprasad v. Imperial Bank of India,* (1933) A.I.R. Nag 330 in which the Court said, in reference to the case of *Mohamed Akbar Khan v. Kasturchand Daga:*

....It is laid down that the mere fact that the debtor is hard pressed or is unable to pay in full at once is not sufficient reason for granting instalments and that ordinarily he should be required to show his bona fide by arranging prompt payment of a fair proportion of the debt. We are in respectful agreement with this interpretation of the law but find great difficulty in constructing the last observation in the way desired by counsel for the plaintiff, i.e. that prompt payment of a fair proportion of the debt is a condition precedent for the exercise of the discretion of granting instalments. Each case has to be decided on its own merits, the predominating factor being of course the bona fides of debtor.

Decree for Possession and Mesne Profits

In a suit for recovery of possession of immovable property and for rent or mesne profits, the court may pass decree: (1) for the possession of the property: and (2) for the rent or mesne profits which have accrued on the property during a period prior to the institution of the suit or, if the same are not certain, a direction in the decree for an inquiry as to such rent or mesne profits from the institution of the suit until (a) the delivery of possession of the property to the decree-holder, (b) the relinquishment of the possession by the judgment-debtor with notice to the decree-holder through the court, or (c) the expiration of three years from the date of the decree, whichever event is the earlier (O.20, r.(1) C.P.C.).

Where an inquiry is directed under (2) or (3) above, a final decree in respect of the rent or mesne profits must be passed in accordance with the result of such inquiry (O.20, r.12(2) C.P.C.).

Decree in Suit for Dissolution of Partnership

In a suit for dissolution of a partnership, or the taking of partnership accounts, the court may, before passing a final decree, pass a preliminary decree declaring the proportionate shares of the partners, fix the day on which the partnership will stand dissolved, and direct such accounts to be taken and other acts done as it thinks fit. When that has been done, the court will then issue a final decree showing the amounts due to each of the partners (O.20, r.15, C.P.C.).

Decree in Suit for Account Between Principal and Agent

As in a suit for dissolution of partnership, in a suit for an account of pecuniary transactions between a principal and an agent, and in any other suit where it is necessary in order to ascertain the amount of money due to or from any party, that an account should be taken, the court must, before passing a final decree, pass a preliminary decree directing such accounts to be taken as it thinks fit (O.20, r.16 C.P.C.).

Decree in Suit for Partition of Property or Separate Possession of a Share Therein

In a case where the court passes a decree for the partition of property or for the separate possession of a share therein, the court may, if the partition or separation cannot be conveniently made without further inquiry, pass a preliminary decree declaring the rights of the several parties interested in the property, and may further give such other directions as may be required (O.20, r.18 C.P.C.).

Decree When Set-off Allowed

As we have seen earlier, a defendant may set up a set-off or counter-claim to a plaintiff's claim. If in such a case the defendant has been allowed such set-off against the plaintiff's claim, the decree must state what amount is due to the defendant and what amount is due to the plaintiff. Such decree, then, must be for the recovery of any sum that appears to be due to either party. (O.20, r.19(1) of C.P.C.).

A question as to costs may arise in such a case. If the defendant succeeds in establishing a set-off exceeding the plaintiff's claim, the correct order for costs is: the defendant is entitled to judgment with costs on the claim, and to judgment for any balance recovered on his counterclaim with costs, in the absence of circumstances depriving him of costs. In the case of *Kiska Ltd. v. De Angelis,* (1969) E.A. 6, Law, J.A., had this to say, at page 11:

> The correct order for costs in a case such as this where the defendant succeeds in establishing a set-off exceeding the plaintiff's claim, is in my opinion as stated in Halsbury's Laws (3rd Edn.), Vol. 34, para 753: the defendant is entitled to judgment with costs on the claim, and to judgment for any balance recovered on his counter-claim with costs, in the absence of circumstances depriving him of costs.

If the successful counterclaim does not exceed the amount due to the plaintiff, the judgment or decree should be: Judgment for the plaintiff for so much on the counterclaim with costs. In the words of Singleton, L.J., in the case of *Chell Engineering Ltd. v. Unit Tool and Engineering Co. Ltd.,* (1951) I All E.R. 378, at page 380:

> I have always thought that where there is a claim and a counterclaim and the plaintiff succeeds on the claim and the defendant on the counterclaim the more convenient course is to enter judgment for the plaintiff for the amount for which he succeeds on the counterclaim, and in the ordinary course, if there are costs both on the claim and on the counterclaim, each party is entitled to the costs which he had to incur to recover the sum recovered on the claim and on the counterclaim respectively.

Any decree passed in a suit in which set-off is claimed is subject to the same provisions in respect of appeal to which it would have been subject had there been no set-off claimed (O.20, r.19(2) C.P.C.).

Decree in Administration Cases

If a suit is for an account of any property and for its due administration under the decree of the court, the court must, before passing the final decree, pass a preliminary decree ordering such accounts and inquiries to be taken and made, and giving such other directions as the court should proceed in respect of a decree in dissolution of partnership and the like. (O.20, r.13(2) C.P.C.).

Decree in Preemption Suit

If a court decrees a claim to preemption in respect of a particular sale of property and the purchase money has not been paid into court, the decree must: (1) specify a day on or before which the purchase money must be so paid; and (2) direct that on payment into court of such purchase money, together with the costs (if any) decree against the plaintiff, on or before the date referred to above, the defendant must deliver possession of the property to the plaintiff, whose title thereto will be deemed to have accrued from the date of such payment, but that, if the purchase money and the costs (if any) are not so paid, the suit must be dismissed with costs (O. 20, r.14(1) C.P.C.).

A suit in preemption here means a suit for a right to purchase property before or in preference to other persons.

Where the court has adjudicated rival claims to preemption, the decree must direct: (1) if and in so far as the claims decreed are equal in degree, that the claim of each pre-emptor complying with the provisions of the above rule must take effect in respect of a proportionate share in respect of which the claim of any preemptor failing to comply with the said provisions would, but for such failure or default; and (2) if any in so far as the claims are different in degree, that the claim of the inferior preemptor must not take effect unless and until the superior pre-emptor has failed to comply with the said provisions (O.20, r.14 (2) C.P.C.).

Certified Copies of Judgments and Decrees

On the application of the parties, copies of judgment and decree must be supplied to them, but at their expense. Such copies must be certified to be true and correct copies of the original (O.20, r.20, C.P.C.)

Interest

As we have seen, after the case has been heard, the court must pronounce judgment and pass a decree (see section 28 C.P.C.). The courts are further empowered to order interest to be paid on the judgment debts up to the date of the judgment at such rates as they may deem reasonable. The rate of the interest to be carried by judgment debts from the delivery of the judgment until it is satisfied will be at the rate prescribed by the Chief Justice under rules made by him in pursuance of the provisions of section 29 of the Civil Procedure Code.

Sub-rule (1) of r.21 of O.20 of the Civil Procedure Code provides that the rate of interest on every judgment debt from the date of delivery of the judgment until satisfaction must be seven per centum per annum or such other rate, not exceeding twelve per centum per annum, at the delivery of the judgment or as may be adjudged by consent. But in any case of a judgment debt that was subsisting on the first day of July, 1964, the provisions of this rule will apply in respect thereto as if there were substituted for the words *"delivery of Judgment"* the words *"on the first day of July, 1964."*

For the purpose of these provisions, the word *"judgment"* in suits relating to mortgages of immovable property means the final decree; and *"judgment debt"* means (1) the principal sum; (2) any interest adjudged on such principal sum for any period prior to the institution of the suit; and (3) interest adjudged on such principal sum for the period between the institution of the suit and the delivery of the judgment (O.20, r.21(2) C.P.C.).

In case of an award for general damages, interest is only due after the delivery of the judgment because it is only then that the amount due is known. As a result, interest would to limited between the minimum of seven per cent per annum and twelve per cent per annum. (see *Kibwa and Another v. Rose Jumbe*, (1993) T.L.R. 175; and *Njoro Furniture v. TANESCO*, (1995) T.L.R. 205.)

TWENTY TWO

COSTS

Civil litigation involves expenses, and in some cases the expenses may be considerable. In order that a successful party should not suffer financial detriment as a result of a litigation, courts are empowered to order the payment of costs by one of the parties to the other, and generally speaking, costs follow the cause, that is, that generally speaking, the successful party is awarded the costs.

Subject to the provisions of any law and to such conditions and limitations as may be prescribed, the costs of and incidental to all suits are warded at the discretion of the court. The court has, besides, full power to determine by whom or out of what property and to what extent such costs are to be paid, and to give all necessary directions for those purposes. The fact that the court has no jurisdiction to try a suit does not bar it from exercising those powers (s.20(1) C.P.C.).

In spite of the general rule that costs should follow the cause, in the exercise of its discretion, a court may decide that the costs in a particular suit must not follow the event. In such a case, such court must give reasons in writing as to why the costs should not follow the event (s. 30(2) C.P.C.).

As pointed out above, the discretion of the court to award or refuse to award costs to any party is subject to the general rule that costs would follow the event, that is, that a successful party must be awarded his costs unless there are circumstances which justify depriving him of costs.

What, then, is the meaning of the phrase *"costs shall follow the event?"* In the case of *Reid Hewitt & Co. v. Joseph,* (1918) A.C. 717, the House of Lords held that the phrase *"costs shall follow the event"* means that the party who on the whole succeeds in the action gets the general costs of the action, but that where the action involves separate issues, whether arising under one cause of action or under different causes of action, the word "*event*" should go to the party who succeeds on the issue, and that an issue in this sense means any issue which has a direct and definite bearing event in defeating the claim to judgment in whole or in part.

In the case of *Shankerdass Mayer and Others v. Trustees of the Rhimtulla Lalji Hirji Charitable Trust*, (22 E.A.C.A. 18), the facts were that on appeal from the Central Control Board to the Supreme Court, the appellants successfully took the point that the appeal was incompetent there having been no "*determination*" by the Board. In dismissing the appeal the trial Judge ordered that each party should bear its own costs stating "*I do not order costs to follow the event, because I doubt if there was any event. By taking his technical objection respondent in the present appeal has prevented all argument on the merits.*" On appeal to the Court of Appeal for Eastern Africa, the Court stated, at page 20:

> As regards the learned Judge's first reason I feel it does not make sense to me. The question before the learned Judge on the preliminary objection was whether an appeal lay and his decision that it did not, amounted, I should have thought, to an effective and conclusive determination of the question before him. Neither does one need a legal dictionary to arrive at the originally and accepted meaning of the word "event." Surely the "event" in this case was the total rejection of the appeal.

In the case of *Devram Nanji Dhathani v. Baridas Kalidas Dawda* (16 E.A.C.A. 35), a successful defendant was deprived of his costs. On appeal, Sir John Gray, C.J., stated, at page 36:

> From the decisions, which were cited to us during the hearing of the appeal, it appears to me to be clear that a successful defendant, who after all is brought into court against his will, can only be deprived of his costs when it it shown that his conduct either prior to or during the course of the action, has led to litigation, which but for his own conduct might have been averted.

The discretion here is a judicial discretion which must, therefore, be exercised judicially. Once a trial court has exercised its discretion on the question of costs, an appellate court will not interfere unless it is shown that the lower court acted on a wrong principle. As was stated by the Court of Appeal for East Africa in *Kiska Ltd v. de Angelis,* (supra) at page 8:

> Thus, where a trial court has exercised its discretion on costs, an appellate Court should not interfere unless the discretion has been exercised unjudicially or on wrong principles. Where it gives no reason for its decision the Appellate Court will interfere if it is satisfied that the order is wrong. It will also interfere where reasons are given if it considers that those reasons do not constitute *"good reason" within the meaning of the rule (see also Donald Campbell v. Pollak,* (1927) A.C. 732, 813; *Hussein Jahmohamed v. Twentsche Trading Co.,* (1967) E.A. 287).

One example of a situation in which a successful litigant could be deprived of his costs is where he files separate actions involving two different causes of action which arose out of the same transaction and which, therefore, could have been joined in a single suit. The case of *Mutungi v. Kabuchi,* (1966) E.A. 458, is a good illustration. In that case, the facts were that the plaintiff was involved in a motor accident, with a vehicle owned by the second defendant and driven by the first defendant. Two separate actions were filed on the same day against both defendants. In the first a consent judgment was entered for the claim for personal injuries. The second suit for damage to his vehicle was defended. One of the questions for determination was whether or not the plaintiff should be awarded costs in both actions. The court held that the plaintiff ought not to be given costs in the second suit, and stated, at page 458:

> In this present matter all the injuries were patent when the two actions were filed on the same day. It is my understanding and experience that in cases of this nature when injury to property and injury to person arise out of an accident claims for damages for each type of injury are included in one suit... I do not propose to award the costs of this action to the plaintiff.

What is the position where, in a suit involving several issues, the plaintiff succeeds in the main purpose of the suit but fails on another issue? In the case of *Dembenictis and Others v. Central Africa Co. Ltd and Another,* 1967) E.A. 310, such a situation arose. The plaintiff sued for cancellation of an agreement, raising two issues, one that the agreement had been extorted by force and the other that it was without consideration.

By an amended defence the defendant, whilst denying that the agreement was extorted, admitted that it was without consideration, and agreed that it should be cancelled. The plaintiff thereupon applied for judgment as prayed. The defendant argued that the plaintiff should be deprived of part of his costs, not having withdrawn the issue of extortion. Otto, J., awarded the plaintiff all his costs, stating, at page 311:

> As pointed out in the cases referred to in *Singh v. Jeram* (1), it is not on every issue in a suit that success will bring a right to the costs of that issue. Clearly costs should follow the event where the plaintiff has succeeded in the main purpose of his suit and I do not consider he should be deprived of costs merely because he has raised another issue which in itself cannot affect the result of the suit even if he loses on that issue. Here he has not only substantially succeeded in the main purpose of the suit, but he has obtained the full relief claimed and that was the cancellation of the agreement. He obtained the precise form of relief he wanted, and it is immaterial that the other issue is left undecided, because whichever way that issue falls to be decided it can not affect the result.

In addition to the court's discretion to award costs, a court has also discretion to give interest on costs, at any rate not exceeding seven per centum per annum, and such interest is added to the costs and is recoverable as such (S. 30 (3) C.P.C. (see also *Njoro Furniture* case (supra) and *City Council v. Taj Mohamed* (1968) H.C.D. n. 287)).

However, where neither party was responsible for the loss sued upon, each party will bear his/her own costs (see *Mwakajinga v. Mwaikambo*, (1967) H.C.D. n. 281).

CHAPTER TWENTY THREE

EXECUTION OF DECREES AND ORDERS

DEFINITION

Execution of decrees means the process by which the decrees of successful parties are satisfied.

Payment Under a Decree

All monies payable under a decree must be paid:
   a) Into the court whose duty it is to execute the particular decree; or
   b) Out of court to the decree-holders; or
   c) In any other manner as the court which made the decree may direct.

If payment of the money under a decree is made into the court, then notice of such payment must be given to the decree-holder. Similarly, where payment of the money is made out of court or the decree is otherwise adjusted to the satisfaction of the decree-holder, such payment or adjustment must be certified to the court by the decree-holder because it is the duty of the court to execute a decree. On receipt of such certificate, the court will endorse in the record of the case that the decree has been satisfied in full out of court.

Which Courts May Execute Decrees?

A decree passed by a court need not necessarily be executed by the same court. It depends on the nature of the decree, the whereabouts of the property of the judgment-debtor and the decree-holder himself.

So, suppose that the decree-holder has applied for execution to Morogoro Resident Magistrate's Court, which passed the decree, by way of attachment of a motor vehicle of the judgment-debtor lying at the judgment-debtor's house at Korogwe. In such a case the Court of Resident Magistrate, Morogoro, may transfer the decree to Korogwe District Court for execution.

In a case in which the decree is to be executed outside the local limits of the court passing it, then such decree must be transferred to the court of resident magistrate within whose local limits of jurisdiction such decree is to be executed. For instance, if a decree is passed by Korogwe District Court and it is sought to have it executed in Kilosa District Court, such decree must be transferred to Morogoro Resident Magistrate's Court and that court will either execute such decree itself or transfer it for execution to Kilosa District Court (see O.21, r.4 and 7 Civil Procedure Code).

Application for Execution

It is the duty of a decree-holder to apply to the court which passed the decree to have it executed. So, if payment or adjustment has not been made out of court, or the decree otherwise remains unsatisfied and the decree-holder desires to execute it, he must apply to the court which passed the decree, or that to which it has been transferred, to execute it (see O.21, r.9 Civil Procedure Code).

Usually an application for execution of a decree is made in writing. But where a decree is for the payment of money, and the judgment-debtor is within the precincts of the court, the court may, on the oral application of the decree-holder, order immediate execution of such decree by arresting the judgment-debtor prior to the preparation of a warrant (see O.21, r.10 Civil Procedure Code). This course, however, must not be resorted to unless there are good reasons for doing so. It is usually preferable to allow the judgment-debtor to pay the decretal sum voluntarily or to leave it to the decree – holder to file a written application for execution of his decree if it remains unsatisfied.

It is the duty of the court to peruse an application for execution of a decree carefully and to be satisfied that it has been properly drawn before filing it. By the provisions of O.21, r.10(2) of the Civil Procedure Code, an application for execution of a decree must contain, in tabular form, the following particulars:

1) The number of the suit;

2) The names of the parties;

3) The date of the decree;

4) Whether or not an appeal has been preferred from the decree;

5) A statement as to whether any, and (if any) what, payment or other adjustment of the matter in dispute has been made between the parties subsequent to the decree;

6) Whether any, and (if any) what, previous applications have been made for the execution of the decree, the dates of such applications and their result;

7) The amount and interest (if any) due on the decree or other relief granted thereby together with particulars of any cross-decree, whether passed before or after the date of the decree sought to be executed;

8) The amount of costs (if any) awarded;

9) The name of the person against whom execution of the decree is sought to be executed; and

10) The mode by which the execution is sought.

Usually the court will require the applicant to furnish a certified copy of the decree. The applicant will usually be the decree-holder himself or his advocate acting on behalf of the decree-holder.

If the application does not comply with the foregoing requirements, in other words, if the application is defective, the court may reject it, or the applicant may be allowed, there and then if given time, to amend it before it is filed (see O.21, r.15 Civil Procedure Code)

Although the rules permit a decree-holder to use more than one mode of executing his decree, the court has the discretion to refuse execution at the same time against the person and property of a judgment-debtor. For example, if an application for the execution of a decree seeks attachment of the person of the judgment-debtor as well as attachment of his property, the court may refuse to sanction it. Instead, it may sanction only the attachment of the judgment-debtor's property.

Modes of Execution

There are several modes of executing decrees. These largely depend on the type and nature of the particular decree. It is usually for the decree-holder to choose the mode of executing his decree. But the court has to satisfy itself that the mode of execution and the application are in accordance with the law and are not intended to be an abuse of court process.

In the case of a decree for the payment of money, such decree may be executed by attachment and sale of the judgment-debtor's property, or by his detention as a civil prisoner, or by both. If it is a decree for any specific movable property (e.g. a motor vehicle), it may be executed by seizure, if practicable, of such movable property and by delivering it to the decree-holder, or by the detention of the judgment-debtor as a civil prisoner, or by attachment of his property, or by all such means.

If it is a decree for specific performance of a contract or for an injunction, and the judgment-debtor has had time to obey it but has wilfully failed to do so, then such decree may be executed by his detention as a civil prisoner or by attachment of his property or by both.

In the case of a decree for the delivery of immovable property, such as a house, execution must be done by delivering such property to the person in whose favour it has been adjudged, and, if necessary, by removing any person bound by the decree who refuses to vacate such property (see O. 21, rr.28 to 34 Civil Procedure Code).

Contents of Warrant of Attachment

The contents of warrants of attachment vary with the nature of the property to be attached. In general, they contain the following:

1) A heading that the same is a warrant of attachment of movable or immovable property in a decree for money, etc.,
2) The name of the court issuing it;
3) The number of the suit;
4) The names of the parties to the suit;
5) The name and address of the person to whom it is directed, that is, the person who is to execute it;
6) The amount of the decree including costs and interest;
7) A command to the executing officer to seize the property named in the warrant unless the judgment-debtor pays to him the sum shown in the warrant;
8) An order that the executing officer shall return the warrant by a particular date; and
9) The seal of the issuing court, date and signature of a magistrate or other authorized officer.

Attachment of Salary, Decree, etc.

If a judgment-debtor is a person receiving a salary, the decree against him may be executed by an order of the court that the amount in the decree must be withheld from such salary by the employer, either in one payment or by monthly instalments, as the court may direct. The amount so withheld will be remitted by the employer to the court for payment to the decree-holder (see O.21, r.47 C.P.C.). However, only one third of the salary is attachable (see s.48 (1) (h) C.P.C.).

Other attachable properties or interest include decree in favour of the judgment-debtor, a share or interest of a judgment-debtor in a firm, negotiable instruments drawn in favour of the judgment-debtor, and attachment of agricultural produce. Properties not liable to attachment are listed in section 48 of the Code.

Objections to Attachments

It often happens that a third party or the judgment-debtor himself objects to the attachment of a particular property or properties, usually on the ground that such property is not liable to attachment on some ground or other. So a party need not file a fresh suit (see *K. Mussa v. Mchodo*, (1984) T.L.R. 348).

In such a situation, it is the duty of the court to investigate such claim or objection. In doing so, the court will deal with the matter as if the objector (if a third party) was party to the suit. The objector will be asked to adduce evidence to show that the property is not subject to attachment, say, on the ground that at the date of the attachment he had some interest in such property, or that, by operation of law, the property is not subject to attachment (see O.21, rr.57 and 58 Civil Procedure Code, and *Nyanza Distributors Co. v. Geita General Stores* (1977) LRT n. 2).

After the objector or claimant has adduced evidence to that effect, the judgment-debtor and/or the decree-holder may adduce evidence to refute the claimant's evidence. Thereafter the court will rule on the matter. The court, however, may decline to entertain an objection or to investigate it if it is of the view that it was designedly or unnecessarily delayed.

If the court is satisfied that the objector did, on the date of the attachment, have some existing interest, the court may make an order releasing the property, either wholly or to such extent as it thinks fit. If, at the time the objection is filed in court, the sale of the property attached has been advertised, the court may postpone such sale pending the result of the investigation.

Resistance to Delivery or Possession to Decree – Holder or Purchaser

Sometimes a third party, who has made no objection to attachment and delivery of the property, may resist possession or delivery of the immovable property to the decree-holder or purchaser or obstruct him. In such an event, the decree-holder or purchaser should apply to the court complaining of such resistance or obstruction.

On such application, the court will fix a date for the investigation of the matter and will summon the person against whom the complaint is made to appear and answer the accusation.

If it is proved to the satisfaction of the court, after such investigation, that the resistance or obstruction has been occasioned without any just cause, the court must direct that the applicant be put into possession of the property. If the applicant is still resisted or obstructed, the court may, at the instance of the applicant, detain the person so resisting or obstructing and commit him to civil prison (see O.21, rr.95, 96, 97, C.P.C.).

CHAPTER TWENTY FOUR

DEATH, MARRIAGE AND INSOLVENCY

The parties to suits may change before a judgment or final order is made owing to change in circumstances. In anticipation of change or circumstances, the Civil Procedure Code has provided for courses of action that may be taken to meet certain eventualities. Among these are death, marriage and insolvency of parties. To these provisions we must now turn.

DEATHS

A plaintiff or defendant in a suit may die before the suit is disposed of, and it occasionally happens. But the fact that the plaintiff or defendant in a suit has died will not, per se, cause the suit to abate if the right to sue survives (see *Kibwana v. Jumbe* (1993) T.L.R. 175.).

So, in a case involving more plaintiffs or defendants than one, and any of them dies, but the right to sue survives to the surviving plaintiff or plaintiffs alone, or against the surviving defendant(s) alone, the court will make or cause to be made entry on the record to that effect, and the suit will proceed at the instance of the surviving plaintiff(s), or against the surviving defendant(s) as the case may be (O.22, rr. 1 and 2 C.P.C.).

In Case of Death of One of Several Plaintiffs or of Sole Plaintiff

As pointed out above, where one of the several plaintiffs dies, but the right to sue survives to the remaining plaintiff or plaintiffs alone, the suit may be proceeded with at the instance of such remaining plaintiffs after an entry has been made on the record to that effect.

But what is the situation where one of two or more plaintiffs dies and the right to sue does not survive to the surviving plaintiff or plaintiffs alone, or where a sole plaintiff or sole surviving plaintiff dies and the right to sue survives? In such a case, the court, on an application in that behalf, will cause the legal representative of the deceased plaintiff to be made a party to the suit and then proceed with the suit (O.22, r.3(1) C.P.C.).

It is the duty of the legal representative of the deceased plaintiff to make an application to be joined as a party in the suit. If no such application is filed within the time allowed by law, the suit will abate so far as the deceased plaintiff is concerned. In such an event and on an application by the defendant, the court may award the defendant the costs which he may have incurred in defending the suit, and such costs would be recovered from the estate of the plaintiff (O.22, r.3(2) C.P.C.)

Let us take a simple example. A and B are joint plaintiffs in a suit against D. A then dies before the suit is disposed of, and the right to sue does not survive to B alone. R, who is A's legal representative, will apply to the court to be made a party. The court will then make the appropriate entry on the record, and the suit will proceed with A and R as plaintiffs against D. If R defaults to make such application within the time limited by law, then the suit will abate so far as A is concerned. Thereupon, D may apply to the court for such costs as he may have incurred in the suit and the court may award such costs, which will be paid from the estate of A. The same procedure will obtain if A, as a sole plaintiff were to die and the right to sue survived.

Where One of Several Defendants or Sole Defendants Dies

Conversely, if one of two or more defendants dies and the right to sue survives against surviving defendant or defendants alone, or if a sole defendant dies and the right to sue survives, the court, on an application made on that behalf will cause the legal representative of the deceased defendant to be made a party to the suit and will then proceed with it (O. 22, r.4(1) C.P.C.)

Any person so made a party to the suit may make any defence appropriate to his character as legal representative (O.22, r.4 (2) C.P.C.).

Should no application be made within the time limited by law, the suit as in the case of death of a plaintiff, will abate as against the deceased defendant (O.22, r.4(3) C .P.C.).

In the case of *Dhanesvar Mehta v. Manilal M. Shah (1956)* E.A. 323, one of the questions that arose was the meaning of the word *"plaintiff"* in r.3 of O.23 of the Kenya Civil Procedure (Revised) Rules, 1948 (cf Tanzania Civil Procedure Code, O.22, r.3), and the Court of Appeal for East Africa stated, at page 327:

> "plaintiff" is not defined in the Civil Procedure Act or, so far as I am aware, in the Rules, but I think that in O.23, r. 3, it must mean the person in whose name the plaint was filed (Per Spry, J.A.).

It is important to note that once an application to implead such party has been made to the court, the court must implead such party. It has no discretion in the matter. All that the party need do is make the application. That would appear to be the effect of the phrase "shall cause the legal representative of the deceased plaintiff to be made a party" in r.4(1) of O.22. The only exception would be where there is a dispute as to who is the legal representative, in which event, the court would first have to decide the question under r.5 of O.22. As stated in *Chitaley and Rao's Code of Civil Procedure* (6th Edition, Vol. 3), at page 3362:

> The court is bound to implead the legal representatives as parties on an application made in that behalf, unless there is a dispute as to who is the legal representative, in which case, the question should be decided by it under r.5. Under the rule all that the person desirous of proceeding with the case has to do is to make an application. The further acts are left to the court. Where no order is passed by the court and the applicant also does not press the need for formal order, the omission on his part will not take away his right to proceed with the case as there is no duty cast on him by the rule to remind the court.

It has been held that the same considerations apply to a deceased defendant. In the case of *Gajender Pal v. Ram B. Sirdaw* (1961) E.A. 344, in which the two quotations above were quoted with approval, the Uganda High Court (Sheridan, J.) said, after quoting the above passage, at page 347:

> The same considerations apply to a deceased defendant. It is sufficient for the application to be made. Thereafter the duty to implead the legal representatives is thrown on the court and the parties are not to be penalized

for any shortcomings in the carrying into effect by the court of this ministerial function.

As pointed out above, should a question arise as to whether any person is or is not the legal representative of the deceased party, such question must be determined by the court before such party can be impleaded (O. 22, r.5 C.P.C.).

What, then, is the period of limitation for such applications. In the case of *Osman v. United India Fire and General Insurance Co. Ltd* (1968) E.A. 102, the Court of Appeal for East Africa held that in Tanganyika, the period of limitation for an application to have the legal representative of a deceased defendant made a party to suit under O.22, r.4 is six months. That case is also authority for the proposition that it is not open to the court to extend the period of limitation in Kenya under the corresponding provisions of O.23, r.491) (See: *Soni v. Mohan Dairy*, (1968) E.A. 58).

Consequence of Death After Hearing

Notwithstanding the foregoing provisions, if death of either party occurs after the conclusion of the hearing of the suit but before the pronouncement of the judgment, and whether or not the cause of action survives, there will be no abatement. Judgment may in such a case be pronounced notwithstanding the death, and will have the same force and effect as if it had been pronounced before the death took place (O.22, r. 6 C.P.C.).

For example, if in a suit between P, the plaintiff and D, the defendant, the hearing is completed on 30th July, 1979 and the judgment is reserved, and P dies before the Judgment is delivered, the court may pronounce the judgment notwithstanding the fact that P has since died, and such judgment will have the same force and effect as if it had been pronounced before P's death.

MARRIAGE

The mere fact that a female party to a suit has married will not cause the suit to abate. The suit may be proceeded with to judgment and, if the decree is against female defendant, such decree may be executed against her alone. However, where the husband is by law liable for the debts of his wife, the decree may, with the permission of the court, be executed against the husband also; and in a case in which judgment is in favour of the wife, the execution of her decree may, with such permission, be issued upon the application of the husband, where the husband is by law entitled to the subject – matter of the decree (O.22, r.4 C.P.C.).

INSOLVENCE OF PLAINTIFF

The insolvency of a plaintiff in a suit which the assignee or receiver might maintain for the benefit of his creditors, will not cause the suit to abate, unless such assignee or receiver declines to continue the suit or (unless for any special reason the court otherwise directs) to give security for the costs thereof within such time as the court may direct.

If the assignee or receiver neglects or refuses to continue the suit or give security within the time fixed by the court, the defendant may apply to the court that the suit be dismissed on the ground of the plaintiff's insolvency, and the court may make an order dismissing the suit and awarding to the defendant the costs which he had incurred in defending such suit. These will be treated as a debt against the plaintiff's estate (O. 22, r.8 C.P.C.).

Effect of Abatement or Dismissal

Once a suit abates or is dismissed under the foregoing provisions, no fresh suit can be brought on the same cause of action. However, the plaintiff or the person claiming to be the legal representative of a deceased plaintiff or the assignee or receiver in the case of an insolvent plaintiff may apply for an order to set aside the abatement or dismissal of the suit. If it is proved that he was prevented by sufficient cause from continuing the suit, the court will have to set aside the abatement or dismissal on such terms as to costs or otherwise as it thinks fit (O.22, r.9(1) (2) C.P.C.).

Any application to set aside an order of abatement or dismissal must be filed within sixty days from the date of the order or from the date on which the applicant became aware of the order (O.22, r.9(3) C.P.C. (see also Part III, item 12 of the First Schedule to the Law of Limitation Act, 1971).

It would appear, however, that if no application is made within the prescribed sixty days, the court may, under the provisions of section 14 of the Law of Limitation Act, 1971, extend the period of limitation for the institution of the application if the court is satisfied that the applicant had reasonable cause for failing to file the application within the period of sixty days.

In what circumstances, then, will an abatement be set aside? It has been held that an abatement ought not to be set aside lightly, because when a suit abates, the person in whose favour the abatement operates obtains a valuable right and so the setting aside of the abatement deprives him of such right. The applicant must satisfy the court that he was prevented by some sufficient cause from making the application to implead the legal representative of the deceased (see *Mohan Dairy v. Ratilal Burabhai*, (1966) E.A. 571, see also Mulla's *Code of Civil Procedure* (12th Edition) at page 959).

Procedure in Case of Assignment Before Final Order in Suit

In other cases of an assignment, creation or devolution of interest during the pendency of a suit, the suit may, by leave of the court, be continued by or against the persons to or upon whom such interest has come or devolved (O.22, r.10(1) C.P.C.).

In the case of attachment of a decree pending an appeal therefrom, such attachment will be deemed to be an interest entitling the person who procured such attachment to the benefit of sub-rule (1) above (O.22, r.10(2) C.P.C.).

This rule is a residuary one. It is intended to cover situations which are not provided for in the foregoing provisions. In *Chitaley and Rao's Code of Civil Procedure* (2nd Edition) the scope and applicability of this rule is described in the following terms, at page 2142:

> The rule is an enabling one. It is based on the principle that the trial of a suit cannot be arrested merely by reason of a devolution of the interest of a party in the subject-matter of the suit; that the person acquiring the interest may continue the suit with the leave of the Court; but that if he does not choose to do so the suit may be continued with the original party and the person acquiring the interest will be bound by, or can have the benefit of, the decree as the case may be.

According to the two learned authors, in order that the rule may apply, the following conditions must be fulfilled:

1) There must be an assignment, creation or devolution of any interest, in the subject mater of the suit;

2) Such assignment, creation or devolution of interest must be by, or from, a party to the suit and not a stranger; and

3) The person to whom the assignment, creation or devolution of interest takes place must be arrayed on the same side in the suit as the person from whom it has passed.

In applying the provisions in this Chapter to appeals, so far as may be, the word *"plaintiff"* is interpreted to include an appellant, the word *"defendant"* a respondent, and the word *"suit"* an appeal (O.22, r.11 C.P.C.). But rules 3,4 and 8 of Order 22 do not apply to proceedings in execution of a decree or order (O.22, r.12, C.P.C.).

CHAPTER TWENTY FIVE

WITHDRAWAL AND DISCONTINUANCE OF SUITS

In general, suits are said to have been disposed of when a final judgment or order has been given by the court either *ex-parte* or after hearing the evidence of the parties on the issues raised in the pleadings. But there are other situations in which suits may be brought to and end. These include withdrawals, abandonment and compromise.

WITHDRAWAL OR ABANDONMENT OF SUIT

After a suit has been instituted, a plaintiff may, at any time, as against all or any of the defendants, withdraw it or abandon part of his claim; where the court is satisfied that a suit must fail by reason of some formal defect, or that there are other sufficient grounds for allowing the plaintiff to institute a fresh suit for the subject- matter or part of a claim, it may, on such terms as it thinks fit, grant the plaintiff permission to withdraw from such suit or abandon such part of the claim with liberty to institute a fresh suit in respect of the subject-matter of such suit or such part of the claim. Should the plaintiff withdraw from a suit, or abandon part of a claim, without the permission of the court as set out above, he will be liable for such costs as the court may award and will be precluded from instituting any fresh suit in respect of such subject-matter or such part of the claim, as the case may be. But a court will not permit one of several plaintiffs to withdraw without the consent of the other plaintiffs O.23, r. 1(1), (2), (3) and (4) C.P.C.).

A plaintiff who seeks to withdraw with leave, therefore, will only be allowed by the court to withdraw from a suit or abandon part of the claim where it is satisfied that the suit will have to fail by reason of some formal irregularity, or where there are other sufficient grounds for allowing him to do so, and in the case of several plaintiffs, the other plaintiffs have consented to his withdrawal.

It should be noted, however, that a fresh suit instituted on such permission is subject to the law of limitation in the same manner as if the first suit had not been instituted (O.29, r.2, C.P.C.). In other words, the time does not stop to run merely by virtue of the court's permission to institute a fresh suit. The time continues to run from the date the cause of action arose or the right to sue accrued.

The provisions of r.1 of O.23 would appear to suggest that a plaintiff has two courses open to him. He can withdraw of his own motion, or with the permission of the court. In the former case he forfeits his right to bring a fresh suit, while in the latter case, he may withdraw with liberty to file a fresh suit. In Mulla's *Code of Civil Procedure* (10th Edition) it is stated, at page 883:

> If a party desires to withdraw from the suit with liberty to institute a fresh suit, he must apply to the court under sub-rule (2) to permit him so to withdraw.... But he cannot withdraw a suit reserving to himself a right to bring a fresh suit.

In the case of *Michael Alexander Ntenda v. Tanganyika Coffee Board.* (Arusha Registry High Court Civil Case No. 50 of 1977 – as yet unreported), the facts were that in an earlier case (Civil Case No. 12 of 1971) the plaintiff sued the defendant company, his former employer, for wrongful dismissal from his work as an Administrative Secretary. In that earlier suit, the plaintiff had given evidence and closed his case. Then witnesses for the defence gave evidence, and the hearing was adjourned to a date to be fixed by the District Registrar. When the mater came up again, this time before a different Judge, the parties, both of whom were represented, applied to the court to record a consent order. The request was granted and an order was recorded in the following terms:

> ORDER: By consent claim and counter-claim withdrawn. No order as to costs.

Some four years later, the plaintiff filed a fresh suit against the defendants on the same cause of action. One of the preliminary points raised by the advocate for the defendants was that the suit was *res judicata* under O.23, r. 1 of the Civil Procedure Code, that is, that the plaintiff's right to institute a fresh suit on the same cause of action had been forfeited by the manner in which the withdrawal was made. It was argued for the plaintiff that since the withdrawal was with the permission of the court, a fresh suit was not barred. The Court held that withdrawal was not, in the circumstances, with the permission of the court. The Court (Mnzavas, J.) stated:

> In the present case the plaintiff, with the consent of the defendant, who also withdrew his counterclaim, withdrew the suit and the learned Judge recorded a consent order of withdrawal of the suit and the counterclaim. Both parties were represented. Neither the learned counsel for the plaintiff nor that of the defendant stated to the court at the time of the withdrawal that he reserved the liberty of bringing a fresh suit. This being the position it therefore follows, as night follows day, that the consent withdrawals of the claim were made under O.23, r.1 of the Civil Procedure Code. This conclusion is the more inescapable taking into account the fact that at the time of the withdrawal the plaintiff had already given evidence and the defendant had gone more than half-way in his defence.

This case underscores the fact that a plaintiff who is desirous of withdrawing from a suit with leave to file a fresh suit must be very careful. He must make sure that his request is in the form of an application to the court for permission to withdraw. Another safeguard: he would be well advised to state that the application is being made under rule 1 sub-rule (2) of O.23 of the Civil Procedure Code.

On the part of the courts, it is advisable that in cases of withdrawal under O.23, the ensuing order should state under which of the two sub-rules the order is being made. If this is done, the difficulty of interpreting the meaning of the order would be forestalled. The problem in *Ntenda's case* (supra) arose from failure by both the learned advocate and the court to state under which of the two sub-rules the applications and ensuing order were being made.

COMPROMISE OR ADJUSTMENT OF SUIT

A suit may also be brought to an end by way of compromise, adjustment or satisfaction. So, if it is proved to the satisfaction of the court that a suit has been adjusted wholly or in part by any lawful agreement or compromise, or where the defendant satisfies the plaintiff in respect of the whole or any part of the subject-matter of the suit, the court will order such agreement, compromise or satisfaction to be recorded, and will pass a decree in accordance with such agreement, compromise or satisfaction so far as it relates to the suit (O.23, r.3, C.P.C.).

Now, what is the consequence of a compromise of suit? In the case of *Hirani v. Kassam*, (1952) 19 E.A.C.A. 131, it was held that where a suit has been settled by a compromise recorded under this rule, the decree is passed upon the new contract between the parties which supersedes the original cause of action. For instance, if A sues B for vacant possession and mesne profits, and subsequently the parties come to a compromise to the effect that B will give vacant possession while A will abandon the claim for mesne profits, on the authority of *Hirani's* case (supra), the resultant decree will be for vacant possession and cause of action for vacant possession and mesne profits will be taken to have been superseded.

The phrase "so far as it relates to the suit" was considered by the Kenya High Court in the case of *Khulshldas & Sons Ltd v. Weinstein and Another* (1964) E.A. 734. In that case the court quoted with approval *Chitaley and Rao's Code of Civil Procedure* (5th Edition, Vol. 2) at page 2787 where it is stated:

> The question whether a particular term in a petition of compromise relates to the suit must be decided from the frame of the suit, the relief claimed and the relief allowed by the decree on adjustment by lawful agreement. The mutual connection of the different parts of relief granted by a consent decree is an important element for consideration in each case in deciding whether any portion of the relief is within the scope of the suit. No hard and fast rule can be laid down and each case must be governed by its own facts. The relief granted in a compromise decree need not to be confined to the relief prayed for in the plant. The fact that a compromise relates to property not the subject – matter of the suit is not in all cases decisive of the question whether the compromise does or does not relate to the suit. Where the suit is merely for the recovery of specific properties, the

compromise must relate to such properties only. But where the suit is not merely for the recovery of the property, but to establish particular rights, the facts have to be looked at as a whole to decide whether matters that do not relate to the suit have been introduced. In such case, all terms which form the consideration for the adjustment of the matters in dispute, whether they form the subject-matter of the suit or not, become related to the suit, and can be embodied in the decree.

Once a court has passed a decree following a compromise, any objection that one of the terms of the compromise decree was not within the scope of the suit can not be considered by the court executing such decree. As was stated by the Bombay High Court in the case of *Ombalal Chunthabhai Patel v. Somabhai B. Patel,* (1944) AIR Bom. 46 (quoted with approval in *Khulshalda's* case – supra), at page 50:

And it may be taken as well settled that the objection that one of the terms of a compromise decree was outside the scope of the suit is not one for the executing court to consider. If there was no right in including that term in the operative part of the decree, it should have been challenged either by way of review or by way of appeal, but the executing court can not go behind the decree.

Indeed the provisions of O.23, r.4 of the Civil Procedure Code expressly provide that the provisions of O.23 do not apply to any proceedings in execution of a decree. This is as it should be because if challenges to compromises were to be allowed freely at that stage it would make decrees or orders of little binding effect. That would be most undesirable.

CHAPTER TWENTY SIX

PAYMENT INTO COURT AND SECURITY FOR COSTS

PAYMENT INTO COURT

If a defendant has been sued for recovery of a debt or damages, he may, at any stage of the suit, deposit in court such sum of money as he considers to be a satisfaction in full of the claim.

When such sum has been so deposited, notice of such deposit must be given through the court by the defendant to the plaintiff. The amount so deposited will then, on application by the plaintiff, be paid to the plaintiff, unless the court should direct otherwise (O.24, rr.1 and 2 C.P.C.).

It is important to note that the requirement that notice be given is not one of form. In the case of *Narshidas M. Mehta & Co. v. The Baron Verheyen* (1956) 2 TLR (R) 300, the defendant, then plaintiff, obtained a judgment against the plaintiff, then defendant, on 5th November, 1952. A decree was not signed and issued until 23rd January, 1953. On 12th December, 1952, an order was made staying execution of the decree, not then signed and issued, upon the condition that the decretal amount be paid into court, and the stay of execution was to become operative upon such payment.

On 24th December, 1952, a sum sufficient to satisfy the judgment was paid into court by the advocates for the plaintiff, then defendant, but no notice of this was given to the defendant, then plaintiff, who applied to the court for execution of the decree by the attachment of the plaintiff's property. The prohibitory order was then taken out by the Court Broker and handed to the plaintiff, but it was taken back on being informed of the payment into court.

The plaintiff then filed a suit against the defendant seeking to recover damages for the wrongful execution of the judgment of the court and for trespass consequent upon the Court Broker entering upon the property of the plaintiff.

Answering the question whether the failure of the plaintiff to give notice of the deposit into court disentitled him to any relief in the second suit, the court answered in the affirmative and stated, at page 308:

> I think it does. If I am right in my reasoning in the answer to the previous issue, it then comes about that by not causing to be issued to the Advocate for the opposite side, a notice of payment, the plaintiff is estopped from benefiting from his own default and so is disentitled to relief in this suit.

It should be noted that from the date notice of payment into court is communicated to the plaintiff, no interest must be charged on the sum so deposited, whether the sum so deposited is in full settlement of the claim or falls short of it (O.24, r.3 C.P.C.).

If the plaintiff accepts such amount as satisfaction in part only of his claim, he may prosecute his claim for the balance. If, in such a case, the court decides that the deposit by the defendant was a full satisfaction of the plaintiff's claim, then the plaintiff will have to pay the costs of the suit incurred after the deposit and those incurred previous thereto, so far as they were caused by excess in the plaintiff's claim (O.24, r.3(1) C.P.C.).

If, on the other hand, the plaintiff accepts the amount deposited as full satisfaction of the claim, he must present to the court a statement to that effect. Once such a statement has been filed in court, the court will pronounce judgment accordingly. In such a situation, in deciding as to who should bear the costs of each party, the court must consider which of the parties is most to blame for the litigation (O.24, r.3(2) C.P.C.).

SECURITY FOR COSTS

If, at any stage in a suit, it appears to the court that a sole plaintiff is or (when there are more plaintiffs than one) that all the plaintiffs are, residing outside Tanzania, and that such plaintiff does not, or that no one of such plaintiffs does, possess any sufficient immovable property within Tanzania other than the property in suit, the court may, either on its own motion or on the application of the defendant, order the plaintiff or plaintiffs, within a time to be fixed by the court, to give sufficient security for payment of all costs incurred and likely to be incurred in the suit by any defendant (O.25, r.1(1) C.P.C.). A person who leaves Tanzania under such circumstances as to give reasonable probability that he will not be forthcoming whenever he may be called upon to pay costs will be deemed to be residing out of Tanzania within the meaning of this sub-rule (O.25, r.1(2) C.P.C.).

When an order for security for costs has been made and such security is not paid within the time fixed by the court, the court will dismiss the suit, unless such plaintiff is permitted to withdraw from the suit (O.245, r.2(1) C.P.C.).

When a suit has been dismissed on the ground that the plaintiff has failed to furnish such security within the time fixed by the court, the plaintiff may apply for an order to set the dismissal aside. If the court is satisfied that he was prevented by any sufficient cause from furnishing such security within the time allowed, it will set aside the dismissal on such terms as to security, costs or otherwise as it thinks fit, and will then appoint a day for proceeding with the suit. But no order setting aside the dismissal must be made unless notice of the application has been served on the defendant (O.25, r.2(2) and (3) C.P.C.).

Under the provisions of the Tanzania Law of Limiteation Act, 1971, an application to set aside such dismissal must be made within 30 days from the date of the dismissal.

What amounts to "sufficient cause" for a plaitniff's failure to furnish security will, of course, depend on the circumstances of each case. But the Court of Appeal for Eastern Africa held, in the case of *Patrick Ngumi v. Muthui*, (22 E.A.C.A. 43) that mere lack of funds is not "sufficient cause" for the purpose of this rule. It will depend on the circumstances of each case. (*Shabir Din v. Anand*, Ibid, 48).

What would be the situation if a plaintiff, residing outside Tanzania and properties elsewhere in East Africa but not in Tanzania. That question arose in the case of *Farrab Incorporated v. Brian J. Robson and Others*, (1957) E.A. 441. There the defendants to the suit filed in Kenya made an application for security for costs under O.35, 1 of the Kenya Civil Procedure (Revised) Rules, 1948, on the ground that the plaintiff was resident abroad. The plaintiff was a corporation registered in Tangier having a place of business at Moshi, Tanganyika. The plaintiff opposed the application on the ground that it owned substantial property in Tanganyika. Granting the application, Connel, J., said, at page 443:

> There may be all sorts of difficulties in obtaining execution in Tanganyika;
> one has no knowledge of what sort of transactions are being carried on in

Tanganyika, who are the employees, what are the terms of the leases, whether a business or firm is registered in Moshi and if so under what name. Moreover, even if there was all that confirmation there is certainly no precedent under which the courts in this colony have followed court decisions under the Judicature Act, 1873, and Judgment. Extensions Act, 1868. Furthermore, in so far as the matter may be one of discretion I think this is a fit and proper case in which to order security for costs.

In the case of *V.H. Kapadia v. Thakersey Laxmidas*, (1960) E.A. 857, the same court (Edmonds, J.) held that *Farrahs* case did not decide that in all such cases, and no matter what the circumstances, security should be given. The facts in *Laxmidas* case were that the defendant applied for security of costs on the ground that the plaintiff was ordinarily a resident of Zanzibar and outside the jurisdiction of the court. The plaintiff submitted that no order should be made as by section 3 of the Judgments Extension Decree, Cap 23, Laws of Zanzibar a decree obtained in any court in Kenya could be transferred to Zanzibar for execution as if the decree had been obtained in Zanzibar. In refusing the application, the learned Judge distinguished *Farrah's* case and stated, at page 853:

The learned judge did not, however, decide that in all such cases and no matter what the circumstances, security should be given. In the instant case, the plaintiff has his principal place of business in Zanzibar with a branch in Dar es Salaam. The defendant will be at no material disadvantage, if successful in this suit, in taking proceedings in the recovery of his costs in Zanzibar or Tanganyika. I will, therefore, and decline the application.

From these two cases, it would appear that where the plaintiff is within East Africa but outside Tanzania, the courts have a judicial discretion whether or not to order security for costs against a plaintiff under the foregoing provisions, but in the wake of the revived East African Community it is reasonable to suppose that East African courts would usually refuse such applications.

CHAPTER TWENTY SEVEN

SUMMARY PROCEDURE

The procedure of framing, filing and disposing of suits which we have dealt with so far is applicable to a majority of suits, but there are exceptions. Suits on bills of exchange (including cheques) or promissory notes, suits for the recovery of income tax, and suits arising out of mortgage, whether legal or equitable, for payment of monies secured by mortgage, sale, foreclosure, delivery of possession of mortgaged property (where such possession is sought otherwise than by foreclosure) to mortgagee by the mortgagor or by any other person in or alleged to be in possession of the mortgaged property, redemption, or retransfer or discharge, may proceed by way of what is called summary procedure.

It should be noted that only suits that fall within the above categories may be proceeded with either by the ordinary procedure or under summary procedure. Suits not falling within this category cannot be instituted under the summary procedure. It was so held by the Court of Appeal for Eastern Africa in the case of *Uganda Transport Co. Ltd. v. Count De La Pasture*, (1954) 21 E.A.C.A. 163.

How Summary Suits are Instituted

Where a plaintiff desires to proceed by way of summary procedure and the nature of the suit falls within one of the categories mentioned above, he must present a plaint in the usual form, but such plaint must clearly be endorsed: "O.35: Summary Procedure" These words are usually shown at the top of the Plaint.

When the plaint has been so filed, the court will issue a summons and serve it upon the defendant.

A summons to be served upon a defendant in a summary suit informs the defendant that unless he obtains leave from the court to defend the suit, a decision may be given against him. It must also inform the defendant the manner in which he may apply to the court for leave to defend (O.35, rr. 1 & 2 C.P.C.).

In other words, in a summary suit, a defendant is not entitled as of right to appear or defend the suit. He can only do so by first obtaining leave from the judge or magistrate to so appear and defend, and such leave may be granted on a proper application made to the court. If he defaults, judgment will be entered against him (O.35, r.2 C.P.C.).

If a defendant who has been served with a summons under O.35 wishes to appear and defend the suit, such defendant must, within twenty one days from the date of servie of the summons, file a chamber application supported by an affidavit or declaration. The affidavit must show that there is a defence to the suit on the merits, or that it is reasonable that the defendant should be allowed to appear in the suit.

On receipt of the application, the court will issue a Chamber Summons to be served on both parties informing them of the date of hearing the chamber application.

There are times when a plaintiff's suit contains some claims which can correctly be brought under summary procedure and others which cannot. What, in such a case, should be done? Can the court in such a case proceed with the entire suit under summary procedure, or can it strike out those claims not falling within the categories of suits that may be dealt with under summary procedure? In the case of *Uganda Transport Co. Ltd. v. Count De la Pasture* (supra) it was held that where a plaint specially endorsed contains other claims, the court may, by O.33, r.3 to 7 and r.10 (Cf. O.35 rr.2 and 3) deal with the claims correctly endorsed as if no other claim had been included therein and allow the action to proceed as respects the residue of the claim and that the court has no power under O.33 (C.f O.35) to strike out any part of the claims.

WHEN IS LEAVE GRANTED?

Where an application, duly supported by an affidavit, has been filed, and such affidavit discloses

1) Such facts as would make it incumbent on the holder to prove consideration, where the suit is on a bill of exchange or promissory note; or

2) Such facts as the court may deem sufficient to support the application, the court must grant leave to appear and defend, and such leave may be given unconditionally or subject to such terms as to payment into court, giving security, framing or recording issues or otherwise as the court thinks fit (O.35, r. 3(1) 92) C.P.C.).

In short, all that the defendant has to show in order to obtain leave to appear and defend is that there is a triable issue of fact or law.

Let us now examine cases in which these provisions have been applied. In the case of *Estratius Karageogelis v. Emmanuel Marvoudis* (I.T.L.R. (R) 479), the plaintiff filed a suit upon a promissory note by way of Summary Procedure. On an application for leave to appear and defend the suit, the defendant averred in his affidavit, *inter alia*, that he never received any consideration whatsoever in respect of the promissory note. Granting leave to defend, Sir Joseph Sheridam, C.J., said, at page 480:

> It is not a question at this stage whether the statement of the application is true or false. I am not entitled to say that he has put forward a sham defence. The truth or falsity of his statement is a matter for trial. If the applicant had merely stated in his affidavit I do not owe the money, I would not listen to him, but he makes a particular statement that he received nothing and the genuineness of that statement he is entitled to have investigated in a trial.

In the case of *Terrazzo Paviors v. Standard Joinery & Building Co.* (1967) E.A. 307, the defendant was given leave to appear and defend on the ground that he had claimed equitable set-off and filed a counterclaim.

In the case of *David Sasson & Comp Ltd. v. Navichandra Patel and Others,* (1972) H.C.D. n. 148, the defendant filed an application upon affidavits brought under r.3 of O.35 for leave to appear and defend. The court stated:

> My role in these proceedings is fairly limited. It is simply to decide upon the affidavits filed by the applicant, whether there is disclosed any issue fit to go for trial and no more.... Now, in the instant case and upon the affidavits filed by the applicant, can this court say to the applicant, "You have no defence whatsoever against the plaintiff's claim?" I do not think so. It would clearly appear on the arguments canvassed by both counsel, that in this suit there is more than one triable issue that should be allowed to go before the appropriate tribunal. What chances the applicant has of succeeding in the end is not for me to say....

That case was quoted with approval by the same court (Mwesiumo, Ag. J., (as he then was) in the case of *Gulamhussein Fazal v. Mustafar Hussein Gulamali* (1976) L.R.T. n. 35 in which an application for leave to appear and defend was granted unconditionally.

In the case of *Kundalal Restaurant v. Devshi & Co.* (1952) 19 E.A.C.A. 77, the plaintiffs sued the detendants on a specially endorsed plaint and filed a motion for summary judgment under O.35, r.1 and 2 of the Civil Procedure Rules. The defendant asked for leave to defend relying on the statement of defence and an affidavit sworn by a partner alleging there was no privity of contract between the plaintiffs and defendants and that the alleged transactions were void for illegality under the Price Control Regulations. On Appeal, Sir Newham Worley – V.P., said, at page 79:

> Turning to the question of merits, I am of the opinion that this appeal should succeed. In *Hasmani Banque Congo Belgeum* (1938) 5 E.A.C.A. 89, Sir Joseph Sheridan, C.J., delivering a judgment, with which the other members of the court concurred, said: "If there is one triable issue contained in the affidavit supporting the application for leave to appear and defend then the appellant is entitled to have leave to appear and defend unconditionally." So far as I am aware, this decision has with one possible exception to which I will refer later, stood unchallenged since 1930 and I do not think we should depart from this general rule therein expressed, though, for my part, I would recognize that this general rule may be subject to some exceptions.

That general rule appears to have been qualified in the case of *Zola v. Ralli*, (1969) E.A. 691 in which Sir Charles Newbold, P. said, at page 694:

> O.35 is intended to enable a plaintiff with a liquidated claim, to which there is clearly no defence, to obtain a quick and summary judgment without being unnecessarily kept from what is due to him by delaying tactics of the defendant.

Zolar's case is also an authority for the proposition that the mere fact that a defendant is claiming or is entitled to indemnity by a third party is no reason for a defendant to prevent a plaintiff in obtaining a summary judgment.

In other words, if the defendant does not raise prima facie triable issues, leave to defend will be refused. It was so held in the case of *Mugambi v.*

Gatururu, (1967) E.A. 196. *(See also Kundalal's* case (supra); *Anand v. Shah* 25 K.L.R. 103;) and *Prabhudas v. The Standard Bank,* (1968) E.A. 670).

In what Circumstances Is Leave Granted Conditionally?

Normally, where the defendant has shown in his affidavit accompanying the application that there is a bona fide triable issue, leave to defend should be given unconditionally. In *Annual Practice,* 1955, it is stated, at page 193:

> The principle on which the courts act is that where the defendant can show by affidavit that there is a bona fide triable issue, he is to be allowed to defend as to that issue without condition *(Jacobs v. Booth's Distillery Co.* (1901) 85 L.R. 262 H.L.)… a condition of payment into court ought to be imposed where no reasonable ground of defence is set up…. Since *Jacobs v. Booth's Distillery Co.* (supra) the condition of payment into court, or giving security, is seldom imposed, and only in cases where the defendant consents, or there is good ground in the evidence for believing that the defence set up is a sham defence and the master "is prepared very nearly to give judgment for the plaintiffs in which case only the discretional power given by this rule (O.14, r.6 of R.S.O.) may be exercised" *(Wing v. Thurlow* 10 T.L.R. 53, 151). It should not be applied where there is a fair probability of a defence *(Ward v. Plumbley,* 6 T.L.R. 198; *Bowes v. Canstic Soda Co.* 9 T.L.R. 328) nor where the practical result of applying it would be unjustly to deprive the defendant of his defence.

This passage was quoted with approval by the Court of Appeal for Eastern Africa in the case or *Kundanlal Restaurant v. Devshi* (supra), which decision was followed by the same court in the case of *Sousal Figuerido & Co. v. Moorings Hotel Co. Ltd.,* (1959) E.A. 425 and in *Camille v. Merali* (196) E.A. 411 in which Spry, J.A. said, at page 419:

> The general rule is, that leave to defend should be given unconditionally unless there is good ground for thinking that the defences put forward are no more than a sham; and it must be more than mere suspicions.

The Tanzania High Court relied on *Kundanlal's* case too in the case of *Thssen-stahlunion Export v. Kibo Wire Industries,* (1973) L.R.T. n. 54 (supra) and reiterated the principle that where the defendant can show that the affidavit discloses a bona fide triable issue, he should defend that issue unconditionally but that a condition can be imposed where the court believes that the defence set up is sham. In *Thssen's* case (supra) the facts were that the applicant, in his chamber application, asked for leave to appear and defend the suit under O.35, r.3 and for an order rejecting the plaint under O.7, r.11 of the Civil Procedure Code. It was a suit instituted under Summary Procedure in which the respondent prayed for summary judgment to be entered in its favour on a set of bills of exchange in respect of which the plaintiff was the drawer and the defendant/applicant the acceptor.

It was the Court's view that although many matters were raised, the only issue that could be conceivably regarded as a triable issue was the issue of the proper stamping of the bills of exchange. However, it also took the issue of non-protest for non-payment to be triable, but not a serious triable issue. The court accordingly granted leave to appear and defend, but on condition that the applicant/defendant deposited into the court, within a month from the date of the order, fifty per cent of the sum claimed in the suit.

Another pertinent observation was made by *Lord Blackburn* in the case of *Wallingford v. Mutual Society* (1880) 5 A.C. 685 in which he said, at page 704:

> I think that when the affidavits are brought forward to raise that defence they must, if I may use the expression, condescend upon particulars. It is not enough to swear, "I say I owe him nothing..." that is not enough. You must satisfy the judge that there is reasonable ground for saying so. So again, if you swear that there was fraud, that will not do. It is difficult to define it, but you must give such an extent of definite facts pointing to the fraud as to satisfy the judge that those are facts which make it reasonable that you should be allowed to raise that defence. And in the like manner as to illegality, and every other defence that might be mentioned.

(See also *Tanzania Saruji Corporation v. Azania Investment and Another*, Dar es Salaam District Registry Civil Case No. 341 of 1999 as yet unreported).

Power to Set Aside a Decree

Ordinarily, after the expiration of twenty-one days from the date the summons is served on the defendant in a suit instituted under Summary Procedure, the court will, on the application of the plaintiff, enter an judgment for the plaintiff as prayed, if by that time the defendant has not filed an application for leave to appear and defend the suit.

However, even after a decree has been issued, the court may, under special circumstances, set it aside and, if necessary, stay or set aside execution, and may give leave to the defendant to appear to the summons and to defend the suit, if it seems reasonable to the court to do so, and on such terms as the court thinks fit (O.35, r.4 C.P.C.).

As the wording of the rule suggests, a decree will only be set aside under these provisions in special circumstances, and where it would be reasonable to do so. Besides, it has been held that, except in exceptional circumstances, a judgment should not be set aside without giving the plaintiff an opportunity to oppose the setting aside (see *N.B. Patel & Co. v. African Cotton Corporation Ltd.,* (1933) 5 U.L.R. 6). This, of course, is in accord with the principle of natural justice which finds expression in the Latin Maxim: *"Audi alteram partem,"* that is, that a man must not be condemned unheard.

Power to Order Bill, Promissory Note etc. to be Deposited With the Court

In any suit instituted under Summary Procedure, the court may order that the bill or note on which the suit is founded should forthwith be deposited with an officer of the court. Besides, the court may order that all proceedings must be stayed until the plaintiff has given security for the costs of such proceedings (O.35, r.5 C.P.C.). It is difficult to justify this provision and courts rarely apply it.

Costs Regarding Noting Non-acceptance of Dishonoured Bill

The holder of every dishonoured bill of exchange or promissory note has the same remedies for the recovery of the expenses he incurred in noting the same for non-acceptance or non-payment or otherwise, by reason of such dishonour, as he has under Summary Procedure for the recovery of the amount of such bill or note (O.35, r. 6 C.P.C.).

CHAPTER TWENTY EIGHT

SUITS IN PARTICULAR CASES

There are certain categories of suits for which there are special provisions as to the manner or by whom they should be prosecuted, processes served, or execution done. We shall now refer to some of them.

Suits by or Against Corporations

In suits by or against a corporation, any pleading, be it a plaint or written statement of defence or reply, as the case may be, may be signed and verified on behalf of the corporation by the secretary or by any director or other principal officer of the corporation who is able to depose to the facts of the case (O.28, r.1 C.P.C.).

As to service of processes, subject to any statutory provision regarding service of process, if the suit is against the corporation, the summons may be served in any of the following modes:

a) On the secretary, or on any director or other principal officer of the corporation, or

b) By leaving it or sending it by post addressed to the corporation at the registered office, or if there is no registered office, then at the place where the corporation carries on business (O.28, r.2 C.P.C.).

In any such suits, however, the court has a discretion to require, at any stage of the suit, the personal attendance of the secretary or of any director, or other principal officer of the corporation who may be able to answer material questions relating to the suit (O.28, r.3, C.P.C.).

Suits by or Against Firms and Persons Carrying on Business in Names Other than Their Own

Any two or more persons claiming or being liable as partners and carrying on business in Tanzania may sue or be sued in the name of the firm (if any) of which such persons were partners at the time the cause of action accrued, and any party to such a suit may in such a case apply to the court for a statement of the names and addresses of the persons who were, at the time of the accruing of the cause of action, partners in such firm, to be furnished and verified in such manner as the court may direct (see 29, r.1(1) C.P.C.).

Notice to be Served on Manager

If persons are sued as partners in the name of their firm, the summons must be served either upon one or more of the partners or at the principal place at which the partnership business is carried on, or upon any person having, at the time of service, the control or management of the partnership business there, as the court may direct; and such service will be deemed to be good service upon the firm so sued, whether all or any of the partners are within or without Tanzania.

If, however, the partnership has been dissolved to the knowledge of the plaintiff before the institution of the suit, the summons must be served upon every person within Tanzania who it is sought to make liable (O.29, r.3, C.P.C.).

What would happen if one of the partners dies either before the institution of the suit or during its pendency in which the partners may sue or be sued or would have sued or been sued? In such an event, and notwithstanding the provisions of section 45 of the Law of Contract Ordinance, it will not be necessary to join the legal representative of he deceased as a party to the suit. However, the legal representative may apply to be made a party to the suit. Besides, he can enforce any claim against the survivor or survivors (O.29, r.4, C.P.C.).

It should be noted that where a summons is issued under r.3 of O.29, then every person on whom it is served must be informed by notice in writing given at the time of service whether he is served as a partner or as a person having control or management of the partnership business, or in both characters. If no such notice is given the person served will be deemed to be served as a partner (O.29, r.5, C.P.C.).

The notice may read thus:

Take notice that the summons served herewith is served on you as the person having the management or control of the partnership business of A, B & C.

Or

Take notice that the summons served herewith is served on you as a partner in the defendant firm A,B & C.

If such persons sue or are sued as partners in the name of the firm as stated above, then, in the case of any pleading or other document required ·by or under the Code to be signed, verified or certified by any one of such persons, any one of them may sign, verify or certify the same.

For instance, if A and B, who are partners in some business under the name and style of *"Mvule Timber,"* want to sue Y, they can file the suit in the name of the firm, that is, *"Mvule Timber,"* and their pleadings or other document relating to the suit may be signed, verified or certified by either A or B; so too if Y were to sue the firm.

Dissolution of a Firm Before Suit

What would be the solution where a cause of action against a firm arises before the firm is dissolved, but the firm is dissolved before a suit is filed against such firm? In the case or *Horra v. Horra and Others* (1959) E.A. 981, the Kenya Supreme Court held that in such a case the suit can be brought against the firm; and that alternatively, the partners can be sued individually and as partners of the firm on their joint liability as partners, but that if the action is to be brought under O.29, r.1, then it must be filed against the firm name. The same court has held that a claim may be enforced against a partnership while making all the partners defendants (see *Sarwan Singh v. Karms Singh*, 1963) E.A. 423).

If the suit is instituted in the name of the firm, the plaintiff or their advocate must, on demand in writing by or on behalf of any defendant, forthwith declare in writing the names and places of residence of all the persons who constitute the firm on whose behalf the suit is instituted. If such demand is not met, then, on application for that purpose, all proceedings in the suit may be stayed upon such terms as the court may direct.

When the names have been so declared, the suit will proceed in the usual manner, and the same consequences in all respects will follow as if the partners had been named as plaintiffs in the plaint. However, since the suit will have been instituted in the name of the firm, the proceedings will continue in the name of the firm (O.29, r.2 C.P.C.). The notice may read thus:

> Take notice that the summons served herewith is served on you as a partner in the defendant firm A, B & Co. and also as the person having the control or management of the partnership business of A, B & Co.

Now, what is the consequence of failure to give such notice? In the case of *The Kenya Tobacco Co. Ltd v. Nairobi Trading Store.* (1954) 27 K.L.R. 37, the plaintiff company instituted a suit against the defendant firm, but without notice as required by O.29, r.4 of the Kenya Civil Procedure (Revised) Rules, 1948. The plaintiff applied in writing, for judgment in default of appearance. The Deputy Registrar, in view of the provisions of the rule, felt unable to enter judgment and referred the application to a Judge. The Supreme Court held that service was not effective. The Court stated, at page 39:

> As the service in this suit was admittedly upon a manager, that is a person, not a partner, who had merely the control or management of the partnership business and no concurrent notice was served, as is required by the rule, I find that the service was ineffective and the application to enter judgment premature and requiring to be dismissed.

Appearance of Parties

If persons are sued as partners in the name of their firm, they must appear individually in their own names, but all subsequent proceedings will continue in the firm name. (O. 29, r. 6, C.P.C.). But where a summons is served upon, say, a manager who has the control or management of the partnership business, no appearance by him will be necessary unless he is a partner of the defendant firm (O. 29, r. 7, C.P.C.).

If one of the partners of the defendant firm appears, and the suit is in the firm name, that constitutes appearance of the firm (see *Lyaght Ltd. v. Clark & Co.*, 1891) 1 Q.B. 552, 556).

It should be noted, however, that appearance in the name of a firm is no appearance at all because a firm is not a legal personality and so cannot appear as such. It was so held in he case of *Smith v. Auto Electric Service Ltd.,* (1951) 24 (2) K.L.R. 22. In that case the partners of the defendant firm at first entered an appearance in the memorandum of appearance in the name of the firm instead of in their individual names but later appeared individually. It was held that under r.5 of O.29 of the Kenya Civil Procedure (Revised) Rules, that earlier appearance was not a valid appearance, but the subsequent one was.

That case was referred to with approval by the Tanzania High Court in the case of *E.A. Posts and Telecommunications Corporation v. M/S Terrazo Paviors* (supra) in which the court held, *inter alia*, that where a partner or partners appear by advocate it is the duty of the advocate to state in court the name or names of the individual partner or partners he is appearing for, and that appearance in the name of the firm amounts to no appearance at all since a firm is not a legal personality and therefore cannot appear as such.

Appearance Under Protest

There are cases where a party who has been served as partner under r. 3 of O.29 denies that he is a partner. In such a case, he may appear under protest, denying that he is a partner. However, such appearance will not preclude the plaintiff from otherwise serving a summons on the firm and obtaining a decree against the firm in default of appearance where no partner has appeared. In other words, an appearance under protest is intended to nullify the service altogether. So, where a person who had been served enters an appearance under protest, that means that the service is nullified as far as the defendant firm is concerned.

What, then, is a plaintiff to do in such a case. In Mulla's *Code of Civil Procedure* it is stated:

> In such a case the plaintiff may disregard the appearance under protest altogether , and have the summons served upon one who is definitely a partner or one who has the control or management of the defendant firm as provided by r.3 above, and having obtained a decree against the firm, he may apply for leave to execute it against such person under O. 21, r.50. But the plaintiff is not bound to adopt this course. He may take out a chamber summons and contend that the party who appeared under protest is a partner or was a partner at the time the cause of action accrued, and apply on that basis to strike out of such appearance the denial of the partnership (page 1355, 13th Edition).

The party appearing, naturally, is not entitled to dispute liability of the defendant firm, for he is not expected to be conversant with the dealings of a firm of which he is not a partner. Indeed, English courts have held that such person is not even allowed to plead in the alternative that if he is a partner in the firm he is to plead in the alternative that he is not reliable (see *Weir & Co. v. McVicar & Co.* (1925) 2 K.B. 127).

Suits Against a Person Carrying on Business in Name Other than His Own Name

There are cases in which a person carries on business in a name or style other than his own name. Such a person may be sued in such name or style as if it were a firm name, and the rules governing suits by or against firms as discussed above will, *mutatis mutandis*, apply to such suit (O.29, r.10 C.P.C.).

The question that sometimes arises is: in what name can such a person sue where the cause of action relates to that business? In the case of *Shariff v. T. Singh* (1961) E.A. 72, the Court of Appeal for East Africa held that such a person can only sue in his own name although he may add such phrase as "trading as...." Dealing with the provisions of r.9 of O.29 of the Kenya Civil Procedure (Revised) Rules, 1948, which is identical with r.10 of O.29 of the Tanzania Civil Procedure Code, 1966, Gould, J.A., had this to say, at page 78:

> It is to be observed that, while r. 1 of the Order which deals with partnership, uses the words "may sue or be used in the name of the firm," r. 9 is confined to "may be sued in such name or style." A person such as the respondent, therefore, the sole proprietor of a business but trading under business name, must sue in his personal name; ... I have no doubt that he is entitled to add some such words as "trading as..." but those are words of description only... The language of O.29 is in any event permissive and the real party is the individual, irrespective of his business names.

If, however, the suit has been wrongly filed in the name or style of the business, then, the East African Court of Appeal has held, he may be allowed to amend (see *Phakey v. World Wide Agencies Ltd.,* 15 E.A.C.A. 1 and *George and Company v. Pritam's Auto Service* (1955) 22 E.A.C.A. 233).

Suits by or Against Trustees, Executors and Administrators

If in a suit concerning property vested in a trustee, executor or administrator the contention is between persons beneficially interested in such property and a third person, then the trustee, executor or administrator must represent the persons so beneficially interested, and it will ordinarily not be necessary to make the persons so beneficially interested parties to the suit. However, the occurt may, if it thinks fit, order them or any of them to be made parties to the suit (O.30, r.1, C.P.C.).

Let us take a simple example. A is the administrator of the estate of X deceased. B, and C are surviving children of X and so are beneficially interested in the property of X which includes a house. Y, who is a third party, claims ownership of the house. In a suit by Y for the ownership of that house, A will be the defendant representing B and C. It will not be necessary to make B and C to be parties to the suit, unless the court should order that both B and C or one of them be made parties/party to the suit.

But if there should be several trustees, executors or administrators of the property, then they must all be made parties to the suit against one or more of them. Here, however, it should be noted that those executers who have not proved their testator's will, and trustees, executors and administrators who are outside Tanzania need not be made parties to the suit (O.30, r.2 C.P.C.).

Now, suppose that two executors disagree as to whether or not to pursue a claim, what course of action should be taken? In the case of *Sargent v. Gautama,* (1968) E.A. 338, it was held that in such a situation, both must be joined.

Suits by or Against Minors and Persons of Unsound Mind

The mentally unsound and minors or infants do have rights and duties in the society within the scope of the law for the time being in force. Although by the very nature of their disabilities, they cannot prosecute their rights in the normal way before the courts, the law of civil procedure provides for various ways in which such people can pursue their civil claims or in which the claim against such people can be pursued.

To that procedure let us now turn.

Suits by or Against Minors

A Minor is defined as a person who is under the age of eighteen years, and the law is that such a person does not have full legal capacity. He cannot, for that reason, conduct legal proceedings himself. So, in every suit by a minor, such suit must be instituted in the name of the minor by a person who is an adult. In other words, an adult must institute the suit and prosecute it on behalf of the minor, but the suit must be in the name of the minor. Such adult is known as a "next friend" of the minor (O.31, r.1 C.P.C.).

If the suit is instituted by or on behalf of a minor without a next friend, the defendant may apply to the court to have the plaint taken off the file, with costs to be paid by the advocate or other person by whom such plaint was presented.

But if a defendant makes such an application, notice of such application must be given to such person. The court will then hear such objections as the person may raise, and it may then make such order in the matter as it thinks fit (O.31, r.2, C.P.C.).

Appointment of Guardian for Minor Defendant

Should a suit be instituted against a minor, that is, if a minor is a defendant to a suit, then the court will make an inquiry as to the fact of such minority, and on being satisfied that the defendant is in fact a minor, will appoint a proper person to be guardian for the suit for such minor. Such order may be obtained upon application in the name and on behalf of the minor or by the plaintiff.

Such an application must be supported by an affidavit verifying: (1) that the proposed guardian has no interest in the matters in controversy in the suit adverse to that of the minor, and (2) that he is a fit and proper person to be so appointed (O.31, r.3 (1) (2) and (3) C.P.C.).

The reason for these requirements is obvious. They are intended to ensure that the interests of that minor are not compromised by the guardian as a result of the guardian's own interest in the matters in controversy in the suit which are adverse to those of the minor, or as a result of the guardian's lack of scruples.

For the same reason, no order must be made on such an application until notice has been given to the minor and to any guardian of the minor appointed or declared by an authority to be competent in that behalf, or, if there is no such guardian of the minor, such notice should be given to the father or other natural guardian of the minor, or, where there is no such father or other natural guardian, to the person in whose care the minor is. Besides, no such order must be made until any objection that may be raised on behalf of any person so served with notice has been heard (O.31, r.3(4) C.P.C.)

Duties and Obligations of a Guardian

A person appointed a guardian for a suit must, unless his appointment is terminated by retirement, removal or death, continue as such guardian for the purpose of all the proceedings arising out of the suit including execution proceedings of a decree arising from the suit (O.31, r.3.(5) C.P.C.).

What, then, are the requisite qualifications for a guardian. He must be a "proper" person, and a proper person is one who is of sound mind, has attained age of majority, and whose interests are not adverse to that of the minor. Besides, he must not, in the case of a next friend, be a defendant, or, in the case of a guardian for the suit, a plaintiff (O.31, r.4(1) C.P.C.)

It should be borne in mind that if a minor has a guardian appointed or declared by competent authority, no person other than such guardian can act as the next friend of the minor or be appointed guardian unless the court considers that it is for the minor's welfare that another person be permitted to act or be appointed, as the case may be. But if the court is of that view, it must give reasons for holding that view (O.31, r.4 (2) C.P.C.).

One more point: no person should be appointed guardian for a suit without his consent (O.31, r.4(3) C.P.C.). In other words, a person, however otherwise qualified to be appointed guardian for a suit, cannot be appointed unless he is willing to be so appointed. A potential guardian, therefore, must first be consulted as to whether he would be willing to act as a guardian in a suit.

It may happen that there is no person who is fit and willing to act as guardian for the suit. In such an event, the court may appoint any of its officers to be such guardian, and may direct that the costs to be incurred by such officer in the performance of his duties as such guardian must be borne either by the parties or by any one or more of the parties to the suit, or out of any fund in court in which the minor is interested, and may give directions for the repayment or allowance of such costs as justice and circumstances of the case may require (O.31, r.4(d) C.P.C.).

Except for an application for stay of proceedings on removal, death or retirement of a next friend of a minor, every application to the court on behalf of a minor must be made by his next friend or guardian for the suit (O.31, r.5(1), C.P.C.).

What, then, would be the position where an order has been made in a suit or on an application before the court in or by which a minor is in some way concerned or affected, without such minor having been represented by a next friend or guardian for the suit? In such an event, such an order may be discharged, and if the advocate of the party at whose instance the order was obtained knew, or might reasonably have known, the fact of such minority, he may be ordered to pay the costs (O. 31, r.5(2) C.P.C.)

Limitations of Powers of Next Friend or Guardian for Suit

To ensure that interests of the minor are safe – guarded, a next friend or guardian for a suit cannot receive any money or other movable property on behalf of the minor either by way of compromise before the decree or order or under a decree or order in favour of the minor unless the court has given leave that he should do so (O.31, r.6(i) C.P.C.)

Where a next friend or guardian of the suit has not been appointed or declared by competent authority to be guardian of the property of the minor, or, having been so appointed and declared, such guardian for the suit or next friend is under any disability known to the court to receive the money or other movable property, the court must, if it gives him leave to receive the property, require him to furnish such security and give him directions as will, in the court's opinion, sufficiently protect the property from waste and ensure that it will be properly applied (O.31, r.6 (2) C.P.C.).

Besides, a next friend or guardian for a suit cannot, without the leave of the court, which must be recorded in the proceedings, enter into any agreement or compromise on behalf of the minor with reference to the suit in which he acts as next friend or guardian (O.31, r.7(1), C.P.C.).

Retirement and Removal of Next Friend

A next friend can retire as such next friend. But he will not be permitted to do so unless he has first procured a fit person to be put in his place, and he must give security for costs so far incurred. His application for the appointment of a new next friend in his place must be accompanied by an affidavit showing that such person has no interest adverse to that of the minor. (O.31, r.8, C.P.C.).

The other way in which a next friend may cease to act as such next friend is by removal. Now, on what grounds can a next friend be removed? A next friend can only be removed when it is sufficiently shown, to the satisfaction of the court, that the interest of the next friend is adverse to that of the minor, or where he is so connected with a defendant whose interest is adverse to that of the minor as to make it unlikely that the minor's interest will be properly protected by him, or where he does not do his duty, or where he ceases to reside within Tanzania during the pendency of the suit. He may further be removed on any other sufficient ground or cause.

When such sufficient cause or causes has/have arisen, an application may be made on behalf of the minor or by the defendant in the suit for the removal of the next friend. If the court is satisfied with the cause or causes given, it may accordingly order the removal of the next friend and make such order as to costs as it thinks fit (O.31, r.9(11) C.P.C.).

Stay of Proceedings after Removal/Retirement of Next Friend

If a next friend has ceased to be such next friend either by retirement, removal or death, the proceedings must be stayed until a new next friend had been appointed in his place. If the case of the minor is being handled by an advocate and such advocate does not within reasonable time take steps to have a new next friend appointed, then any person interested in the minor or in the matter in controversy may file an application to the court for the appointment of one, and the court may appoint such person as it thinks fit (O.31, r.10, C.P.C.).

Retirement, Removal or Death of Guardian for Suit

Should a guardian for the suit wish to retire, or should he fail to do his duty, or if there is other sufficient cause, the court may allow such guardian to retire or it may remove him, and may there and then make such order as to costs as it thinks fit (O.31, r.11 (1) C.P.C.).

Should the guardian for the suit retire, die or be removed by the court during the pendency of the suit, the court must appoint a new guardian in his place (O.31, r.11 (2) C.P.C.)

Minor Plaintiff/Applicant on Attaining Majority

A minor plaintiff or a minor who is not a party to a suit on whose behalf an application is pending must, on attaining age or majority, elect whether or not he will proceed with the suit or application. If he elects to proceed with the suit or application, he must apply for an order discharging the next friend and for leave to proceed in his own name. When an order of discharge has been made, and the minor given leave to proceed in his own name, the title of the suit or application must be altered so as to read thereafter thus:

A.B. late a minor, by C.D., his next friend, but now having attained majority.

If on the other hand, he elects to abandon the suit or application, he must, if he is the sole plaintiff or sole applicant, apply for an order to dismiss the suit or application on payment of the costs incurred by the defendant or opposite party or which may have been paid by his next friend (O.31, r.12(1), (2) (3) and (4) C.P.C.).

Any application by a minor plaintiff or applicant may be made ex-parte, but an order discharging the next friend and permitting a minor plaintiff to proceed in his own name must not be made without notice to such next friend (O.31. r.12(5) C.P.C.).

If on yet the other hand, the minor is a co-plaintiff and on attaining the age of majority wants to repudiate the suit, he must apply to have his name struck out as co-plaintiff, and if the court finds that he is not a necessary party, it must dismiss the suit on such terms as to costs or otherwise as it thinks fit. In such a case, it must be remembered, notice of the application of such minor to repudiate the suit must be served to the next friend, on the co-plaintiff and on the defendant. As to costs of the parties of such an application and of all or any proceedings thereto have had in the suit, it is for the court to direct by whom they should be paid. But if the minor is a necessary party to the suit, the court may direct him to be made a defendant to the suit (O.31, r.13, C.P.C.).

But suppose the suit filed by the late minor's next friend is improper or unreasonable? In such a case, a minor may, on attaining age or majority, and if he is a sole plaintiff, apply that the suit instituted by his next friend in his name be dismissed on the ground that it is improper or unreasonable (O.31, r.14(1) C.P.C.). Notice of the application, however, must in such a case be served on all the parties concerned. If the court is satisfied that the suit is in fact unreasonable or improper, it may grant the application and order the next friend to pay the costs of all the parties in respect of the application and of anything done in the suit, or it may make such other order as it thinks fit (O.31, r.14(2) C.P.C.).

This, perhaps, should be a warning to all those who are potential next friends. A next friend must be sure, before instituting a suit on behalf of a minor, or before agreeing to act as such next friend, that the suit is proper and has a reasonable chance of success. He has to do this not only because he must live up to the reputation of having been selected as *"a fit and proper person"* to be appointed as a next fried, but also because he stands to lose if the suit is improper or unreasonable.

Suits by or Against Persons of Unsound Mind

The rules regarding suits by or against persons who are minors apply also to persons who have been adjudged to be persons of unsound mind, or , though not so adjudged, whom, on inquiry, the court finds to be incapable of protecting their interests when suing or being sued by reason of unsoundness of mind or mental infirmity (O.31, r.15, C.P.C.).

CHAPTER TWENTY NINE

ARREST AND ATTACHMENT BEFORE JUDGMENT

We have so far discussed attachment of movable and immovable property in the execution of decrees and orders and the arrest and detention of judgment – debtors in civil prison in execution of decrees and orders. We have also looked at provisions regarding security for costs where one or all the plaintiffs resides or reside outside Tanzania. There is yet another situation in which there can be an attachment. We may call that attachment the *"pre-emptive attachment"* or *"attachment in anticipation."* It is what is called arrest and attachment before judgment. The provisions regarding arrest and attachment before judgment are pre-emptive: they are intended to statutorily empower the courts to prevent the ends of justice from being defeated by some unscrupulous defendants. To those provisions we now turn.

ARREST BEFORE JUDGMENT

In any suit, other that suits referred to in section 14(a) to (d) of the Civil Procedure Code, and at any stage of such suit, the court may issue a warrant to arrest the defendant and bring him before it to show cause why he should not furnish security for his appearance.

A court, however, will only issue such warrant for the arrest of the defendant where it is satisfied, by affidavit or otherwise, that the defendant, with intent to delay the plaintiff, or to avoid any process or to obstruct or delay the execution of any decree that may be passed against him-

a) Has absconded or left the local limits of the jurisdiction of the court; or

b) Is about to abscond or leave the local limits of the jurisdiction of the court; or

c) Has disposed of or removed from the local limits of the jurisdiction of the court his property or any part of it.

The court will also issue such a warrant where it is satisfied that the defendant is about to leave Tanzania under circumstances affording reasonable probability that the plaintiff will or may thereby be obstructed or delayed in the execution of any decree that may be passed against the defendant in the suit.

Once the warrant to arrest the defendant has been issued and given to an arresting officer, the arresting officer will not arrest the defendant if the defendant pays to him any sum specified in the warrant as sufficient to satisfy the plaintiff's claim. The officer entrusted with the execution of the warrant will then deposit the money with the court where it will be kept until the suit is disposed of or until the further order of the court (O.36, r.1 C.P.C.)

It is for the plaintiff to satisfy the court that there is reasonable and probable cause that the defendant will act or has so acted.

But what amounts to "reasonable and probable cause?" In the case of *Fernandes v. Commercial Bank of Africa Limited* (1969) E.A. 482, the Kenya High Court referred to the meaning of that expression in a criminal process in the English case of *Hicks v. Faulkner* (1881 Q.B.D. 167 and said: "*Altering the words of Hawkins, J., in Hicks v. Faulkner defining reasonable and probable cause to suit the present context of abuse of civil process...* I think they would read as follows:

An honest belief based upon a full conviction, founded upon reasonable grounds, or the existence of a state of circumstances which assuming them to be true would reasonably lead an ordinary prudent and cautious man placed in the position of the defendant (former plaintiff) to the conclusion that the plaintiff (former defendant) was about to leave Kenya under circumstances affording reasonable probability that the defendant will or may thereby be obstructed or delayed in the execution of any decree that may be passed against the plaintiff in the suit.

It would, therefore, appear that a plaintiff need not prove the actual intention of the defendant to obstruct or delay the execution of any decree that may be passed against him. It is sufficient for him to show that the circumstances under which he is about to leave the jurisdiction of the court or the country, or the manner in which he has disposed of his property, afford a reasonable probability that the execution of the decree that may be passed against the defendant will thereby be obstructed or delayed. The plaintiff, however, must bring out adequate material on which he bases his belief that unless his prayer is granted there is real danger that the ends of justice will be defeated.

In addition, before a court can act on such a prayer, it has further to be satisfied that the suit is *bona fide* and not *mala fide*.

Should the defendant be outside the local limits of the court in which the suit is filed, the court issuing the warrant may, by telegram, request any district court within the area of whose jurisdiction the defendant is believed to be to arrest him and cause him to be taken under escort to the court which issued the warrant. Such telegram must state the number and title of the case, the full name of the defendant and the place where he is believed to be, the amount of money upon payment of which the defendant may be released, a statement to the effect that the person applying for the arrest has given security for the expenses of and transport of the defendant and his escort to the court which issued the warrant, and the date when the warrant was issued (O.36, r.2(1) and (2) C.P.C.).

On receipt of such telegram, the court to which it is addressed must issue a provisional warrant in accordance with the particulars in the telegram and cause it to be executed (O.36, r.2(3) C.P.C.).

If at the time of the execution of the warrant the defendant does not pay to the officer executing the warrant the amount shown in the warrant, he must be escorted to the court which sent the telegram.

When the defendant is brought before the court which issued the original warrant, such court will inform him, if not already served with a copy of the plaint, the nature of the claim and the contents of the affidavit on the strength of which the warrant of arrest before judgment was issued, and then call upon him to show cause why he should not be made to furnish security for his appearance.

If he fails to show cause, the court will have to order him either to deposit in court money or other property sufficient to answer the claim against him, or to furnish security for his appearance at any time when called upon while the suit is pending and until satisfaction of any decree that may be passed against him in the suit, or make such order as it thinks fit in respect of the sum which may have been paid by the defendant at the time of the arrest (O.36, r.3(1) C.P.C.).

A defendant may also furnish security in the form of a bond to be executed by a surety. The surety will guarantee the appearance of the defendant. In default of such appearance, the surety binds himself to pay any sum of money which the defendant may be ordered to pay in the suit (O.36, r.3(2) C.P.C.).

It is, however, open to a surety at any time to apply to the court in which he became such surety to be discharged from the obligation (O.36, r.4(1) C.P.C.). On receipt of such an application, the court must summon the defendant to appear or, if it thinks fit, may issue a warrant for his arrest in the first instance. When the defendant appears in answer to the summons or warrant, or if he voluntarily surrenders himself, the court will direct that surety to be discharged from the obligation and call upon the defendant to furnish fresh security (O.36, r.4(2) and (3) C.P.C.).

What if the defendant should fail to furnish security? In such a case, the court may commit him to civil prison until the decision of the suit or, where a decree is passed against him, until the decree has been satisfied. However, no person must be detained in civil prison in such a case for more than six months, nor more than six weeks where the amount or value of the subject-matter of the suit does not exceed T.Shs. 150/=. But if he complies with the order he will not, of course, be committed to prison (O.36, r.5, C.P.C.).

Attachment Before Judgment

If, at any stage of a suit, the court is satisfied, by affidavit or otherwise, that the defendant, with intent to delay or obstruct the execution of any decree that may be passed against him in the suit, is about to dispose of the whole or any part of his property from the local limits of the jurisdiction of the court, the court may direct the defendant, within a time to be fixed by it, either to furnish security, in such sum as may be specified in the order, to produce and place at the disposal of the court when required, the said property or value of it, or such portion of it as may be sufficient to satisfy the decree, or to appear to show cause why he should not furnish security (O.36, r.6(1), C.P.C.).

Unless the court should direct otherwise, the plaintiff must specify the property to be attached and its estimated value, and the court may also order the conditional attachment of the whole or any portion of such specified property. (O.36, r.6(2) and (3) C.P.C.).

The provisions regarding attachment before judgment differ from those regarding arrest before judgment in one important respect: arrest before judgment does not include suit set out in section 14(a) to (d) of the Civil Procedure Code, while attachment before judgment can be in any suit.

But no agricultural produce in possession of any agriculturist may be attached (O.36, r.13, C.P.C.).

When, then, will a court exercise the power to attach property before judgment? In the case of *Raphael Dibogo v. Prablamus Wambura* (1975) L.R.T. n. 42, Lugakingira, Ag. J., (as he then was) had this to say:

> First of all before he (the magistrate) can order an attachment of disputed property he must be satisfied that the property is in danger of being destroyed, hidden, wasted, damaged, alienated or otherwise injuriously dealt with. In this case none of these was alleged.

In the case of *Mtale v. January Kapembwa*, (1976) L.R.T. n. 7, the same Court (Sisya, Ag. J., (as he then was), said at page 27:

> No doubt, the main object of this rule is to enable the plaintiff to realize the amount of decree, if one is eventually passed, from the defendant's property. However before invoking the provisions of this rule the court must be "satisfied by affidavit or otherwise, that the defendant, with intent to obstruct or delay the execution of any decree that may be passed against him" is about to commit the mischief about which the complaint is made. It is my considered opinion that power to attach, in these circumstances, should not be exercised lightly and without proof of the mischief aimed at.

The Court added:

> The mere fact that suit has been filed against a person should not be a warrant to debar him from dealing with his property.

(See also *Gulamhussein Fazal v. Muzafar Hussein Gulamali*, (No. 2) (1976) L.R.T. n. 64).

Should the defendant fail to show cause or furnish security within time fixed by the court, the court may order that the property specified or such portion of it as appears sufficient to satisfy the decree which may be passed in the suit, be attached.

CHAPTER THIRTY

TEMPORARY INJUNCTIONS AND INTERLOCUTORY ORDERS

TEMPORARY INJUNCTIONS

It not infrequently happens that a situation arises necessitating a restraint order against a party or property of a party before the suit or matter is finally determined. Such restraint orders are referred to as temporary injunctions. To that end, the law provides that where in any suit it is proved by affidavit or otherwise either, that any property in dispute in a suit is in danger of being wasted, damaged, or alienated by any party to the suit or suffer loss of value by reason of its continued use by any party to the suit or wrongly sold in execution of a decree, or that the defendant threatens or intends to remove or dispose of his property with a view to defraud his creditors, the court may grant an order of a temporary injunction to restrain such act; or it may make such order for the purpose of staying and preventing the wasting, damaging, alienation, sale, loss in value, removal or disposition of the property as the court thinks fit, until disposal of the suit or until further orders (see O.37, r.1 C.P.C.).

Similarly, in any suit for restraining the defendant from committing a breach of contract or other injury of any kind, whether compensation is claimed or not, the plaintiff may, at any time after the suit has been filed, and either before or after judgment, apply to the court for a temporary injunction to restrain the defendant from committing such breach of contract or injury complained of, or any breach of contract or injury of a like nature arising out of the same contract or relating to the same property or right (see O.37, r.2(1) C.P.C.). If the court is satisfied that the defendant might commit the breach or injury complained of by the plaintiff, it will grant the temporary injunction sought on such terms as it thinks fit.

If, after an order of temporary injunction has been made or issued, the defendant is guilty of disobeying the order, or is in breach of any terms of such order, the court which granted the injunction may order that the property of such person guilty of disobedience or breach of the terms of the order be attached. It may also order such person to be detained as a civil prisoner for a term not exceeding six months, unless the court should earlier direct that he be released (see O. 37, r.2(2) C.P.C. as amended by G.N. No. 508 of 1991)

In addition, in making orders of temporary injunctions, the court may order such terms as to the keeping of account and giving security. Such orders given under rule 1 or r.2 of O.37, must remain in force for a period specified by the court, but such period must not exceed six months. However, the court granting the injunction may, from time to time, extend such period for a further period which in aggregate must not exceed one year. But the court will only give such extension if it is satisfied that the person in whose favour the earlier injunction was granted had diligently been taking steps to settle the matter complained of and, if the court is further satisfied that the extension sought is in the interests of justice, necessary or desirable (see O.37, r.3 C.P.C. as amended by G.N. No. 508 of 1991) (see also *Knitwear v. Esmail* (1989) T.L.R. 48).

Ex-parte orders of temporary injunctions must not be made at the whim of a court. R.4 of O.37 of the Code (as amended) provides that before granting an injunction, the court must in all cases direct notice of the application to be given to the opposite party. The court before whom such an application is made can only proceed *ex-parte* where it appears that the giving of such notice would cause undue delay and that such undue delay would defeat the object for which the application has been made – (see also *Golcher v. G. Manager M.C.M.* (1987) T.L.R. 78; and *Mrema and Others v. Abdallah Majengo and Others*, CAT Civil Appeal No. 41 of 1999).

The requirement that notice should be given to the other party before an order of temporary injunction can be issued in mandatory, save in cases covered by the exception to the rule. As was stated by the Court in *Mrema's* case (supra):

The effect of r.4 of O.37 is to make it compulsory for the giving of notice to the opposite party in all cases except in situations covered by the exception to the rule.

As to the onus of showing that a particular case falls within the ambit of the rule, that is, before the court can dispense with the giving of notice, the Court stated:

It is up to the respondents to satisfy the court that there was a good cause for dispensing with the mandatory requirement to serve the notice of the application to the appellants.

The Court also quoted with approval the case of *Noor Mohamed Jan Mohamed v. Kassamali Virji Madhani*, (1953) 20 E.A.C.A. 8 in which it was stated, at page 11:

The requirement to give notice is clearly mandatory and it cannot be disputed that the onus of satisfying the court that there is good cause for dispensing with it will lie with the applicant.

Mrema's case (supra) is also authority for the proposition that the rule covers temporary injunctions as well as interim injunctions. This is as it should be because the rule talks of *"in all cases."*

It is important to note that ordinarily, temporary injunctions must be made, in the language of O.37, r.1, against a party to the suit. It ought not to be made against strangers to a suit (see also *N.B.C. v. Education and Office Stationery*, (1995) T.L.R. 272)., and *Mrema's* case – supra).

An order for an injunction can be varied, discharged or set aside by the court on application by any party who is dissatisfied by such an order (see O.37, r.5 C.P.C. as amended by G.N. No. 508 of 1991). The court has discretion in the matter, which discretion, however, must be exercised judicially.

In the case of an order for an injunction against a corporation, such order is binding not only on the corporation itself, but also on all members and officers of the corporation whose personal action it seeks to restrain (see O.37, r.6 C.P.C.).

The principles on the basis of which applications for temporary injunctions are granted or refused are well settled. In the case of *Attilio v.*

Mbowe, (1969) H.C.D. n. 284, George, C.J., restated the principles in the following terms:

> It is generally agreed that there are three conditions which must be satisfied before such an injunction can be issued:
>
> i) There must be a serious question to be tried on the facts alleged, and a probability that the plaintiff will be entitled to the relief prayed,
>
> ii) That the court's interference is necessary to protect the plaintiff from the kind of injury which may be irreparable before his legal right is established, and
>
> iii) That on the balance there will be greater hardship and mischief suffered by the plaintiff from withholding of the injunction than will be suffered by the defendant from the granting of it... the court must be satisfied that the damage which the plaintiff will suffer will be such that mere money compensation will not be adequate.

He added that a temporary injunction will normally be granted only if the whole point of the perpetual injunction claimed would be defeated if the temporary injunction is not granted.

In the case of *Ibrahim v. Ngaiza*, (1971) H.C.D. n. 249, it was held that it is a question of discretion of the court, which discretion must be exercised judicially by appreciating the facts and applying them to the principles governing issuance of temporary injunctions.

INTERLOCUTORY ORDERS

Sale Before Judgment

There are cases where the subject-matter of a suit or property which has been attached before judgment may be ordered to be sold at once pending the finalization of the suit. Such could be the case where the subject – matter or the attached property is movable property which is subject to speedy and natural decay, or which, for any sufficient reason, it is desirable that such property be sold at once (see O. 37, r.7, C.P.C.). Such an order is an interlocutory order in that it is made in the course of the proceedings before the suit is finally determined. A couple of examples will suffice.

Example 1:

A.B. and C.D. are exporters of fish fillets from Tanzania to Europe. While a consignment of fish fillets, which is in the name of A.B. as the consignor, is waiting to be loaded on a transport aeroplane at Mwanza Airport for transportation to Holland, C.D. files a suit against A.B. in the High Court at Mwanza claiming that he is the owner of the consignment. In such a case, C.D. may, after filing the suit, make an application to the court for an order for immediate sale of the fish. The court could, in such a situation, grant such an order because the subject-matter is movable property which is subject to speedy and natural decay.

Example 2:

In a suit between Jane and James, the dispute is over ownership of a car which, by an order of the court, has been attached before judgment. James, in whose name the car is registered, is about to go for studies abroad for three months and so fears that during that period, while the case is pending, the car could be exposed to waste and/or that the costs of its storage would needlessly be exorbitant. In such a situation, James may apply to the court to order that the car be sold at once. The court could, in its discretion, make such an order.

By the language of the rule, such an application should be made after institution of the suit. If the application is made by the plaintiff, an order will only be made after notice has been given to the defendant. If the application is made by the defendant, the plaintiff is likewise entitled to such notice, and no order will be made until after such defendant has entered an appearance (see O.37, r.9 C.P.C. as amended by G.N. No. 508 of 1991).

Detention, Preservation or Inspection

For the purpose of obtaining full information or evidence in any suit, the court may, while a suit is pending, make an order for the detention, preservation or inspection of any property which is the subject-matter of the suit, or as to which any question relevant to the suit may arise. But such an order will usually be made by the court on an application by any party to the suit, and it will be made on such terms as the court thinks fit. When such an order has been made, and for the purpose of carrying it out or executing it or any part of it, the court may authorize any person to enter upon or into the building or land or any other party to the suit or may authorize that any observation be made, or samples taken, or experiment to be tried as may seem to be necessary for the purpose (see O.37, r.8 C.P.C. – as amended by G.N. No. 508 of 1991).

One example will suffice. John and Charles enter into an oral agreement by which John agrees to build a residential house for Charles at a labour cost of ten million shillings with all materials supplied by Charles, and it is agreed that the work must be up to reasonably acceptable standards and must be completed within twenty months. Charles terminates the contract on the grounds that John is in breach of the contract for failing to complete the construction within twenty months and only 50% of the work was completed within the agreed twenty months. John claims that he has done 95% of the work, that the delay was caused by Charles' failure to supply materials in time and that the work done is up to reasonably acceptable standards. So John sues Charles and claims nine Million shillings for work done. In such a case, John could file an application for an interlocutory order for the inspection of the property and experiment to be tried so as to determine the amount of work done and the quality of the work before Charles takes over and proceeds to finalize the construction of the house.

If the subject-matter of the suit is money or some other thing capable of being delivered and any party to the suit admits that he is in possession of such money or thing as a trustee for another party, or if he admits that such money or thing belongs or is due to another party, the court may order the same to be deposited in court or delivered to such last-mentioned party, with or without security subject to further directions of the court (see O.37, r.10 C.P.C. – as amended by G.N. No. 508 of 1991).

CHAPTER THIRTY ONE

APPEALS

To state the commonplace, in many cases the unsuccessful party is dissatisfied with the judgment of the trial court, and in others both the parties may be dissatisfied with the outcome of the case. In such a case the dissatisfied party may appeal or cross-appeal (as the case may be) from the decision of the trial court to a superior court (see *Mariki v. Ngomuo,* (1981) T.L.R. 143. Indeed, this is a right granted by no lesser a law than the Law of the Land, that is, the Constitution of the United Republic, under Article 13.

As we have seen earlier, every suit must be instituted in the court of the lowest grade competent to try it, and by the provisions of the Civil Procedure Code, 1966, the district court and court of resident magistrate, which are deemed to be courts of the same grade, are the lowest courts competent to try suits, if they otherwise have jurisdiction. So, unless otherwise provided by any law, an appeal from every appealed decree of a court of resident magistrate or district court in the exercise of its original jurisdiction, lies to the High Court.

It should be noted that an appeal may lie from an original decree passed after a full trial and also from an original decree passed *ex-parte*. However, no appeal lies from a decree passed by the court with the consent of the parties (S.70, C.P.C.).

An Appeal may also lie from a preliminary decree. Indeed, if any party aggrieved by a preliminary decree does not appeal from such a decree, he will be precluded from disputing its correctness in any appeal which may be preferred from the final decree (see S.71 C.P.C.).

Let us now proceed to consider the various types of appeals which may be preferred, and the mode in which they are preferred and dealt with.

APPEALS FROM ORIGINAL DECREE

To start with, what is an original decree? We may define an original decree as a decree issued by a court of first instance, that is, a decree issued by a court in the exercise of its original jurisdiction as opposed to a decree issued in the exercise of its appellate or revisional jurisdiction.

Papers Essential for an Appeal

It is a general rule that every appeal must be preferred in the form of a memorandum signed by the appellant or his advocate and presented to the appellate court or to such officer as it appoints in this connection.

For our purposes, in this Chapter, we shall deal with the question of appeals with regard to appeals that lie to the High Court from subordinate courts.

The memorandum of appeal is usually presented to the Registrar or District Registrar or some senior officer in the High Court Civil Registry. It is important to remember that the memorandum of appeal must be accompanied by a copy of the decree appealed from and, unless the High Court dispenses with it, the judgment on which such decree is founded (O.39, r.1(1) C.P.C.).

What, then, is the consequence of failure to include a copy of a decree in an appeal? In the case of *Adams v. Adams* (1959) E.A. 777, the appellant filed the record of appeal without including therein a copy of the preliminary decree with which the appeal was concerned. The preliminary decree had not then been extracted but this was done later and the appellant applied for and obtained without objection leave to file a supplementary record including the decree. At the hearing of the appeal the respondent took a preliminary objection that since the decree had not been extracted when the appeal was filed, the appeal was incompetent. The Court of Appeal for East Africa held that the rule requiring a copy of a decree to be filed with an appeal applies to any appeal and not merely to appeals against a judgment, and that the requirement was mandatory. The preliminary objection, however, was overruled on the ground that if leave to amend the record were granted, any breach of the rule would have been cured.

In the case of *Kotak v. Kooverji,* (1967) E.A. 348, in an appeal to the High Court from an order made in the District Court of Dar es Salaam a preliminary point was taken by the respondents that no certified copy of the order accompanied the memorandum of appeal (although a certified copy of the ruling was attached) as required by O.39, r.1 (1) of the Civil Procedure Code, 1966, read with O.40, r.2 of the Code. Dismissing the appeal, the High Court held that the rules were mandatory, and that where an appellant has failed to comply with this provision, the appeal is incompetent for in such a case there has been no legal presentation of a memorandum of appeal. The court also dismissed the appellant's argument that a decree order must be taken to be in the judgment or order; it distinguished a judgment/ruling from a decree or order. In that case, the court quoted with approval the decision in the Kenya case of *Munshiram & Co. v. Star Soda Water Factory* (1934), KLR. 50, in which the Kenya Supreme Court held that O.39, r. 1 is mandatory in requiring every memorandum of appeal to be accompanied by a copy of the decree or order appealed from, and that where an appellant has failed to comply with this provision, the appeal is not properly before the court and must be dismissed.

The court also quoted with approval the Indian case of *Bashir Ram & Others v. The Municipal Committee Chiniot* (1922), AIR Lah. 191, in which the court said:

> Presentation of memorandum of appeal not accompanied by a copy of decree is no legal presentation (see also *Masha v. Shija,* (1997) T.L.R. 41; *Bakhressa v. Ngume,* (1997) T.L.R. 312; *Stanley v. Kunyamale* (1988) T.L.R. 250); and *Mtale v. Karmali,* (1983) T.L.R. 50.

And what is the position where an appellant presents a copy of the decree together with the memorandum of appeal, but omits to present a copy of the judgment without the court having dispensed with the requirement of filing a copy of judgment. It is submitted that the wording of the rule being mandatory and not permissive, the appeal would likewise be incompetent, unless the High Court has dispensed with it (see *Mariki's* case − supra).

Form and Contents of a Memorandum of Appeal

As pointed out above, every appeal must be preferred in the form of a memorandum signed by he appellant or his advocate. And what is a memorandum of appeal? We may define it as a concise statement of the grounds on which the judgment, ruling, decree or order appealed from is sought to be varied or reversed.

The memorandum of appeal must set out, concisely and under distinct heads, the grounds of objecting to the decree appealed from without setting out any argument or narrative, and such grounds must be numbered consecutively (O.39, r.1(1) and (2) C.P.C.).

What this means is that a memorandum of appeal must not be a narrative or detailed exposition of the arguments to be made at the hearing of the appeal. For instance, if one of the grounds of appeal is that the trial court erred in accepting the evidence of one side and disbelieving that of the other in spite of contradictions in the evidence accepted, you do not need to set out in your memorandum of appeal that evidence and point out the various discrepancies. That would be tantamount to setting out argument or narrative which the rule prohibits. Leave argument and narrative till during the hearing of the appeal.

In the example given above, a paragraph stating:

> That the learned trial magistrate erred in believing the evidence of the plaintiff's witnesses in view of the serious discrepancies in their evidence

would suffice. Similarly, if one ground of appeal were to be that the trial magistrate misdirected himself on the question of the burden of proof, it is sufficient to state merely:

> That the learned magistrate misdirected himself on the question of the burden of proof

without setting out whole paragraphs in the judgment which constitute the misdirection complained of.

It is important that before presenting the memorandum of appeal, the appellant must be fully satisfied that his memorandum of appeal contains all points that need to be argued in the appeal. This is because an appellant will not, except with the leave of the court, urge or be heard in support of any ground of objection which has not been set out in the memorandum of appeal. But in deciding the appeal, the court will not confine itself to the grounds of objection set out in the memorandum of appeal or taken by leave of the court. However, a court ought not to base its decision on any other ground unless the party who may be affected by so doing has had sufficient opportunity of contesting the case on that ground (O.39, r.2 C.P.C.).

The question that arises, then, is: in what circumstances will an appellate court exercise its discretion to allow an appellant to take a new point on appeal? In the case of *Tanganyika Farmers Association v. Unyamwezi Development Corporation* (1960) E.A. 620, at the trial in the High Court, the appellants' defence had been that there had been no privity of contract between them and the respondents (the former plaintiffs) and that they (the appellants) had bought the goods in question from a different party whom they had fully paid. The trial Judge dismissed both these defences and found for the respondents. On appeal, counsel for the appellants attempted to treat the evidence of certain witnesses in a way which was the reverse of that adopted by counsel who had appeared for the appellants in the High Court. This was objected to. On this point, Gould, Ag. V-P, said, at page 626:

> The objection to this submission is that it raises a question which was never in the contemplation of the parties in the court below. It was not argued there, nor was it ever mentioned in the correspondence between the parties. An appeal court has a discretion to allow a new point to be taken on appeal but it will permit such a course only when it is assured that full justice can be done to the parties.

His Lordship then referred with approval to several English authorities, among them the case of *North Staffordshire Railway Co. v. Edge* (1920) A.C. 254, in which Lord Buckmaster said, at page 270:

> Upon the question as to whether the appellants should be permitted to raise here a contention not raised in the court of first instance I find myself most closely in accord with the views just stated by my Lord Atkinson. Such a matter is not to be determined by mere consideration of the convenience of this House but by considering whether it is possible to be assured that full justice can be done between the parties by permitting new points of controversy to be discussed. If there be further matters of fact that could possibly and properly influence the judgment to be formed, and one party has omitted to take steps to place such matters before the court because the defined issues did not render it material there, leave to raise a new stage ought to be refused, and this is settled practice.

In an earlier case, which was also quoted with approval in the *Tanganyika Farmers'* case, namely, *The Tasmania* (1890) 15 A.C. 223, Lord Herschell said, at page 225:

My Lords, I think that a point such as this, not taken at the trial, and presented for the first time in the Court of Appeal, ought to be most jealously scrutinized. The conduct of a cause at the trial is governed by, and the questions asked for the witnesses are directed to, the points then suggested. And it is obvious that no care is exercised in the elucidation of facts not material to them.

It appears to me that under these circumstances a Court of Appeal ought only to decide in favour of an appellant on a ground there put forward for the first time, if it be satisfied beyond doubt, first that it has before it all the facts bearing upon the new contention, as completely as would have been the case if the controversy had arisen at the trial; and next, that no satisfactory explanation could have been offered by those whose conduct is impugned if no opportunity for explanation had been afforded them when in the witness box.

In the case of *Connecticut Fire Insurance Co. v. Kavanagh (1892)* A.C. 473, Lord Watson had this to say, at page 480:

When a question of law is raised for the first time in a court of last resort, upon the construction of a document or upon facts either admitted or proved beyond controversy, it is not only competent but expedient, in the interests of justice to entertain the plea. The expediency of adopting that course may be doubted, when the plea cannot be disposed of without deciding nice questions of fact, in considering which the court of ultimate review is placed in a much less advantageous position than the courts below. But, their Lordships have no hesitation in holding that the course ought not, in any case, to be followed, unless the court is satisfied that the evidence upon which they are asked to decide establishes beyond doubt that the facts, if fully investigated, would have supported the new plea.

This passage was quoted with approval in the case of *Warehousing & Forwarding Co. v. Jafferali & Sons Ltd.,* (1963) E.A. 385, in which the Privy Council advised that a new point ought not to be taken on appeal where it would take the other side by surprise and mislead him as to the case his opponents were making at the first instance (see also *Visram & Karsan v. Bhatt & Others* (1965) E.A. 789).

Rejection and Amendment of Memorandum of Appeal

If a memorandum of appeal is not drawn up in the manner discussed above, it may be rejected or returned to the appellant for the purpose of being amended within a time to be fixed by the court, or it may be ordered that it be amended there and then. If the court rejects the memorandum of appeal, it must record its reasons for such rejection. If the memorandum of appeal is rejected, it must be duly endorsed and signed by the Judge or such officer as may be appointed in this behalf (O.39, r.3 C.P.C.).

When, then, will a memorandum of appeal be rejected? It would appear that a memorandum of appeal may be rejected if it is discursive, that is, that it does not precisely show what are the grounds of appeal (see *Visram & Kartan's case* (supra) at page 792, letter C.).

An appeal will also be rejected or returned, as stated above, if it does not comply with the revisions of O.39, r.1 and 2 of the Code (see *Bhakhressa v. Ngume*, (1997) T.L.R. 312).

Should there be more plaintiffs or defendants than one in a suit, and the decree appealed from proceeds on any ground common to all plaintiffs or to all defendants, any one of the plaintiffs or of the defendants may appeal from the whole decree, and thereupon the court may reverse or vary the decree in favour of the all plaintiffs or defendants as the case may be (O.39, r.4 C.P.C.).

Stay of Proceedings in Execution

To state the obvious, a decree or order issued or made by a court of competent jurisdiction remains valid unless and until varied or set aside by a superior court; and as a general rule, an appeal from a decree or order does not operate as an automatic stay of execution proceedings under the decree or order appealed from. Similarly, execution of a decree will not be stayed merely because an appeal has been preferred from such decree. The court, however, may order stay of proceedings under a decree, and it may, for sufficient cause, order stay of execution of such decree (O.39, r. 5(1), C.P.C.).

What this means, therefore, is that the unsuccessful party must not assume that execution of the decree will be stayed by reason only of the fact that he has filed an appeal from the decree. If he desires that execution proceedings under the decree or order of the execution of it be stayed, he must file an application for such stay, and such application has to be made before the expiration of the time allowed for appealing from the decree or order. On such application, the court which passed the decree may, if sufficient cause is shown, order the execution to be stayed pending the determination of the appeal or intended appeal (O.39, r.5(2) C.P.C.).

A stay of execution, however, will not be granted as a matter of course. Under the provisions of sub- rule (3) of rule 5 of Order 39 of the Civil Procedure Code, neither the High Court nor the court which passed the decree will order stay of execution under the foregoing provisions unless such court is satisfied: (1) that substantial loss may result to the party applying for stay of execution if the order is not made: (2) that the application has been made without unreasonable delay; and (3) that security has been given by the applicant for the due performance of such decree or order as may ultimately be binding upon him (see *Lekule v. Independent Power,* (1997) T.L.R. 58 and *Braganza v. Braganza,* (1992) T.L.R. 307).

When an application for stay of execution has been made, the court may exercise its discretion and make an ex-parte order for stay of execution pending the hearing of the application (O.39, r.5 (4), C.P.C.).

If an order is made for the execution of a decree from which an appeal is pending, and the appellant shows sufficient cause, the court which passed the decree must require security to be taken of the restitution of any property which may be or has been taken in execution of the decree or for the payment of the value of such property and for the due performance of the decree or order of the court; or the High Court may for a similar cause direct the court which passed the decree to take such security (O.39, r.6(1) C.P.C.).

These provisions are the reverse of the provisions of rule 5 of Order 39. While those of rule 5 are intended to protect the interests of the decree-holder, those in rule 6(1) are intended to protect the appellant in the event of the appeal succeeding. But unlike provisions of rule 5, those of rule 6 only apply; (1) when there is an order made for the execution of a decree, and (2) when there is an appeal pending from that decree.

From the language of rule 6(1), it would appear that the application may be made to the court which passed the decree or to the appellate court itself. The only difference would appear to be that whereas it is mandatory for the court which passed the decree to order such security on sufficient cause being shown, on an application to the appellate court, that court may, in its discretion, require security to be given.

In a case where an order has been made for the sale of immovable property in execution of a decree, and an appeal is pending from such decree then, on application of the judgment-debtor, the sale must be stayed on such terms as to giving security or otherwise as the court thinks fit until the appeal is disposed of (O.39, r.6(2) C.P.C.).

The court, it would appear, has no discretion in this regard. All that is required for the court is to satisfy itself; (1) that an order for sale of immovable property in execution of a decree has been made; (2) that an appeal is pending from such decree; and (3) that the judgment-debtor has filed an application for stay of such sale. The only discretion the court has in such a matter in the nature of the security which should be given.

It should be noted, however, that no security as is referred to in r.5 and 6 of O.39 may be required of the Government or, where the Government has undertaken the defence of the suit, from any public officer sued in respect of an act alleged to have been done by him in his official capacity (O.39, r.7 C.P.C.).

Stay of proceedings of execution and security are also exercisable where an appeal may be or has been preferred not from the decree itself but from an order made in execution of such decree (O.39, r.8 C.P.C.).

Procedure on Admission of Appeal

When a memorandum of appeal is admitted, the High Court or the proper officer (usually the Registry Officer) must endorse on it the date of presentation, and then register it in a book called the Register of Appeals (O.39, r.9 C.P.C.).

The High Court may, in its discretion, either before the respondent is called upon to appear and answer or afterwards on the application of the respondent, demand from the appellant security for the costs of the appeal, or of the original suit or both. However, in every case in which the appellant is residing outside and does not possess sufficient immovable property within Tanzania other than the property (if any) to which the appeal relates, the court must demand that security be furnished within the time fixed by the court, otherwise the court will reject the appeal (O.39, r.20).

The requiring of security, it should be obvious, is designed to afford some measure of protection to the other party in the event of dismissal of the appeal. In the case of *Noormohamed Abdulla v. Patel and Another,* (1962) E.A. 447, the facts were that the appellant's claim for damages for wrongful distress against the first respondent was dismissed by the Supreme Court with costs subsequently taxed at T.Shs. 8,640/50. The first respondent then issued execution by notice to appellant to show cause against arrest and committal on the hearing of which the appellant was ordered to pay the costs by monthly installments of T.Shs. 100/= and that in default a warrant of arrest should issue. The appellant paid the installments regularly. About fifteen months after filing of the appeal but three months before the appeal was to be heard, the first respondent applied for an order that the appellant should give security for the past costs relating to the matters in question in the appeal and that such past costs should be paid within such time as the court thought fit. The appellant was undisputedly a man of little substance. The court there stated, at page 451:

> The order for security in such a case as this is not directed towards enforcing the payment of the costs as such, but is designed to ensure that a litigant who by reason of near insolvency is unable to pay the costs of the litigation when he loses, is disabled from carrying on the litigation indefinitely except upon the terms and conditions which afford some measure of protection to the other parties.

The court, however, dismissed the application on the ground, *inter alia*, of dilatoriness of the first respondent in making the application which it was for the applicant to show that the dilatoriness did not prejudice the appellant. The court went on to say that the mere poverty of an appellant was no warrant for hindering a party from pursuing his litigation, and that the power to order security in respect of costs ordered to be paid in the Supreme Court was one which should be sparingly exercised (see also *Gunning v. Motor Mart & Exchange Ltd.* L.R.S. 1 of 1962; page 5).

When the memorandum of appeal has been duly filed, the court will send for the record of the trial court. On receipt of the record, the Registrar or the District Registrar, will then submit the record together with the memorandum of appeal, to a Judge. The Judge will then peruse the record and the memorandum of appeal. If after such perusal, the Judge is satisfied that the appeal raises nothing of substance and so is devoid of any merit, he will certify accordingly and summarily reject the appeal. In other words, a Judge has the power to reject an appeal *in limine* without calling upon or hearing the parties (see Section 28 of the Magistrate's Courts Act, 1984 and O.39, r.11 (1) C.P.C.). If, on the other hand, the Judge finds merit in the appeal he will order that the appeal be admitted to hearing.

When the appeal has been admitted to hearing, a day will be fixed for hearing the same, and notices will be sent to the parties.

If on the day fixed, or on any other day to which the hearing is adjourned, the appellant does not appear and there is evidence that the was duly notified, the court may dismiss the appeal and notify the trial court accordingly (O.39, r.11(2) and (3) C.P.C.), or it may adjourn the hearing to some other day. In fixing a hearing date, the court will have regard to the current business of the court, the place of residence of the parties and the time necessary for service of the notices of appeal, so as to allow the respondent sufficient time to appear and answer the appeal on the day so fixed (O.39, r.12 C.P.C.).

The notice of appeal will be sent to the trial court for service on the parties. On receipt of the notices, such court must, with all practicable speed, send to the High Court all material documents in the case (such as exhibits), or such papers as may be specifically called for by the court (O.39, r.13 (1) and (2) C.P.C.).

Notices of appeal are served in the same manner as summonses are served on defendants, and a notice must declare that should the respondent fail to appear in court on the date fixed for hearing as shown in the notice, the appeal will he heard *ex-parte* (O.39, rr.14 and 15 C.P.C.).

In some cases, the High Court may itself serve the notices instead of sending them for service to the court from whose decree the appeal is preferred (O.39, r.14 C.P.C.).

Procedure of Hearing

When the appeal comes up for hearing, the appellant will be heard in support of the appeal. In other words, the appellant has the right to begin. Thereafter, the court may dismiss the appeal at once without calling on the respondent to reply. If it does not so dismiss the appeal, it will call upon the respondent and hear him against the appeal. In such an event the appellant is entitled to reply (O.39, r.16 C.P.C.).

As pointed out earlier, if the appellant, duly served with the notice, fails to appear on the hearing date, the appeal may be dismissed. If, on the other hand, the appellant appears but the respondent, having been duly served with the notice, fails to appear, the court will proceed to hear the appeal *ex-parte* (O.39, r.17 C.P.C.).

If on the day fixed for hearing it is found that notice was not served on the respondent owing to failure by the appellant to deposit within the time fixed by the court the sum required to defray the cost of serving the notice, the court may dismiss the appeal.

However, such order should not be made if, in spite of the fact that the respondent has not been served, he appears when the appeal is called on for hearing (O.39, r.18 C.P.C.).

Where the appeal has been dismissed as a result of such appellant's default, he may apply to the court to have the appeal re-admitted and if it is proved to the court that he was prevented by any sufficient cause from appearing or from depositing the sum required, as the case may be, the court will re-admit the appeal on such terms as to costs or otherwise as it thinks fit (O.39, r.19 C.P.C.).

If, at the hearing of the appeal, it appears to the court that any person who was a party to the suit in the court from whose decree the appeal is preferred, but who has not been made a party to the appeal, is interested in the result of the appeal, the court may adjourn the hearing to a future day to be fixed by it and direct that such person be made a respondent (O.39, r.20 C.P.C.).

Under this rule, it would appear, an appellate court has the discretion to make or not to make an order that a party to the original suit who has not been made a party to the appeal, be joined. In Mulla's *Code of Civil Procedure* it is stated, at page 1203 (12th Edition):

> It is a question for the court in its discretion to determine in each case whether or not it will make an order for the addition of a party as contemplated by this rule. A party will not be added merely in order to enable the respondent to file cross-objection against him.

But a party who was not a party to the proceeding will not be made a party on appeal (see *Mariki's* case – supra).

Before these previsions can apply, it must be shown: (1) that the person in question was a party to the suit in the court from whose decree the appeal is preferred; (2) that such a person has not been made a party to the appeal; and (3) that the person is interested in the result of the appeal. The phrase "interested in the result of the appeal" would appear to mean "who may be affected by the result of the appeal."

If an appeal is heard *ex-parte* and judgment is pronounced against the respondent, the respondent may apply to the court to re-hear the appeal, and if he satisfies the court that the notice was not duly served on him or that he was prevented by sufficient cause from appearing when the appeal was called on for hearing, the court must re-hear the appeal on such terms as to costs or otherwise as it thinks fit to impose upon him (O.39, r.21, C.P.C.).

A respondent who has not appealed from any part of a decree may file an objection within one month from the date of service on him or his advocate of notice of the day fixed for hearing the appeal, or within such further time as the court may see fit. Such cross-objection must be in the form of a memorandum and the rules governing memoranda of appeals govern cross-objections also. Such a respondent is at liberty not only to support the decree on any of the grounds decided against him in the lower court, but to take any cross-objection to the decree which he could have taken by way of appeal (O.39, r.22910 and (2) C.P.C.).

On receipt of such cross-objection, the court will, as soon as practicable after the filing of the objection, cause a copy of it to be served upon the party who may be affected by such objection or his advocate at the expense of the respondent, unless the respondent has filed with the objection a written acknowledgment from the party who may be so affected (O.39, r. 22(3) C.P.C.).

As with counter claims, if, in any case in which any respondent has filed memorandum of objection under the foregoing provisions, the original appeal is withdrawn or is dismissed for default, the objection so filed may nevertheless be head and determined after such notice to the other parties as the court thinks fit (O.39, r.22(4) C.P.C.).

In some cases, a trial court may dispose of a suit on a preliminary point. What, in such a case, is the remedy of the unsuccessful party? He can appeal from such trial court's resulting decree. If the decree is reversed in appeal, the High Court may, if it thinks fit, order the case to be remanded, and will send a copy of its judgment and order to the trial court, with direction to re-admit the suit under its original number in the register of civil suits, and proceed to determine the suit.

In such an event, the evidence (if any) recorded during the original trial will, subject to just exceptions, be evidence during the trial after remand (O.39, r.23, C.P.C.). Let us take one example. A sues B for damages resulting from a motor accident. The defendant raises preliminary points, namely, (1) that the suit is time-barred, and (2) that it is *res-judicata*. The trial court upholds B's preliminary points and so dismisses the suit. A appeals against the trial court's order of dismissal to the High Court. In the appeal, the High Court holds that the suit was neither time-barred nor *res-judicata*, and so reverses the decree. In such a case, the High Court may, if it thinks fit, remand the case. It may further direct what issues should be tried in the case, and will send a copy of its judgment to the trial court with directions that the suit be restored to the file under its original number in the register and that the trial court should proceed to determine the suit. If any evidence was recorded at the time of hearing the preliminary objections, such evidence will, subject to all just exceptions, be evidence during the trial after remand.

It also sometimes happens that although the pleadings raised a particular issue or issues in addition to others, a trial court omits to decide an issue or issues. In such a case, and if the evidence on the record is sufficient to enable an appellate court to pronounce judgment, the appellate court may, after resettling the issues, if necessary, finally determine the suit, notwithstanding that the judgment of the trial court proceeded wholly upon some ground other than that on which the appellate court proceeds (O.39, r.24 C.P.C.). But there must be sufficient evidence on record before an appellate court can exercise its discretion to pronounce judgment.

Besides, if the court from whose decree the appeal is preferred has omitted to frame or try any issue, or to determine any question of fact, which appears to the appellate court to be essential for the right decision of the suit on the merits, the appellate court may, if necessary, frame the issues, and refer the same for trial to the court from whose decree the appeal is preferred. In such a case, it will direct such court to take the additional evidence required, and such court will proceed to try such issues, and return the evidence to the appellate court together with its findings thereon and the reasons for such findings. Such evidence and findings will form part of the record, and either party may, within a time fixed by the appellate court, present a memorandum of objections to any findings. When that has been done, the appellate court will proceed to hear and determine the appeal (O.39, rr.25 and 26, C.P.C.).

When Additional Evidence May be Required

Generally speaking, the parties to an appeal are not required to adduce additional evidence, whether oral or documentary. It is generally assumed that all the evidence that was necessary to prove or disprove matters in issue at the trial was adduced during the trial. An appeal, therefore, usually proceeds upon the questions of findings of fact arrived at by a trial court and applicable principles of law in the light of the evidence on record.

However, in a case where the court from whose decree the appeal is preferred has refused to admit evidence which out have been admitted, or if the court requires any document to be produced or any witness to be examined so as to enable it to pronounce judgment, or if there is any other substantial cause, the court may allow such evidence or document to be produced, or witness to be examined. If it so rules, it must give reasons for so doing (O.39, r.27(1) and (2) C.P.C.).

Having ruled that such additional evidence should be produced, the court may either take such evidence itself, or direct the court from whose decree the appeal has been preferred, or any other subordinate court, to take such evidence and send it, when taken, to the court (O.39, r.28 C.P.C.).

If additional evidence is directed or allowed to be taken, the court must specify the points to which the evidence is to be confined and record on its proceedings the points so specified (O.39, r.29, C.P.C.). It is, therefore, the duty of the court recording such evidence to ensure that in recording or receiving such additional evidence, it confines the evidence to the points so specified. So, any evidence that is outside the scope of the points specified will he ignored by the court.

In what circumstances, then, will the reception of additional evidence be ordered? In the case of *Karmali Termohamed v. Lakhani & Co.* (1958) E.A. 567, the court quoted with approval a passage in the judgment of Denning, L.J. (as he then was) in the case of *Ladd v. Marshall,* (1954) I W.L.R. 1389, which states at page 1491:

> In order to justify the reception of fresh evidence or a new trial, three conditions must be fulfilled, first, it must be shown that the evidence could not have been obtained with reasonable diligence for use at the trial; second, the evidence must be such that, if given it would probably have an important influence on the result of the case, although it need not be decisive; third,, the evidence must be such as is presumably to be believed, or in other words, it must be apparently credible, though it need not be incontrovertible.

In the *Annual Practice*, 1953, this principle is enunciated in the following terms, at page 1252:

> It is an invariable rule in all courts... that if evidence which either was in the possession of the parties at the time of a trial, or by proper diligence might have been obtained, is either not produced, or has not been procured, and the case is decided adversely to the side to which the evidence was available, no opportunity for producing that evidence ought to be given

by the granting of a new trial (See also *Paryani v. Choitram*, (1963) E.A. 464, 467).

Shredded of all its niceties, the principle may be stated simply thus: an appellate court will not order the taking of additional evidence merely in order to allow an unsuccessful party to fill in gaps in his weak case. It will only order additional evidence when, after perusing the evidence before it and considering the questions to be decided, it comes to the conclusion that the evidence as it stands is defective in that some piece or pieces of evidence which ought to have gone on the record for a just decision of the case to be made did not go on the record; and that a court must not lightly order the production of additional evidence on appeal: it must only do so where the trial court improperly refused to admit such evidence or for some "substantial cause."

Judgment in Appeal

After hearing the parties or their advocates and referring to any part of the proceedings to which it is considered necessary to refer, the court will pronounce judgment either then and there or at some future day, notice of which must be given to the parties or their advocates, and such judgment must be in writing and must be pronounced in open court (O. 39, r.30 C.P.C.).

Now, what should a judgment of an appellate court contain? It must, in the first place, state what points are for determination. For instance, an appeal may raise questions such as whether the evidence on the record justified the trial court's findings of fact and whether there was misdirection or non-direction on any point of law. Those points must be set out. Secondly, the judgment will contain a decision on those points and reasons for that decision. Thirdly should the decree be reversed or varied, the judgment must contain the relief to which the appellant is entitled, and this usually includes costs. The Judge or Judges pronouncing the judgment must sign and date it at the time it is pronounced.

The judgment may confirm, vary or reverse the decree from which the appeal is preferred. In some cases, if the parties to the appeal agree as to the form which the decree in the appeal should take, or as to form the order to be made in appeal should take, the court may pass a decree or make the order in terms agreed upon by the parties (O.39, r.32, C.P.C.).

The High Court, moreover, has power to pass any decree and make any order which ought to have been passed or made by the trial court, or to pass or make any further or other decree or order as the case may require. This power may be exercised notwithstanding that the appeal is as to part only of the decree, and may be exercised in favour of all or any of the respondents or parties notwithstanding that such respondents or parties may not have filed any appeal or objection (O.39, r.33, C.P.C.).

In an appeal heard by more judges than one, any judge dissenting from the judgment of the court must state in writing the decision or order which he thinks should be passed on appeal, and may give his reasons for the same (O.39, r.34, C.P.C.).

Decree in Appeal

A decree in appeal must contain the number of the appeal, the names and descriptions of the parties, the day on which the judgment was pronounced, and a clear specification of the relief granted or other adjudication made. It must further state the amount of costs incurred in the appeal, and by whom, or out of what property, and in what proportions such costs and the costs in the suit are to be aid. It must then be signed and dated by the Judge or Judges who passed it, but a dissenting Judge need not sign it (O.39, r.35, C.P.C.).

Should parties to the suit require certified copies of the judgment and decree in appeal, they must apply for the same which will be furnished to them at their expense (O.39, r.36, C.P.C.). A copy of the judgment and decree duly certified by an authorized officer of the court (usually a Registrar of the High Court) will be sent to the court which passed the decree appealed from, and the same will be filed in the original record of proceedings in the suit. An entry of the judgment must then be made in the register for civil suits (O.39, r.37 C.P.C.).

APPEALS FROM ORDERS

Under the provisions of section 74 and r.1 of O.40 of the Civil Procedure Code, an appeal lies from the following orders:

1) An order under r.10 of O.7 returning a plaint to be presented to the proper court;
2) An order pronouncing judgment against a party under r.24 of O.8;
3) An order under r.9 of O.9 rejecting an application (in a case open to appeal) for an order to set aside the dismissal of a suit;

4) An order under r.13 of O.9 rejecting an application (in case open to appeal) to set aside a decree or judgment passed *ex-parte*;
5) An order under r.4 of O.10 pronouncing judgment against a party;
6) An order made under r.18 of O.11;
7) An order made under r.10 of O.16 for the attachment of property;
8) An order under r.20 of O.16 pronouncing judgment against a party;
9) An order under r.32 of O.21 on an objection to the draft of a document or of an endorsement;
10) An order under r.9 of O.22 refusing to set aside the abatement or dismissal of a suit;
11) An order under r.10 of O.22 giving or refusing to give leave;
12) An order under r.70 or r.90 of O.21 setting aside or refusing to set aside a sale;
13) An order under r.3 of O.23 recording or refusing to record an agreement, compromise or satisfaction;
14) An order under r.2 of O.25 rejecting an application for an order to set aside the dismissal of a suit;
15) An order under r.3 or r.8 of O.32 refusing to extend the time for the payment of mortgage – money;
16) Orders in interpleader-suits under r. 3, 4 or 6 of O.33;
17) An order under r.3, and 4 or r.7 of O.36;
18) An order under r.1, r.2, r.4 or r.9 of O.37;
19) An order under r.1 or r.4 of O.38;
20) An order of refusal under r.19 of O.39 to re-admit, or under r.21 of O.39 to re-hear an appeal;
21) An order under r.23 of O.39 remanding a case, where an appeal would lie from the decree of the High Court;
22) An order under r.4 of O.42 granting an application for review (see also ss.74, 75 and O.40 C.P.C. and *Mariki's* case – supra).

The rules that govern appeals from decrees also govern, *mutatis mutandis*, appeals from orders. It should also be noted that unless otherwise provided by any law, no appeal lies from any order other than those stated above.

It is submitted that the wording of subsection (2) of Section 74 of the Civil Procedure Code is misleading in the sense that it gives the impression that a defendant against whom an ex-parte judgment has been given may appeal against such judgment. The correct position is as stated in O.40, r.1(a) of the Civil Procedure Code.

CHAPTER THIRTY TWO

REVIEW

Apart from the mode of challenging a judgment, decree or order of a court by way of an appeal to a higher court, an aggrieved party may challenge such judgment, decree or order by some other way in certain circumstances, and that is by way of what is called Review. An application for review may be made in cases where no appeal lies or in cases where the judgment, decree or order is appealable. The provisions of O.42 of the Code are the applicable provisions with respect to review.

Rule 1(1) of the Order provides that any person who considers himself to be aggrieved with a judgment, decree or order of the court, whether or not an appeal lies to a higher court may apply for a review of the judgment, decree or order. Such an application, however, must be made to the same court which passed the judgment, decree or order.

In an application for a review, the applicant must show: (1) that there has been a discovery of new and important matter or evidence which, after the exercise of due diligence, was not within his knowledge or could not be produced by him at the time when the decree was passed or order made; or (2) that there is a mistake or error apparent on the face of the records; or (3) that there is any other sufficient reason (see O.42, r.1(1) C.P.C.).

In a case where the party is not appealing, he may nevertheless apply for a review of the judgment, decree or order even if an appeal by some other party is pending, unless the ground of such an appeal is common to him and such appealing party, or where as a respondent, the party applying for review could present to the court the case on which he applies for a review (see O.42, r.1(2) C.P.C.).

On the question of discovery of new matter or evidence, one example will suffice. Amina and Hamisi lock horns over the inheritance of the estate of the late Juma, a wealthy businessman. Amina claims that Juma was her only son who was sired by Hussein, Amina's late husband. Hamisi, on the other hand, claims that Juma was his only brother born out of wedlock by their late mother, Fatuma, who was a sister of Amina. Amina brings evidence of witnesses to the effect that since they knew Amina and her late husband, Hussein, Juma had been their only child. Hamisi fails to bring any independent evidence other than his own assertion. The court then enters judgment for Amina. Subsequently, Hamisi finds a birth certificate in the name of Juma showing that Juma was born of the late Fatuma and was sired by one Konda, who was sentenced to life imprisonment many years ago, but he is alive and well enough to give evidence on behalf of Hamisi to the effect that he is the father of Juma who was born out of wedlock by Fatuma who took the child to her sister Amina after he, Konda, was imprisoned for life only a few weeks after the birth of Juma.

In such a situation, Hamisi could file an application for review of the judgment upon discovering that new and important matter or evidence as to the true parentage of Juma.

An example of a case with "an error on the face of the record" is where, in the concluding remarks to a judgment on appeal, the judgment were to read thus:

> For the foregoing reasons, this appeal cannot succeed. It is accordingly hereby allowed.

In such a case, any of the parties could apply for a review of the judgment on the ground of an error apparent on the face of the record because, if the appeal *cannot succeed*, it should be *dismissed* and not *allowed*. That was more or less the situation in the case of *Ramadhani Mbegu v. Kijakazi Mbegu* (see *infra*).

It should be noted that an application for a review can be based on any of the three conditions or a combination of them. In the case of *N.B.C. v. Cosmas M. Mukoji* (1986) T.L.R. 27, the applicant had failed to show that the fact that the subject-matter of the case, a house, was a residential house as envisaged in section 48(a) of the Civil Procedure Code, was *"discovery of new matter of evidence,"* because the applicant had all along been aware of such fact. The High Court, however, granted the application for review. The court stated, at page 129:

> I agree that the fact that the house is residential was within the knowledge of the applicant at the first trial. But nevertheless the application is competent. There are two other legs under which an application for review can be made:
>
> a) if there is an error apparent on the face of the record;
> b) if there is any other sufficient reason.

An application for review of a decree or order of a court, other than the High Court, on some ground other than the discovery of new and important matter or evidence or the existence of a clerical or arithmetical error apparent on the face of the record, must be made only to the same magistrate who passed the decree or made the order sought to be reviewed. But if such magistrate has already been of the view that the application for review should be granted and has issued a notice to the other party, then the application may be heard by such magistrate's successor (see O. 42, r.2 C.P.C.).

As stated above, an application for review must be made to the same court which passed the decree or made the order. But once an appellate court has rendered its decision in the matter then the lower court cannot review its own decision which was appealed against. Such court then becomes *functus officio* for purposes of review, and any application for a review thereafter would have to be made to the appellate court (see *Mjasiri v. Joshi*, (1995) T.L.R. 181; *Zee Hotel v. Minister of Finance*, (1997) T.L.R. 265; *Lema v. Chuma*, (1989) T.L.R. 130; and *Benedict v. Benedict*, (1993) T.L.R. 1).

R.3 of O.42 of the Code provides that the provisions as to the form of preferring appeals must apply, *mutatis mutandis*, to applications for review. This rule had been a subject of some controversy as to its meaning and scope. One school of thought took the view that the rule refers to form only and not the entire application of O.39, r.1(1) of the Code which governs appeals. Another school of thought took the view that an application for review must in every sense comply with the rules governing appeals, including the requirement that such an application must be accompanies by a copy of the decree sought to be challenged in the application for review. The position was clarified by the Court of Appeal of Tanzania in the cases of *Chiku Hussein Lugonzo v. Brunnids F.S. Lugonzo*, Civil Application No. 30 of 1999 and *Ramadani Mbegu v. Kijakazi Mbegu and Others*, Civil Application No. 46 of 1999 (supra) (both of them as yet unreported). In *Chiku Lugonzo's* case, the Court had this to say:

> With great respect, it appears to us that the learned judge got mixed up in applying O.42, r.3 in relation to the form of preferring appeals *mutatis mutandis* to applications for review without the important limitation and restriction to formality.... Simply stated, mutatis mutandis means that when dealing with cases of a similar type and circumstance, applicable principles would, in similar manner, apply to the case with the necessary changes and modification. In this case, ... from the very wording of r.3 of O.42 even with the necessary changes and modification, the application of the rule mutatis mutandis was to be applied only in so far as the form of the memorandum for review was concerned. The learned judge, with respect, went beyond the form of the Memorandum for review in dealing with what to accompany the memorandum.

The Court added:

> "In our view, ... the requirement for a drawn order to accompany the memorandum for review does not also accord with logic in an application for review. The reason is that unlike the situation in an appeal, in the case of an application for review involving the same file and the same court as was the case here, it was not necessary to require the attachment of a drawn order to the memorandum for review."

In *Mbegu's* case (supra), the facts, in brief, were that in the body of a judgment on appeal, the learned judge held that three out of four grounds of appeal filed were properly founded. However, in his final order of the judgment, the learned judge said:

> From the foregoing reasons the appeal succeeds. It is dismissed with costs.

In an application for review of that judgment, the applicant did not attach a copy of the decree sought to be challenged in the review nor did he attaché the proceedings. The learned judge held that the omission constituted a fatal irregularity and so dismissed the application for review. In an application for revision of the order dismissing the application for review, the Court of Appeal reiterated its decision in *Lugonzo's* case (supra).

After reproducing O.42, r.3 and O.39, r.1 of the Civil Procedure Code, the Court stated:

> With respect, the learned judge, it seems to us, does not appreciate any distinction between the two and the requisite documents to accompany the memorandum for review or appeal. A close scrutiny of these provisions, would show that O. 39, r.1(1) covers the form of the memorandum of appeal and other requirements for accompanying the memorandum. However, as regards an application for review, it is our view that O.42, r.3 is restricted to matters of form, that is to say the structure, such as title, names of parties, date of decree, number of suit and the numbering of paragraphs. Apart from this stipulation on an application for review, we are unable to find any provision in Civil Procedure Code which requires the memorandum for review to be accompanied by a copy of the decree as the learned judge held in this case. In the light of these provisions of the law we are with respect, satisfied that the learned judge misconstrued and misapplied O.42, r.3 and O.39, r.1 to the instant case.

The Court added:

> It is now settled that in an application for review, it is not a legal requirement to have the memorandum for review accompanied by a copy of the decree... We hasten to observe here that if circumstances permit and the applicant is in a position to avail such documents to accompany the application, it would facilitate the processing of the application although as already indicated it is not a necessary requirement under the law.

It *Mukoji's* case (supra), the High Court granted the application for review although the Chamber Application was not supported by an affidavit but was supported by statements made by the applicant in Court.

After the application has been filed, the court will issue a notice and cause it to be served on the opposite party to enable him to appear and be heard in support of (or even against) the decree or order for which a review is sought. If it appears to the court that the application does not have sufficient ground for a review, it will reject the application (see O. 42, r.4(1) and (2) (a) C.P.C.).

If the application for review is founded on an allegation that there has been a discovery of new matter or evidence which the applicant claims was not within his knowledge or could not be produced by him when the decree was passed or the order made, the applicant must strictly prove such allegation before his application for review can be granted (see O. 42, r.4 (2) (b) C.P.C.).

If a judge or magistrate or any number of them is/are still attached to the court which passed the decree or made the order sought to be reviewed, then that same judge or magistrate (or judges or magistrates) must hear the application for review and no other (see O.42, r.5 C.P.C.). The point here is that as far as possible the same judge or magistrate who passed the decree or made the order sought to be reviewed must hear the application for its review.

In the case of an application for review heard by more than one judge or magistrate, and the court is equally divided, then the application must be dismissed; but where there is a majority, the decision will be that of the majority (see O.42, r.6 C.P.C.).

If the court rejects an application for review, such order of rejection is not appeallable. But where the application for review has been granted, it may be challenged on appeal on any of the following grounds, namely, (1) that the application was made contrary to rr. 2 and 4 of O.42, of the Code; or (2) that it was made out of time and without sufficient cause (see O.42, r.7 (1) C.P.C.).

An application for review, like other applications, may be rejected by reason of failure by the applicant to appear when the matter is called on for hearing. In such an event, the aggrieved applicant may apply to that same court for restoration of the application to the file. Before any decision can be made in the matter, however, notice must be served on the opposite party so that he too may be heard in the matter. If the applicant satisfies the court that he was prevented from appearing by any sufficient reason when the application was called on for hearing, the court will order restoration of the application to the file on such terms as to costs or otherwise as it thinks fit, and it will fix a day for the hearing of the earlier application (see O.42, r.7(2) and 3 C.P.C.).

Where a court grants an application for review, it will make such correction of the decree or make such other order as it thinks just in the circumstances of the case (see O.42I, r.8 C.P.C.).

It is also important to note that no application to review an order made on an application for review or a decree passed or an order made on a review must be entertained (see O.42, r.9 C.P.C.).

CHAPTER THIRTY THREE

INHERENT POWERS OF THE COURT

Section 95 of the Civil Procedure Code Act, 1966 provides that nothing in the Code must be deemed to limit or otherwise affect the inherent power of the Court to make such orders as may be necessary for the ends of justice or to prevent abuse of the process of the court.

The language of the section could give an impression that courts can do anything or make any orders in applying the provisions of the Code or any other statutory law. That is not quite so. There are some limitations to the application to those provisions.

In the case of *Hassan Karim & Co. v. Africa Import and Export*, (1960) E.A. 396, Simmons, J. dealt with the application of section 151 of the Indian Code of Civil Procedure, 1908, which is *in pari matria* with section 95 of the Tanzania Civil Procedure Code Act, 1966. He had this to say, at page 399:

> The attitude to s. 151 of the Code of Civil Procedure suggests a misconception. No application could ever be brought "under" it. It confers no power on the courts nor rights on litigants. It provides no more than that in so far as the courts may have certain inherent powers the Code does not abrogate them. To find out whether those powers exist one must look elsewhere than at S. 151, for they must exist independently of that section.

The Court of Appeal for East Africa held that inherent powers of courts can be brought in aid where a given provision of a given law is found not to have been intended to be exhaustive (see *Rawal v. Mombasa Hardware Ltd.*, (1968) E.A. 392, 393). In the case of *Ryan v. U.S.A.* (1970) E.A. 675, the same Court held that where a summons has been irregularly issued, it can be challenged by invoking the court's inherent jurisdiction. That was a case in which the summonses did not adequately state what documents were required to be produced. The appellants applied to the High Court to have the same set aside. There was, however, no specific provision for such an application to be made. Amplifying the point, Law, Ag. V. – P., stated, at page 677:

> In the absence of specific legislative provision, I consider that he (the Judge) should have set aside the summonses in the exercise of his inherent jurisdiction. Strictly speaking, the judge was correct in saying that no application can be made under section 9 of the Civil Procedure Act (cf. S. 95 C.P.C.), as it does not create jurisdiction but merely makes it clear that the inherent powers of the court are not affected by the enactment of the Act. It was apparent that the application in fact invoked the exercise of the court's inherent powers. Such an application can be made if no remedy is available, and a remedy should be provided if the interests of justice so require.

In the case of *Adonia v. Mutekanga,* (1970) E.A. 429, the Court was more explicit. There, Spy, J.A., stated, at page 432:

> On the other hand, there is no rule of law... that inherent powers cannot be invoked where another remedy is available. The position, as I understand it, is that the courts will not normally exercise their inherent powers where a specific remedy is available and will rarely if ever do so where a specific remedy existed but, for some reason, such as limitation, is no longer available.

The Learned Judge added:

> The matter is, however, not one of jurisdiction. The High Court is a court of unlimited jurisdiction, except so far as it is limited by statute, and the fact that a specific procedure is provided by rule cannot operate to restrict the court's jurisdiction.

The purport and scope of this section appears to have been aptly condensed in Mulla's *Code of Civil Procedure* in which it is stated, at page 576:

> The Civil Procedure Code is not exhaustive. The court has, therefore, in many cases – where the circumstances require it, acted upon the assumption of the possession of an inherent power to act *ex debito justionis,* and to do

that real and substantial justice for the administration of which alone it exists. The law can not make express provisions against all inconveniences... that may possibly happen, and it is, therefore, the duty of a Judge to apply them not only to what appears to be regulated by their express provisions, but to all the cases to which a just application of them may be made and which appears to be comprehended either within the express sense of the law or within the consequences that may be gathered from it (13th Edition, Vol. 1.).